Girlfriends and Postfeminist Sisterhood

Girlfriends and Postfeminist Sisterhood

Alison Winch
Middlesex University, UK

First published 2013 by
PALGRAVE MACMILLAN

Palgrave Macmillan in the UK is an imprint of Macmillan Publishers Limited, registered in England, company number 785998, of Houndmills, Basingstoke, Hampshire RG21 6XS.

Palgrave Macmillan in the US is a division of St Martin's Press LLC, 175 Fifth Avenue, New York, NY 10010.

Palgrave Macmillan is the global academic imprint of the above companies and has companies and representatives throughout the world.

Palgrave® and Macmillan® are registered trademarks in the United States, the United Kingdom, Europe and other countries.

ISBN 978–0–230–34875–2

This book is printed on paper suitable for recycling and made from fully managed and sustained forest sources. Logging, pulping and manufacturing processes are expected to conform to the environmental regulations of the country of origin.

A catalogue record for this book is available from the British Library.

A catalog record for this book is available from the Library of Congress.

For Erika Winch (1921–2013)

Contents

Acknowledgements

I am deeply grateful to my friends Anna Webster and Laura Hamilton for their support, wit and laughter. Chapter 8 is partly constituted out of a journal article that I wrote with Anna, and our chats about feminism, branding and popular culture are inspirational. A special thank-you goes to Helen Hester who read the whole manuscript and gave me invaluable and perceptive feedback, making this a much, much better book: Cheers! Thanks also to Sarah Baker for her wise, perceptive and informed comments, as well as for our conversations on popular culture. Daniel Sellers and Agnes Davis were immensely encouraging and I am thankful for their beady editorial eyes. Sophie Mayer's enthusiasm was, as ever, motivational. Paolo Gerbaudo gave important suggestions on the introduction. Any flaws and mistakes are, of course, mine.

Much of the media in this book was watched with friends. I have been particularly energized by evenings shared with Nicola Parsons, Jo Taylor and Jess Cook, as well as Kate Potts. I am grateful for Nicola's advice on parts of the manuscript. I'm also indebted to Akaam for enduring the romantic comedies.

A warm thank-you to Sophie Herxheimer, Soonita Ramtohul, Nia Davies, Claire Boulton and Jennie Tsai for their friendship, as well as Pamela Ramtohul, Maureen Ni Fiann and Alison Little for sharing their insights on relationships. Thanks also go to my students at Middlesex University for talking about their experiences.

I am deeply grateful to those who have let me house sit in times of precarity, especially Rachel Malik, Rick and Wendy Webster, and Martin Little. Wendy gave essential early feedback and invited me to speak at Huddersfield University about my work. Thank-you to my colleagues at Middlesex University, especially Jamie Hakim, Merja Makinen and Lawrence Normand. I am also grateful to participants at various conferences, especially 'Forthcoming Feminisms' at the University of Leeds and 'Talking Bodies' at the University of Chester. Parts of Chapter 4 are derived from my essay ' "We can have it all": The Girlfriend Flick' published in *Feminist Media Studies*, 2012. Sections of Chapter 2 appeared in a different form as ' "Your new smart-mouthed girlfriends": Postfeminist Conduct Books' in *Journal for Gender Studies*, 2011. The chapter 'The

Friendship Market' is partly constituted out of an article co-written with Anna Webster, 'Here Comes the Brand: Wedding Media and the Management of Transformation' which was published by *Continuum: Journal of Media and Cultural Studies*, 2012. I am especially grateful to the editors and anonymous reviewers for their invaluable comments and suggestions, especially Cindy Carter and also Sally Davidson at *Soundings*, where I published earlier work.

The writing of this book has been sustained and encouraged by my family, especially Chris, Cathy, Paul and Ravina. It may never have seen the light of day if it wasn't for Ben's belief in the project – and the fun, happiness and joy that he generates in our life.

Gratitude goes to my grandmother who I lived with through much of the writing. She taught me so much about care, love and friendship and this book is dedicated to her.

Introduction: Girlfriend Culture

> You must begin to think of yourself as becoming the person you
> want to be.
>
> (http://thinspiration-pictures.blogspot.co.uk/)

The *Thinspiration* blog showcases photographs of 'real girls, models,
and celebrities' and has 8659 members (http://thinspiration-pictures.
blogspot.co.uk). The blogger is a young Australian called Erin whose aim
is to motivate women to lose weight by posting photographs of 'super
skinny girls in fashionable clothes'. She made the site 'for girls who were
like me that needed something to motivate them'. Erin explains that
previously, 'I thought I was curvy and looked like any other "healthy
girl" ', but the images of these women inspired her to become thinner.
The women in the photographs are the size that we normally expect
from models and celebrities. However, because celebrity is marketed
as democratic, all women can aspire to be like them. *Thinspiration* is
a friendly, feminine, and intimate blog where the ideal body is trafficked among a homosocial group of women. The images are employed
to incite comparison, competition, envy, identification and aspiration.

Losing weight is depicted as empowering, whereas not striving for
transformation is a sign of weakness. Erin advises her users:

> Stay positive! In moments of weakness remember everyone who has
> lost weight has had the same weak moments as you they just didn't
> give in to the negative thoughts, tell yourself you can do it and
> believe in it. I hope this helps you guys! Stay strong. Xx

Women engage with the blog through thanking Erin, posting photographs and asking questions. 'CANNOT thank you enough!' writes

1

one user. The blog contains motivational statements such as 'You must begin to think of yourself as becoming the person you want to be' and 'I'd rather say "I did it!" than say "I gave up".' The body is held up as a project to be worked upon. The *Thinspiration* blog exemplifies an emerging 'girlfriend culture' with its emphasis on peer control. It is demarcated from other women cultures because of its yoking of an intimate friendliness with a mutual body regulation that is configured as entrepreneurial and empowering. In this culture, men are absent whereas girlified women are hypervisible to each other across a convergent media culture.

This book intervenes in contemporary debates about feminism. More specifically, it locates itself within a critique of postfeminism that has analysed the ways in which feminism has been paired with individualism. This framing understands postfeminism as harnessing the Anglo-American liberal feminist rhetoric of agency, choice and empowerment to generate bonds between consumers and brands (Banet-Weiser, 2012). It is intricately bound up with a conservative and neoliberal political economy in which feminism is being 'undone' (McRobbie, 2009). I understand neoliberalism as an aggressive form of capitalism that opens up every area of life to exploitation for profit and limits democratic restraints on corporate and financial freedoms (Harvey, 2005). It is a political project that dominates social and economic norms by enabling a culture where the individual is prized above society and choice is placed in conflict with collective action. This book looks at the way neoliberalism penetrates the intimate relations between women.

In such a culture where the focus is on the individual, why is there a proliferation of locations within the media that place primary emphasis on female sociality? The focus on an expressive and aspirational lifestyle and the capacity to select the correct consumer options to achieve it is, according to Angela McRobbie and Diane Negra, anti-connectivity. For them, the ideal feminine subject is girly and flawless, and her desire for hypervisibility is exclusive. This means that solidarity among women is foreclosed. For this reason, I understand 'girlfriendship' to be strategic. Identifying how female sociality is represented, evoked, created and mined across popular culture, I look at how girlfriends support each other in striving for 'representability' (Negra, 2009) and the perfect self. Girlfriendship is an investment in the individual as girlfriends are essential in enabling feminine normativity. Their intimate networks of comparison, feedback and motivation are necessary in controlling body image. It is not enough to be normative, however, as a girlfriend must also stand out from her peers. She must do so in such a way as to sustain the friendship group, preserve her friends' dignity and validate their striving for skinniness; she must be normatively distinctive. The normative postfeminist subject is white, straight, able-bodied and middle class. Strategic friendships ossify certain power structures and these prohibit women from investing in relationships that might devalue one's femininity. Drawing on the research of Bev Skeggs and Helen Wood, I look at how female networks are constructed through symbolic violence, whether this is through the power dynamic between a middle class expert and a working class subject demonstrated to be in need of fixing, or by the deliberate erasure of all working class signifiers. I also look at how women are represented as relating across racial difference. McRobbie argues that contemporary popular culture insists on erasing 'almost all signifiers of racial difference' and subsuming 'ethnicity into the dominant repertoire of normative white femininity'. Consequently, 'the idea of complete perfection [...] is elusive, unviable, and beyond reach [...] for non-white women' (McRobbie, 2009, 70–71). In girlfriend culture women of colour are either absent or are situated in a position of subordination, where they are often depicted through the signifiers of authenticity.

Girlfriendships are located in a popular culture that markets the self as an entrepreneurial project that should be constantly worked upon. The self is intricately connected to networks of mutual governance where citizens are 'never finished with anything' (Deleuze, 1992, 5). Gilles Deleuze maintains that in societies of control, individuals are in 'perpetual training' (Deleuze, 1992, 7). This is evident in the *Thinspiration* blog where being skinny must be continually attained. Successful women are in the constant process of *'becoming'*, which is characterized as 'more desirable than *being*' (Jones, 2008, 12). Fat, or rather the fascination with fat, becomes the signifier of letting go of the self as project, but also of letting go of the surveillance networks of female sociality in which the body is enmeshed.

Girlfriendship is an affective social relation. I draw on the psychosociological research of Jessica Ringrose (2013) and Valerie Walkerdine (2011), who argue for the significance of the affects of shame, jealousy and competition in female relations. I understand affect to be social, psychological and embodied. It is 'a substrate of potential bodily responses, often autonomic responses' (Ticineto Clough, 2007, 2). It covers a range of feelings but before they have been differentiated and objectified in relation to a particular object or source (Kavka, 2008, 29, 31). Affect is dynamic and mobile so that feelings such as shame can unconsciously saturate situated experiences. Self-help or therapeutic communication models are dependent upon the separation and objectification of a particular emotion in order for it to be talked about but, as I argue in Chapter 3, affect precedes commodification.

I apply these theoretical frames to a reading of media convergence culture where new media have taken up and embedded old media (Jenkins, 2006). I examine representations and interventions into friendship networks since the television series *Sex and the City* (HBO, 1998–2004). I identify these texts (which loosely make up girlfriend media) as 'remediations' of *Sex and the City* which itself dramatized the consumer and sexual advice of the woman's magazine, as well as the television sitcom, to create a specifically girlfriend comedy (Bolter and Grusin, 1999; Arthurs 2004, 134). 'Girlfriend media' is a porous term that illuminates instances across media platforms where (predominantly heterosexual) female sociality is used as representation and/or a marketing strategy, as well as an affective social relation. Its books, television and digital platforms are 'interconnected resources for self-work' (Oullette and Wilson, 2011, 559). UK texts are analysed in parallel to US media as part of a portfolio of contemporary British consumer options.[1]

Girlfriend media appropriate the intimate rhetoric of belonging and recognition that typifies 'intimate publics'. Lauren K. Berlant notes how the private intrudes into the public sphere of women cultures, thus creating affective and intimate spaces (Berlant, 2008). This intimate culture is feminine and assumes the commonality of women who are in need of conversation. In particular, it privileges the sharing of conventionality to produce deep affinities, offering solutions to the desire 'to be *somebody* in a world where the default is being nobody or, worse, being presumptively *all wrong*' (Berlant, 2008, 3). Typically, intimate publics configure sociability, belonging and recognition through the narrative of love and desire, where women are cast as the wounded in a heterosexual power structure. Women are portrayed as searching for a simpler and more visible version of themselves, and this is frequently achieved through the resolution of a love plot. The figure of the friend who prioritizes her girlfriends over a man demarcates girlfriend culture as a niche within, or as an extension of, intimate publics. In a postfeminist landscape where women are regulating each other's bodies, the man is cast as an accessory in proving a girl's worth to the most important people in her life – a circle of girlfriends. Girlfriend culture does not rely on the hope generated through a heterosexual 'happy ever after'. Instead, it takes pleasure in the presence of girlfriends.

Relations between women are often complex, knotty and ambivalent. Developing the ethnographic research of Ringrose and Walkerdine I understand them to be made up of an assemblage of affect, including 'ugly feelings': inferiority, jealousy, rivalry, competition and desire (Ngai, 2005). I suggest that these are harnessed in popular culture in order to cultivate a sphere of intimacy. However, they are also used to regulate normative femininities. Significantly, the affective social relations evoked and courted in girlfriend media are extended to viewers and users in order to engage them in systems of surveillance. In a neoliberal postfeminist culture, women mutually control each other through policing networks. The desire for intimacy, normativity and belonging often means submitting oneself to regimes of looking by the girlfriend gaze.

This book offers a complex understanding of patriarchy. It argues that hegemonic power structures are both perpetuated and obfuscated through girlfriend culture where women are complicit in the regulation and policing of female bodies. They do this through a 'gynaeopticon' – a gendered, neoliberal variation on Bentham's panopticon – where the many girlfriends watch the many girlfriends. My argument is that girlfriend culture revolves around homosocial forms of control where women bond through the bodies of other women. This element is significant because the male gaze is veiled as benign, and instead it is women who are represented as looking at other women's bodies. Popular culture marketed to women has always positioned the female body as an object of scrutiny, anxiety and aspiration. However, this homosocial surveillance is marketed as solidarity through the rhetoric of girlfriendship. It is promoted as entitlement and strength. I understand this regulation of the body to be particularly insidious because it is located in a female sphere, and is marketed as intimate and enabling. I understand it to be a process of slut-shaming where the traditional misogynist fear of the female libido is translated into a fear of fat. The images of women in *Thinspiration* – especially their bellies – are both eroticized and de-libidinized, as their aim is to evoke feelings of inferiority, diminishment and worthlessness.

This book comprises nine chapters. Each chapter loosely centres on a particular medium: magazines, conduct books, television, film and digital networking sites. It moves from representation in the beginning chapters, through to evocation and intervention into female sociality on reality television, and it ends with a discussion of the co-participatory practices of digital media. Chapter 1 looks at the UK's *Heat* magazine, the celebrity figure of Josie Gibson, as well as the film *Mean Girls* (2004) and the US sitcom *Cougar Town* (ABC, 2009). It identifies how the non-normative body is slut-shamed by a 'girlfriend gaze' that regulates through discourses of class. Chapter 2 investigates conduct books written by best friends who become co-brands in the marketing and selling of a particular classed and raced discourse of expertise. This includes books by best friends Fearne Cotton and Holly Willoughby, Susannah Constantine and Trinny Woodall, as well as *Skinny Bitch* co-authors, Kim Barnouin and Rory Freedman (a book enthusiastically recommended by *Thinspiration*).

Chapter 3 examines the representation of female friendship networks in US television Manhattan dramedies, *Sex and the City*, *Lipstick Jungle* (NBC, Living TV, 2008–2009) and *Cashmere Mafia* (ABC, 2008), where female sociality is conceived as social capital in order to consolidate women's power base and to enable the feminine masquerade. These friendships are depicted as exclusive, and homosexual desire is prohibited or marginalized as libidinal relations threaten the strategic transaction at the heart of the girlfriends' intimacy. I also look at *The L Word* (Showtime, Living TV, 2004–2009), which offers a knottier, deeper and more ambivalent representation of women's relationships.

Chapter 4 brings these issues to 'the girlfriend flick', where men are largely absent and the central relationship is between heterosexual women. Friends relate with and through the branded cultures of the 'wedding imaginary' (Sgroi, 2006, 114), where homosexuality is foreclosed whereas the commercial spaces are eroticized. I conceive this portrayal of intimacy as depicted in *In Her Shoes* (2005), *Bride Wars* (2009), *Baby Mama* (2008) and *The Women* (2008) as a 'womance'. Because women in popular culture are often cast as indices of the economy, so this chapter also examines the figure of the bridezilla, whose desire for perfection makes her the ideal scapegoat for contemporary anxieties over deregulated market forces. I look at *Bridesmaids* (2011) and *Your Sister's Sister* (2011) as alternative, more complex, representations of female relating. In Chapter 5 I take this argument further to examine the unequal power dynamic that structures women's relations across racial difference, especially in *The Help* (2011) and the spin-off films *Sex and the City 1* (2008) and *Sex and the City 2* (2010). Although there are attempts to bridge the divide of normative distinctiveness through the consumption of high-end consumer goods, women of colour are positioned within the narrative as a means to make 'white lives better' (Springer, 2008, 84). Rarely do we see women as relating across cultural difference, and non-white identities are reified. This is also evident in the US television programmes *2 Broke Girls* (CBS 2011) and *Girls*

(HBO, Sky Atlantic, 2012–) which otherwise offer a complex and critical negotiation of postfeminism.

In chapters 6 and 7, I take this analysis further to look at US and British reality television. Affects of competition, envy and rivalry are harnessed as necessary forms of feedback and comparison in the cultivation of the ideal postfeminist woman in programmes such as *The Hills* (MTV 2006–2010), *Paris Hilton's My New BFF* (MTV, ITV 2, 2008) and *Sorority Girls* (E4, 2012). This is especially apparent in British reality television where women are subject to the white middle class gynaeopticon. Programmes looked at include *What Not to Wear* (BBC, 2001–2005), *Cook Yourself Thin* (Channel 4, 2010–2012) and *Wife Swap* (Channel 4, 2003–2009).

Chapter 8 brings us to digital media and the way in which female sociality is enabled and mined in order to extend the reach of control. Through wedding media sites such as youandyourwedding.co.uk and hitched.co.uk, it looks at the cultivation of the self-brand. In this context, a celebrity subjectivity is marketed as empowering and attainable.

The conclusion attempts to look at the implications of a critique of girlfriend culture. It argues that this critique allows us to understand postfeminism in a new frame where women do have more agency within the popular culture of the global North, but this very empowerment has become a tool of conservative governance. To unpack this has important ethical and political ramifications in terms of liberating the female body from patriarchy. In addition, this chapter looks forward to how feminism can provide a collective space for a productive exploration of the ambivalence of affective social relations. Untangling the knottiness of sociality, especially through a frame of intersectionality, can be used as a regenerative force to create alliances and aggregations among women who are typically recognized to be in conflict. Indeed, dis-identification can be a dynamic force within the movement (Perrier, 2012). In addition, it argues that the ugly feelings that are evoked and manipulated in postfeminist popular culture in order to cement relations between consumers and brands can also be employed to expose the ways in which women are accultured into needing thinspiration.

1
The Girlfriend Gaze

Being mean is such a rush. It is like that feeling you get when
someone loses weight and then they brag about it and then
they gain it all back.

(Ellie, *Cougar Town*)

Halloween is the one night a year when girls can dress like a
total slut and no other girls can say anything about it.

(Cady, *Mean Girls*)

The film *Mean Girls* (2004) is a teen comedy representing girls' high
school cliques. The heroine, Cady (Lindsay Lohan), has been home-
schooled by her zoologist parents and at the beginning of the film she
moves back to the US after living on the African continent for 12 years.
At school, the innocent Cady is confronted with a variety of in-groups,
including The Plastics: so-called because of their Barbie doll aesthetic.
The Plastics are ruled by the Queen Bee, Regina (Rachel McAdams), who
is blonde, wears pink and is the most powerful girl in the school. She
controls her girlfriends – and the other students – through regulating
body image and style; no one can be as perfect as her. Her attitude
towards other girls is revealed when one of The Plastics, Gretchen,
asserts that 'seven out of ten girls have a negative body image'. Regina
replies, 'Who cares? Six of those girls are right.' She abuses the students
by denigrating their weight, and she also participates in slut-shaming
by calling the other girls sluts and whores. These forms of regulation
intersect with misogyny. As one of the teachers, Ms Norbury (played by
Tina Fey, who is also the writer and therefore a privileged mouthpiece
for certain ideas) warns: 'you all have to stop calling each other sluts
and whores. It just makes it OK for guys to call you sluts and whores.'

The Plastics are intrigued by Cady and they befriend her. However, after Cady falls for Regina's boyfriend, she enacts revenge on Regina by cutting off her 'resources', including the way that she looks. Cady fools Regina into eating high-calorie weight gain bars. As a result, the Queen Bee receives her just deserts as getting fat teaches her about humility. Nevertheless, through the film's narrative, Cady must also learn her own lessons about what it means to be a good friend.

Mean Girls represents the pleasures and terrors of high school friendship groups. Partially based on Rosalind Wiseman's self-help book *Queen Bees and Wannabes: Helping Your Daughters Survive Cliques, Gossip, Boyfriends, and Other Realities of Adolescence* (2002), the film reveals the bitchiness prevalent among female cliques. It portrays how the lure of belonging, and therefore being normal, can also mean subjecting oneself to cruelty by friends. Cady confesses, 'The weird thing about hanging out with Regina was that I could hate her, and at the same time, I still wanted her to like me.' Cady notes how Gretchen also submits to punishment in her quest for hypervisibility:

> the meaner Regina was to her, the more Gretchen tried to win Regina back. She knew it was better to be in The Plastics, hating life, than to not be in at all. Because being with The Plastics was like being famous... People looked at you all the time and everybody just knew stuff about you.

I have used *Mean Girls* here to illustrate the complex emotions and systems of control that permeate female sociality in a postfeminist context. The schoolgirls' bitchiness and their desire for visibility are brought to excess and satirized. The bullying is, to some extent, exaggerated. However, the affect of friendship that the film depicts and evokes is pertinent to the media I am examining in this book. Girlfriend media both reproduce these social pleasures of belonging to an intimate group, while also holding up the female body for analysis and scrutiny. They are sites that induce pleasure and belonging, while also enacting surveillance and cruelty. Moreover, girlfriend media offer the possibility of achieving hypervisibility through participating in these friendship networks. Indeed, part of the desire to partake in this intimate female sphere is the recognition and distinctiveness that it might bring. In this chapter, I look at the UK's *Heat* magazine and its representation of the reality TV celebrity Josie Gibson, as well as (to a lesser extent) the representations of friendship in the US television sitcom *Cougar Town* (ABC 2009–) and the film *Sex and the City 1* (2008). I identify the ambivalence located in their evocations of female sociality. In other words, these media texts both promote the intimacy of female networks and the pleasures of belonging to a 'we'. Simultaneously, however, they regulate their consumers around body image by inducing feelings of shame and humiliation. I also introduce the idea of the 'girlfriend gaze'. Developing Foucault's configuration of the panopticon I argue that women are regulating each other's bodies through affective networks of control which constitute a gynaeopticon where the many girlfriends survey the many girlfriends.

Normative cruelties: *Mean Girls*

Female friendships are complex and formative in the production of feminine identities. As the psychosociological ethnographic research of a number of theorists demonstrates, meanness pervades many girls' intimacies. Terri Apter and Ruthellen Josselson examine the psychological impact of friendship in the lives and identity formations of girls in both the UK and the US. Rather than focusing on the role of the mother or the family in shaping feminine norms, they argue that codes of acceptable femininity 'are established anew in each generation' and consequently 'the power of friends to shape values is enormous' (Apter and Josselson, 1999, 211). This suggests that, although familial relations are primary, friends and their gaze disseminate and negotiate much of the normative (and subversive) discourses that constitute a feminine skills set. Women and girls look to their peers to secure appropriate behaviour and looks. Apter and Josselson theorize a 'female gaze' which is formed in childhood but then internalized. They argue that women and girls search for what is feminine 'in the mirror of her girlfriend's gaze'. This can be confirming and comforting, but if 'she sees criticism or rejection, she can be struck with panic' (Apter and Josselson, 1999, 4). In addition, Apter and Josselson suggest that female friendship can be 'a school of correction' where the rules about what is and is not acceptable are meted out (Apter and Josselson, 1999, 66). Friends are punished and rewarded according to the rules of the clique.

As illustrated in *Mean Girls*, school friends can regulate each other through controlling body image. Apter and Josselson note how the rules of belonging are intertwined with food and the body: 'Try to persuade a teenage girl to resist the social obsession with how she looks or how much she weighs, and one will run headlong into the brick wall of the norms of her friendship circle' (Apter and Josselson, 1999, 66). Conforming to the standards of the group is essential to guard against ostracism. Furthermore, belonging can be achieved by mocking and humiliating others; cruelty can be a means to develop bonds among girls. What is of particular interest here is that girls' hunting packs often locate the changing body of adolescence as a site of abuse. The anxiety that attends puberty can be projected on to a girl who is less popular and whose physical changes are more noticeable. These experiences of bullying are part of the complex rules of friendship 'which may go unnoticed because they are sometimes implicit and subtle, but are nonetheless controlling' (Apter and Josselson, 1999, 63).

Educational sociologists Jessica Ringrose and Emma Renold investigate school friendships in the UK. They argue that although girls describe their ideal friends as nice, they often perceive real girls to be mean, two-faced and unable to keep secrets. Moreover, their interviewees reveal how they are 'systematically betrayed and talked about by one another. Meanness is therefore part of the normative cruelties of "doing" girl' (Ringrose and Renold, 2010, 585). Ringrose's data illustrate how the ideal girlfriend is not only expected to be 'supportive' and 'there for you', but also non-competitive and 'friends with everybody' (Ringrose and Renold, 2010, 584). Nevertheless, the reality is often more complex than this and Ringrose and Renold propose a nuanced understanding of what bullying constitutes. Rather than perceiving schoolgirl relationships through the binary logic of bully and victim, they explore how 'a range of "normative cruelties" inhere in the social and cultural processes of becoming a recognizable gendered subject' (Ringrose and Renold, 2010, 575).

'Normative cruelties' is a powerful phrase that neatly encapsulates the affective power dynamics of friendship groups, as well as the girlfriend media that I am looking at. Ringrose and Renold demonstrate how girls employ cruelty in order to discipline feminine identities. Significantly, they identify how these forms of control are linked to regulating sexuality:

> A primary way girls are socially sanctioned to express meanness is through subtle and direct regulation of other girls' sexuality [...] it is normative for girls to position themselves and others in sexual hierarchies, invoking regulative discourses around sexuality, appearance and behaviour in the private spaces of their friendship groups as a mode of constructing idealised femininity.
>
> (Ringrose and Renold, 2010, 585–586)

What is pertinent here is that the school where they were conducting the research did not perceive this as bullying. Indeed, Ringrose and Renold note that the figure of the bully is often pathologized as *transgressing* normative gendered behaviours, rather than imposing them. Consequently, we can read girls' mutual controlling through shame and humiliation around the body and sexuality as institutionally acceptable; the friends both channel normative feminine discourses and police them. As Ringrose notes in *Postfeminist Education?*:

> I want to emphasize that sexual regulation of other girls provides the *primary* means through which girls are socially sanctioned to express their assertiveness, aggression and rage (against other girls), usually against a particular member of their affective networks (friendships) at school. When jealousy and competition emerge they are legitimately allowed to discipline other girls' sexual subjectivity, a dynamic that works to bring some of the friendship group closer together while other girls are projected onto as objects of hatred, shame and/or disgust.
>
> (Ringrose, 2013, 95)

Consequently, conflicts based on gendered and sexualized regulation demand the recouping of the traditional feminine qualities of being nice and good in order to maintain female friendship (Ringrose and Renold, 2010, 587). This is pertinent as conflict in girlfriend culture, especially the girlfriend flick, is resolved through this childhood fantasy of 'just being friends'. Consequently, sexual power relations and hierarchies are subsumed under a sentimental understanding of girlhood and idealized feminine relationships – and sexual regulation by girlfriends is glossed as friendship.

Slut-shaming is a concept recently theorized to account for how girls discipline each other's sexual conduct. Indeed, Ringrose and Renold identify that the most pressing and affectively charged conflicts between girls at school relate to sexualized status, identity and competition (Ringrose, 2013, 87). Friends, therefore, not only police each other's normative feminine conduct around sexuality, but this mutual governance originates from feelings of envy and competition. Ringrose suggests that 'slut-shaming appears to express a dynamic where jealousy gets sublimated into a socially acceptable form of social critique of girls' sexual expression' (Ringrose, 2013, 93). Ostensibly, girlfriend media eschew an overt condemnation of female sexuality. Indeed, the normatively cultivated feminine body is admired for its erotic capital; girlfriends who have harnessed their sexuality for empowerment within a normative paradigm are celebrated. However, a girlfriend must know how to correctly regulate her libido in a postfeminist market, and this regulation is partly enacted through monitoring the consumption of food. Women's eating habits and body image are obsessively scrutinized, analysed and judged, and those who 'let go' are critiqued. These affective forms of control are constituted out of a complex web of envy, competition and friendliness. In other words, the mutual disciplining of body size is apparently supportive in an individualized postfeminist culture which privileges normativity. On the other hand, these forms of control can also be cruel as they channel the ugly feelings also experienced between women. As Ellie from *Cougar Town* states, 'Being mean is such a rush. It is like that feeling you get when someone loses weight and then they brag about it and then they gain it all back.'

Experiences in childhood and adolescence – 'the threshing floor of friendship' (Apter and Josselson, 1999, 7) – also affect the performance of identity in adulthood. This has a number of implications for the girlfriend media that I am looking at. It means that feminine identities, shaped in the playgrounds and private spaces of adolescence, are still susceptible to, and shaped by, girlfriends in older life. It also means that these formative relationships can evoke powerful feelings in adulthood; the wounds inflicted by girls are still vulnerable to further exploitation, and this includes the shame of unbelonging. Significantly, Apter and Josselson argue that childhood traumas around friendship are re-lived through adult relations with other women: 'behind the most confident and powerful woman is a girl who wants a friend, and a girl who has learned to be terrified of a friend's abandonment and betrayal' (Apter and Josselson, 1999, 5). This search for confirmation and comfort does not dissipate with age; it is part of the need for, and popularity of, women cultures, intimate publics and girlfriend media. These sites of popular culture exploit and build on the joys and scars of adolescent friendships. The pain and anguish of being excluded, of being not quite right, are played and replayed.

Valerie Walkerdine (2011) examines the affect of shame through the framework of class and gender in the context of reality television. She maintains that provoking shame functions effectively on reality television because it is already embodied by the female viewer. In particular, Walkerdine perceives shame as variously experienced, depending on class. For example, middle class women wield it as a means to subjugate and distance themselves from working class women. Indeed, fat is conventionally linked to working class or 'chav' culture throughout popular culture and in the press. Consequently, just as policing eating habits is a means to control sluttishness, so it is also a way in which symbolic violence is legitimately enacted. In other words, the working class body is configured as pathological through its association with excessive sexuality, which itself is marked on the body through fat; exploiting the fear of fat is a strategy of class exploitation in an aspirational popular culture. I discuss this further in chapters 6 and 7, but here I want to suggest that shame is employed as a governing weapon, that it can be experienced as trauma by women across class lines, and that these emotions are learnt and absorbed in childhood. Indeed, like Susie Orbach in *Bodies*, Walkerdine discusses how women's experiences of their bodies (as culturally regulated and disciplined) are passed among women. In particular, she argues that shame is intergenerational and passed down from mothers to daughters. If we extend this transmission to friendship groups, we can understand friends as sharing, controlling and disciplining each other through embodying and inflicting shame; friends are like sisters perpetuating the rules of maternalism and patriarchy. In turn, girlfriend media exploit, court and activate these formative affective social relations.

Friendship has a complex and subjective affect depending on one's experiences and history of female relating. The work of Ringrose, Renold, Apter and Josselson usefully reveals how friendship networks imprint traumatic experiences of shame and exclusion on the body, while simultaneously codifying these phenomena as expressions of friendliness and sisterhood. Girlfriend culture cultivates this dual affect. In her work on makeover television, Brenda R. Weber conceptualizes the term 'affective domination' to capture the ways that 'experts point out flaws in a combined gesture of humiliation and care' (Weber, 2009, 30). Drawing on Richard Brodhead's works on childrearing, Weber identifies 'a disciplinary regime structured through intimacy'. Authority here dons a human face – the makeover experts – and sentimentalizes the disciplinary relation between the participant and the expert. Consequently, the participant appears to be bathed, not in rules, but in the power of love. It is this love-power that has the authority to control behaviour (Weber, 2009, 97). This is pertinent to girlfriend culture which also produces affective domination but through the representation and signifiers of friendship. Girlfriend culture generates an affective girlfriendliness, a loving meanness.

Who cares about letting go? *Heat* magazine

In June 2012, the front cover of *Heat* zoomed in on the apparently round bellies of five female celebrities. They included the 2010 winner of UK *Big Brother*, Josie Gibson, as well as the wife of footballer Wayne

Rooney, Colleen. The strapline reads 'In Love & Ditching the Diet: Who cares about letting go? They're loved up!' Colleen is 'eating more & Wayne likes her bigger' while Josie '[l]oves her curries with boyfriend Luke'. Among the omnipresent glossy and airbrushed flat stomachs, these curves are an anomaly. But *Heat* understands what has happened:

> We've all been there. You get a new boyfriend, and suddenly the gym doesn't seem as inviting as the sofa [...] suddenly you've gained half a stone.

The 'we' speaks to a (mainly) female group who are aware of body image and the rigours involved in attempting to maintain an ideal look. The readers are on the same plane as the loved-up women, who are 'just as guilty of scoffing junk with their new men as we are'. The democratization of celebrity, as evidenced in the figures of Josie and Colleen, means that all women now have the potential to be hypervisible (Tyler and Bennett, 2010). Consequently, *Heat* includes its readers in its sphere of body analysis. And it also includes its readers in its apparent celebration of that unaspirational and class-coded vice – the eating of junk food.

The photographs of Josie were taken while she was on holiday in Ibiza and were subsequently posted across the internet and throughout the press. Josie is working class and apparently spent her childhood in traveller communities. When she won the UK *Big Brother* in 2010 she received 77.5 per cent of the votes. The publicity work that she has done since winning has focused on her 'ordinariness', including the irreverent down to earth performance of her farting, laughing and eating in public. However, her class and her body are highly problematic markers in girlfriend culture. *Heat* ostensibly celebrates Josie's (and the other celebrities') 'happier' bodies – 'Ladies, we salute you' – and insists there is no need to apologize for them. In doing so it pokes fun at the mechanics of celebrity culture, as well as the contemporary obsession with body image. However, the magazine wants to have it all: the glamour of skinniness as well as the animalistic pleasure of letting rip into a takeaway pizza. It wants humiliating photographs of Josie caught with a slow-speed shutter that captures her cellulite mid-wobble, as well as the delicious revelling in her rebellious weight gain. And, of course, it *can* have it all. But through doing so, *Heat* promotes a volatile and insecure attitude towards the body. Its contradictions encourage 'loosening the reins' of food control as the route to health and happiness, while at the same time touting skinniness as the ultimate ideal.

Popular culture marketed to women has always positioned the female body as an object of scrutiny and anxiety, offering consumers the aspirational possibilities of image change, makeover and reinvention. It has also always employed intimacy as a powerful affect. Here, however, I want to focus on the role played by the 'girlfriend gaze' in constructing contemporary mainstream femininity, which generates its affect from the visual and rhetorical signifiers of friendship and girlhood. This is frequently executed through a nostalgic rebranding of the closeness of adolescent intimacy. The starkest examples of the surveillance of the female body are in celebrity culture, particularly in its proliferation of gossip blogs and magazines. However, it is pervasive across media platforms. The UK magazines, *Heat*, *Closer* and *Now*, all position celebrities as subjects of scrutiny within a world of women. *Heat* veils the misogynist gaze at the heart of these gender-marked popular texts through its friendly copy. Moreover, through appropriating the affect of intimacy and the girlfriendliness of its 'we', *Heat* summons the possibility of belonging to a normative group.

The volatility of *Heat*'s attitude towards women's consumption of food presumably reflects the ambivalences of the (female) editor and journalists. Through apparently celebrating the appetites of celebrities, it refuses to maintain a stable position vulnerable to critique: it colonizes both the conventional and the nonconformative. Its instability helps to keep its brand innovative; its irony and lack of fixity means that it is always in process, always becoming, and therefore always distinctive. In addition, it complicates the possibilities of dissent through its own ironic ambivalence, and this insecurity marks the fascination with fat as well as the intimacy of girlfriend networks as pervasive and powerful. The copy appears to be understanding, knowing and empathetic, but the images are cruel, analytical and scrutinizing. The photographs wilfully destabilize the text as they are culturally coded to produce disgust. This text/image disjunction unfastens our interpretation, and thus allows magazine and reader to indulge in the pleasures of benevolence and bitchiness simultaneously. *Heat* embraces the junk-food-eating or otherwise imperfect section of its demographic and suspends them between sisterly love and normative cruelty. It mimics the swing between belonging and exclusion that attends many school-age friendship networks.

The issue here is not so much whether *Heat* celebrates or condemns fat. What is important is that the female body is the subject of analysis and consequently control. Across girlfriend media, the female body – as represented by the icon of celebrity – becomes what Foucault terms a 'docile body'. That is, a body that is subjected to the analytical gaze that is 'alert everywhere' (Foucault, 1991). The technologies enforcing these docile bodies take on different forms across media platforms, but they are enacted by and for groups of women. In this particular feature, the women's weight gain is collected as data. The copy details the women's dress size, weight and 'love gain'. Josie, for example, weighs 14st 7lb, her 'love gain' is 2st, and her dress size is recorded as 16. Her diet consists of takeaway curries. As evidenced in *Heat's* ambivalent address, Josie is both celebrated and attacked for her transgression of the white, thin, middle class postfeminist norm. This is partly played out through signifying her class through fat, and then courting and activating prurience.

Susie Orbach writes that we have become hypercritical of our bodies, objectifying our faults, and consequently producing 'volatility and instability' which makes the quest for perfection 'unsustainable' (Orbach, 2009, 73). Susan Bordo concurs, stating that consumer culture 'continually excites and encourages us to "let go," indulge in our desires – for sugar, fat, sex, mindless entertainment'. Simultaneously, 'burgeoning industries centered on diet, exercise, and body enhancement glamorize self discipline and code fat as a symbol of laziness and lack of will-power'. Bordo identifies the difficulty in finding a place of moderation in this culture (Bordo, 2003, xxi). The celebrities' apparently fluctuating bodies are a way of writing large contemporary society's inconsistent messages about consumption. Indeed, this is part of their appeal as celebrities' weight gain reveals and mirrors consumers' own lack of knowledge about how to have it all. Celebrity narratives reflect women's failure to make correct choices. This failure of discernment is marked on the body. The female belly signifies a woman who does not know how to negotiate her own identity in the market, both in terms of being a discerning shopper and in terms of being a successful self-project. That is, the belly represents sexual appetite, evidencing the devouring of food, menstrual bloat or motherhood. It is libidinal.

Heat is not an obvious example of girlfriend media as it is marketed to both men and women (although it only directly addresses women in its copy). It does not obviously promote girlhood and there is little nostalgic sentimentalization of girlfriendships. However, it does participate in girlfriend culture through a number of indices. It relentlessly surveys bellies – that grotesque marker of womanhood – and it also obfuscates the straight male gaze. In this article the men are benign and friendly as they feed their beloveds takeaway pizza regardless of the monstrous consequences. *Heat's* rhetoric of belonging and exclusion, bitchiness and inclusion, is typical of girlfriend culture. The shamed girl in the school playground is replayed in *Heat* as she recasts herself as a celebrity brand and consequently participates willingly in her own humiliation. Because the ever-visible celebrity has tacitly agreed to permanent scrutiny, her body exists in the market economy of popular culture and is available to all. She has allowed herself to be dissected, admired and admonished; her weight loss/gain is essential to her celebrity narrative and its 'emotion work' (Nunn and Biressi, 2010). Josie, for example, is complicit in her own surveillance, talking 'exclusively' to *Heat*, and insisting she is comfortable in her new relationship with Luke. The delicious pleasures of the playground's normative cruelties are given free rein in the production, circulation and consumption of the magazine as part of Josie's self-marketization in a mediated convergence culture.

Across media platforms, the curved stomach is a source of shame. It also betrays what happens when you become dependent on men: you let go. The only way out of this trap is to have girlfriends who will advise on the right choices and offer support through a calculating gaze. In magazines such as *Heat* the female gaze is honed: it is trained, guided and informed so that it can always locate the spectacle of the female body as subject to calculation by other women. But it is not just celebrities who are held up for analysis in this way, and such detailed body scrutiny is not confined to the most obvious outlets like the weight-loss brands such as Weight Watchers or Slimming World, for whom the calculations of dimensions of the body are central. As I will explore further in Chapter 8, it is also prevalent in internet forums marketed to women, particularly those targeting mothers and brides – and their bellies. The girlfriend gaze is collaborative as it is produced through the many watching the many.

Gynaeopticon

To illustrate formations of power in a disciplinary society, Foucault invokes the architectural design of the prison or panopticon. At the centre of the panopticon is a tower from where the supervisor can monitor the inmates in the cells. Permanently visible, the prisoners perform their lives, knowing that they are under constant surveillance. Instead of physical force, power is exerted through the prisoner being 'subjected to a field of visibility' from which it is impossible to hide. Foucault argues that the subject not only submits to these constraints of power but, more importantly, he spontaneously lives under the internalization of the constantly watching eye. That is, 'he inscribes in himself the power relation in which he simultaneously plays both roles; he becomes the principle of his own subjection' (Foucault, 1991, 202–203). The panopticon is also designed to experiment, mould and discipline people's behaviours. This disciplining practice is primarily enforced through the prisoner's submission to the watching eye that is willingly enacted. Beauty and lifestyle industries can be understood as specifically gendered panoptical industries that ensure the internalization of control through the ubiquitous perfected images of women. The supervisor in the tower is masked through the 'visual muzak' of flawless bodies that saturate public and domestic space, and which ensure self-regulation (Orbach, 2009).

In 'The Viewer Society' Thomas Mathieson extends the image of Foucault's panopticon to include the symbol of the synopticon. He argues that technology and mass media generally, but radio and television especially, have enabled an environment where instead of the 'few seeing the many', 'the many see the few' (Mathieson, 1997). This is certainly the case in *Heat* where consumers watch celebrities relentlessly put themselves up for scrutiny. Their watching, however, takes place through the already internalized panoptical gaze and its technologies of control over the female body. In the case of *Heat* both the images of the panopticon and the synopticon are valuable in recognizing how control is internalized, and how this discipline is reinforced through the repetitive and voyeuristic surveillance of celebrity bodies. In the context of the panopticon or the synopticon metaphors, the phrase 'letting go' is a revealing one. It suggests letting go of the internalized systems of control through which neoliberal society governs its citizens. Moreover, it implies letting go of the policing gaze and, in doing so, releasing the corseted belly. It reveals the subject as letting go of their self-surveillance, as well as – in the context of *Heat* – the surveillance of the few other celebrity women. This is why its front cover has a seductive and rebellious emotive draw – it teases potential consumers with images of women who are apparently absenting themselves from girlfriend surveillance. However, the story of letting go can only be a front-page event because the networks of control are so powerful. Celebrity bellies are only fascinating because the discourses of aspirational thinness are so pervasive.[1]

The celebrity bodies in this *Heat* article are mesmerizing because the magazine positions them so that they appear imperfect. They are an anomaly in the visual muzak, but their bulging bellies also make them 'like us'. This, in turn, means that we can be 'like them'. Josie and

Colleen are examples of working class women who have succeeded in celebrity culture. Consequently they signify aspiration and fame in an apparently meritocratic society. Through these celebrity figures, readers are transmogrified from being passive consumers in thrall to celebrity stardom to subjects that might themselves become hyper-visible. This means that the practices of celebrity body analysis are potentially universally applicable. Moreover, because celebrity media proliferate across multiple platforms that encourage users to interact, engage and participate, so the bar of feminine perfection is raised for all. Oullette and Wilson identify how women's cultures no longer provide time out. Instead, we are experiencing the transition from traditional televisual women's cultures designed 'to be watched in a state of distraction' to 'the purposeful, multiplatform, "on demand" domestic media' (Oullette and Wilson, 2011, 550). Focusing on the US-based Dr. Phil multimedia self-help franchise, they argue that:

> women's interactivity can be mobilized as a gendered requirement of neoliberal citizenship, an ongoing, mundane regimen of self-empowerment that does not intensify the pleasure of the text as much as it intensifies a 'second shift' of familial and affective labour historically performed by women in the home.
>
> (Hochschild, [1989] 2003) (Oullette and Wilson, 2011, 549)

Maintaining and controlling body image can be understood as part of the 'second shift'. Consequently, being a good mother and wife also means preserving one's visibility. Contextualized within this 'second shift' convergence culture, *Heat* is both a source of escapist entertainment, and part of the active project of the entrepreneurial neoliberal self.

It is through the figure of the celebrity that expertise is disseminated. Readers can consume or emulate their haircuts, maple syrup diet or favourite cocktails. Celebrity lifestyles can be our lifestyles. In this way, celebrity culture becomes an important constituent of the self as entrepreneurial project. Because the successful self is a thing to be worked on, so we must become experts at managing 'human capital to maximum effect' (Fraser, 2003, 168). And consuming celebrity media can be a significant component of this self-management. The importance of celebrity media is intensified in a convergence culture. Part of the labour of being a female celebrity, as evidenced through the figure of Josie, is to have one's body held up for analysis and to put oneself under media surveillance. Therefore, if a celebrity subjectivity is marketed as available to all, then this also means setting *oneself* up for scrutiny and surveillance. Whether girlfriend media are celebrating or condemning the body in 'letting go', they speak within a tacit understanding of the female body as a potential object of humiliation which is therefore in need of policing. Indeed, Mark Andrejevic theorizes digital interactivity as 'productive surveillance' or 'the work of being watched' (Andrejevic, 2003). Women are not just watching celebrity bodies, they are also watching their own and each others'. Indeed, the fragmentation of media audiences into niche markets and the evolution of a Web 2.0 world where women co-produce and participate in brand spreading, means that the image of synopticon and the panopticon needs development in order to illustrate the ways in which the many participate in the cultivation and control of the bodies of the many. The panopticon, the synopticon and the paradigm of the many watching the many, work in harmony. That is, the panoptical gaze disseminated through the health and beauty complexes and utilized as a system of control is still pertinent as means of subjugating citizens through the internalization of surveillance. As evidenced in *Heat* and celebrity gossip culture, this internalized gaze is honed, perfected and given the opportunity to indulge (unlike the body) through synoptic practices. In digital media this surveillance is then harnessed as a means through which women can relate and express intimacy as they all turn their eyes on each other in tightly bound networks where they gaze and are gazed upon. It means subjecting oneself to the gynaeopticon of the girlfriend gaze where the many girlfriends watch the many girlfriends.

'How I went from fat to fit': Erotic capital

In girlfriend culture the gaze objectifies women's bodies but it functions differently from the male gaze. Here, the straight male gaze is rendered inadequate or redundant and, instead, regimes of looking are promoted between women. The long tradition of the commodification of women for male desire is internalized, redirected and utilized by girlfriends. The female body still remains at the centre of the gaze, but it is strategically subjected to analysis, calculation and control. In the hypervisible landscape of popular culture the body is recognized as the object of a woman's labour: it is her asset, her product, her brand and her gateway to freedom and empowerment in a neoliberal market economy. Although it is glossed as 'me-time', managing the body is also the means by which women acquire their cultural capital. In this context, dependency on a man is represented as a high-risk scenario, whereas investing in the self – and especially one's body – is the pathway to self-actualization, coherency, and success. A collaborative enterprise between women, the girlfriend gaze enables the mutual development of hypervisibility. Women are encouraged, enticed or coerced into experimenting with the pleasures of converting their bodies into more appropriate and visible commodities or feminine brands. John Berger argues that:

> Men look at women. Women watch themselves being looked at. This determines not only most relations between men and women but also the relation of women to themselves. The surveyor of the woman in herself is male: the surveyed female.
>
> (Berger, 1972, 47)

In this paradigm the male gaze is internalized and as a result women look at their bodies through the eyes of men. It echoes and genders Foucault's panoptical internalization of surveillance and discipline. Eve Kosofsky Sedgwick develops this understanding and identifies how patriarchal heterosexuality is achieved through 'the use of women as exchangeable, perhaps symbolic, property for the primary purpose of cementing the bonds of men with men' (Kosofsky Sedgwick, 1985, 25–26). She argues that the bodies 'traffic' among a homosocial cohort of men. Mary Ann Doane also notes the commodification of female bodies in the context of film where women's 'susceptibility to processes of fetishization' situates them 'in a relation of resemblance to the commodity form' (Doane, 1987, 22).

In girlfriend culture women's bodies 'traffic' among the women themselves. Just as the male gaze is part of the apparatus that produces patriarchal heterosexuality, so the girlfriend gaze contributes to the creation of a heterosexual and normatively distinctive feminine identity. Significantly, the girlfriend gaze converts women's to-be-looked-at-ness (Mulvey, 1975) into erotic capital. Whereas the male gaze, as conceived by Laura Mulvey or Doane, takes the female body as sexualized and rapeable object, the girlfriend gaze *cultivates* women's control over her own libido and turns it into 'hotness'. The girlfriend gaze functions through calculation and care where sexuality is configured as strategic. Floating on the de-regulated market of a self-promotional and celebrified culture, women are encouraged to relate to their bodies as both product and brand, and in this system they are brand manager.

This is evident in the case of Josie who, six months after being flashed by the paparazzi with her 'love gain', has a 'world exclusive' in *OK!* alongside the strapline: 'MY FANTASTIC SIX STONE WEIGHT LOSS: HOW I WENT FROM FAT TO FIT!'. The copy writes her original weight as a symptom of an 'addiction' to sugar that Josie has finally confessed. It gushes: 'She looks like a different person with cheekbones you could shave Parmesan off' (Fraser, *OK!*, 30 October 2012). The way her weight loss is framed intersects with normative cruelty as her previous weight is (overtly and covertly) condemned across the tabloid and celebrity press. We see the affect of the mean girl being harnessed in the depiction of Josie's body. In addition, the narrative of Josie's weight in *OK!* mirrors the erasure of her class. Imogen Tyler contends that popular culture is invested in 'the screening of the disenfranchised white poor from view; they are rendered invisible' (Tyler, 2008, 32). Part of this exclusion is enacted through denoting working class bodies as fat and therefore uncontrollable and slutty. Class hatred is reconfigured through the regimes of makeover and weight loss.

Josie confesses, in the context of the *Heat* photographs, 'I look like a total beast' and this self-disgust is approvingly cited through the popular media (cited in Dadds, *Mail Online* 12 October 2012). Although she still laughs and speaks loudly and irreverently, her language mimics that of, for example, *Skinny Bitch* (which I examine in the next chapter). She has appropriated the language of health and happiness as she regales how she 'was like junkie for sugar': 'It's disgusting stuff. It's toxic. It's a drug. It's the most addictive drug on the market.' The article in *OK!* again situates her body as an analysed text as it lists her weight loss, her waist size, as well as her diet and fitness routines. All this is presented as 'before and after' with professionally choreographed photographs of a thin, groomed and stylized Josie juxtaposed with the photographs originally shown in *Heat*. Her new diet is more middle class. That is, it is more expensive, involves more time, and is informed by fashionable discourses of what constitutes healthy eating, including the vilification of sugar, dairy and wheat. Josie now eats porridge sweetened with tree bark sugar and soya milk for breakfast. She has grilled salmon for dinner and only drinks champagne. Typically for a postfeminist girlfriend, Josie is delighted with her new weight and strives to lose more. In other words, she is not content with being, she must always be becoming and consequently never letting go of the reins of control. Whereas before Josie appeared to be refreshingly free of the regulatory and disciplining signifiers of body image, she now performs the neoliberal entrepreneurial self through the marketing of a normatively distinctive 'hot new body' (Fraser, *OK!*, 30 October 2012). She has learnt the mechanics of self-branding by erasing all the popular cultural signifiers of class. She has learnt how to regulate her body as erotic capital.

Pierre Bourdieu conceives forms of capital – cultural, social and symbolic – as grounded in an individual's (inherited or generated) economic capital, but which are expended or reinvested to establish social advantage and disadvantage. Cultural capital is primarily transmitted through the family and is consolidated and embodied through institutionalized forms of knowledge (Bourdieu, 1984). For him, it is women's role to convert economic capital into symbolic capital for their families through the markers of taste. In this way women are *capital-bearing objects* whose value accrues to the family and its patriarchal structures, rather than *capital-accumulating subjects*. Through this paradigm, women are conceived as repositories (Lovell, 2000; Skeggs, 2004). This analysis has been challenged (Skeggs, 1997; Adkins and Skeggs, 2004). However, what is pertinent for girlfriend culture is the way in which the feminine 'hot new body' is produced as erotic capital. That is, a woman can accumulate value from both the commodification of the hypervisible body but also through being the entrepreneurial manager of her own representability. On the one hand, this can be understood as patriarchy with a kinder feminine face (and I discuss this below), which sells commodification as postfeminist empowerment, but is in fact a fragile attempt to live with powerlessness (Skeggs, 1997). On the other hand, women in popular culture are *accumulating* capital, as evidenced by Josie, however exploitative, short-term and provisional this might be. This is capital that is legitimated by the dominant symbolic. Furthermore, the middle class women who are involved in Josie's promotion also profit from the trafficking of her body, as well as the marketing of their own classed taste which is repurposed as 'expertise'.

What is not legitimated by the dominant symbolic is the female libido that threatens the business logic of the self-brand. This is where slut-shaming is harnessed as a powerful regulatory force. Slut-shaming in the form of female groups and the girlfriend gaze is particularly effective as a tool of control. Catherine Hakim is a pertinent example of a figure who advocates femininity as erotic capital and yet denounces female libidinal energies. She maintains that men have a higher sex drive than women and so suffer from a 'sex deficit' (Hakim, 2011, 6).

Hakim argues for a positive recognition of the power of femininity, which she defines as erotic capital. She asks: 'Why not champion femininity rather than abolish it? Why does no one encourage women to exploit men whenever they can?' (Hakim, 2011, 3). She criticizes patriarchy and radical feminists for devaluing erotic capital, and argues that women should put their energies into its cultivation in order to benefit society and themselves.[2] Nevertheless, we can see that women are already being encouraged to make this investment through refining themselves into self-brands. Erotic capital – in the context of girlfriend culture – is not about having sex. It is about promoting a normative sexual self who is in control of her sexuality and who appears not too sluttish and not too dowdy. Indeed, it is about promoting the ideal of a woman who has a smaller libido than her male counterpart, but who gains advantage through her higher visibility.

Girlfriend culture does not overtly centre the male gaze or male desire. Patriarchal structures are obfuscated by the gynaeopticon. Indeed, its slut-shaming boundaries (codified through body image) register and reinforce (self) control among networks of women. What is striking about Hakim's configuration of the male and female libido is her insistence on women's lower sex drive (which she backs up with apparently scientific evidence). She defines what is normative for women in terms of sexual appetite and, by definition, those women who experience the same levels of desire as men are therefore transgressive or abnormal; they have not correctly produced their feminine selves. Hakim is a spokesperson for girlfriend culture. She privileges a particular kind of visible (and de-libidinized) femininity as a weapon against men; she perceives it as a means to accumulate money, power and status in a patriarchal culture.

In a de-regulated market economy where a woman's primary asset is her erotic capital, being possessed by a man is a problem. The celebrities whose over-indulgences are documented in the pages of *Heat* have had their bodies privatized by the love of one man – and this has made them fatter. Sex and emotions have made them let go of the reins of control (especially if they have to compensate for his sex deficit). In girlfriend media men are depicted as incapable of acting; they are either conspicuously absent or have withdrawn from the tyranny of skinny discipline. The male gaze in the *Heat* article, for example, is linked to love and indulgence. Men are the friendly gaze: 'Jack adores her sexy new body' and Wayne loves Colleen's curves. They are represented as outside the preserve of anxiety about female body image and this means that they are loveable, but they are also high-risk and undependable. Straight men do not have the expertise to recognize the labour and strategy that has been invested in the body. Moreover, they can purloin women's erotic capital and render it exclusively theirs. Trapped in the privatized space of the heterosexual couple, a woman's body is no longer marketable. Because she has relinquished the controlling networks of her girlfriends and been seduced by the love of a man, her body has let go into corpulence.

Twenty-first-century women apparently exercise ownership over their body, and so can profit from its commodification through the processes of branding. Consequently, the control and trafficking of bodies in girlfriend media is sold as enabling. In a relentlessly visual culture, the spectacle of the female body is necessary for self-promotion and therefore success. Moreover, the collaborative practices formed between women in the cultivation and maintenance of the normatively distinctive body is marketed as sisterhood. As the practices of beautifying and 'girling' become more complex, it is women who are able to recognize and appreciate the work spent and expertise accumulated. Because the body is represented as integral to success in the labour market, this surveillance of women by women through friendship is represented as entitlement; it is 'girl time' as women can survey each other through a rhetoric of empowerment. In girlfriend media, women do not overtly compete for male attention. Instead, the commodification and marketing of the body is circulated among a homosocial world of women through a tacit and strategic understanding of its leveraging power. Eroticism is capital, so the gaze as disseminated in girlfriend culture intersects with discourses of class, race, sexuality and disability. These factors affect one's selling power. For example, women's bodies are regulated through symbolic violence where fat is pathologized and configured as working class, or where the mechanics of taste are governed through networks of women. Consequently, as evidenced in 'social work' reality television (see Chapter 7), women's control over their erotic capital is proved through adhering to middle class norms around consumption.

The girlfriend gaze does not straightforwardly objectify women's bodies in order to produce heterosexual identities as in the case of homosocial bonding between men. This is because the gaze is strategic and analytical as it is an important constituent in the development of the self as an entrepreneurial subject. However, it is also produced from a complex assemblage of affect. The gaze is intricately bound up with feelings of envy, desire for status and identification. Indeed, in girlfriend culture the emotions of envy and comparison are harnessed, exploited and perpetuated in order to encourage women to participate in the creation of brands. If we want to 'be like them' we must also enjoin in the processes of comparison, judgment and assessment. Moreover, evoking feelings of shame, guilt and unbelonging are effective in yoking consumers into the practices of normativity. Apter identifies how heterosexual women experience 'simultaneous feelings' towards other heterosexual women and these feelings includes both love and hate, identification and jealousy (Apter, 2007). Girlfriend culture gains its powerful affect through exploiting these complex and simultaneous emotions, which are difficult to unpack and make sense of because they are so formative and personal.

In her new forward to *Unbearable Weight*, Bordo describes a teenage girl watching MTV:

> Self-hatred and shame start to burn in the girl, and other things too. When the video goes on, the singers' bodies are like magnets for her eyes; she feels like she's in love with them. But envy tears at her stomach, it is enough to make her sick.
>
> (Bordo, 2003, xiv)

The combination of the democratization of celebrity with the intimate rhetoric of friendship, as well as the commercialization of these relations, means that women and girls are encouraged to both admire and envy celebrities in order to buy into the brands that they are selling. The way that envy is appropriated in a neoliberal culture is a means to negate the self through branding practices. It sabotages bonds and solidarities through promoting the individual.

This is not to assert that the male gaze is no longer pervasive and objectifying. Indeed, preserving and critiquing the concept of the male gaze is necessary and productive in challenging corporate invasion. It is also useful in locating female oppression through the history of patriarchal sexualization and subjugation of women's bodies. After all much of the affect of the girlfriend gaze is generated by the inescapable legacy of this gaze. It is also relevant in contemporary visual culture which relentlessly eroticizes women's bodies for heterosexual male consumption in magazines such as *Zoo* or *Nuts* (although female bodies marketed to straight men are often more curvaceous than those aimed at heterosexual women). Nevertheless, the gaze conceived in girlfriend culture is complicated as its power is achieved through female complicity. The girlfriend gaze is a handmaiden to the male gaze. It is powerful because the handmaiden mocks and plays with the rules of patriarchy within the intimate space of a female cohort, while simultaneously being complicit in the enforcement of its power. Girlfriend media internalize and perpetuate male regimes of looking while acknowledging and humorously disrupting this appropriation. The fact that shame and misogyny are evoked at all as a means to regulate reveals that homosocial bonding through bodies is not as empowering as it is marketed to be.

School girls to cougars

The representation of mutual surveillance over body image in *Mean Girls*, as well as its attendant misogyny, is also employed in texts depicting mothers and older women. In these texts this surveillance is configured through the gestures and signs of friendship and its attendant normative cruelties. In the film *Sex and the City 1*, one of the four core girlfriends, Samantha (Kim Cattrall) puts on weight as a result of an unfulfilling sexual relationship. The camera zooms in on her apparently expanding belly and one of the gay male characters cries, 'Mother of God! What's with the gut?' Samantha replies, 'I guess I didn't realize how big I was until I saw it on your faces.' Her girlfriend Carrie tells Samantha, 'How? And I say this with love. How could you not realize it?' and insists, 'Now, listen, this isn't about the weight...but are you happy?' Female intimacies are portrayed as intersecting with body control through the rhetoric of loving meanness. As Weber points out in the context of reality television, control is disseminated through the power of love.

In *Sex and the City 1*, and within girlfriend culture as a whole, weight gain is linked to emotional imbalance caused through the loss of control. In contrast, thinness is equated with health, serenity and normativity. In particular it is a signifier for girliness. Women must be cast as girls, and older or professional women are 'made safe' through masquerading in the desirable attributes of adolescence: a flat belly, a fresh demeanour (McRobbie, 2009, 24; Negra, 2009, 12; Kaklamanidou, 2012). Indeed, girlification is a result of a discomfort with female adulthood and power. This privileging of girl-women is manifest in films like *13 Going on 30* (2004) and *Enchanted* (2007) that 'depict female childhood as a space of epic fantasy' (Negra, 2009, 12). This fantasy is a potent one because it speaks to an evocative desire for simplicity, intimacy and friendship. In the relentlessly visual landscape of contemporary popular culture, the feminine ideal is the girl, and the girled body is an asset. Freed from the marriage market, it is invested in as an essential part of self-branding. The labour undertaken to achieve this body is glossed as 'me-time', and portrayed as a strategic means of achieving self-coherency, empowerment and autonomy. A body image that matches the adolescent norm is temporarily a signifier of success. It is only temporary, however, as the body is always fluctuating and a postfeminist subject is in a continuous state of becoming (thin and flawless). The marketing of the eternal girlhood masquerade functions in a number of ways. It is necessary for the health and beauty complexes that women are provoked into striving for youth, as this means they will spend more on veiling the inevitable. However, the idealization of adolescence also forecloses the possibility of *not* appearing youthful. The mediated girl is waxed pre-pubescent, flat-stomached; she is fresh-faced and happy. As we will see in relation to *Cougar Town*, to look like a mature woman becomes a failure of self-marketing. The possibilities of looking like a girl are promoted to all women, so anxieties over aging become means through which female friends are represented as relating to one another. What is significant is that girlfriends not only share their body hatred, but their identities depend upon mutual governance. Moreover, this reciprocal regulation over the site of the body is presented as an expression of love. The girlfriends' system of body control is delivered through the gestures of loving meanness: 'I say this with love'. Samantha is in need of friendship intervention in order to address her relationship and get her body back into an appropriate shape. Consequently, girlfriends are essential in monitoring recalcitrant flesh and any apparent deviation from the postfeminist norm. They deliver normative cruelties through their scrutinizing gaze. Without the strategic love of her girlfriends, Samantha's hypervisibility, which is vital to her career, could be destroyed. Indeed, in a landscape where these women are dependent on the success of their self-brand – of which body image is a necessary part – the friends' surveillance is crucial.

Cougar Town (ABC, 2009–) is a US sitcom that centres on Jules (Courtney Cox) who is recently divorced and has a teenage son. She is in the process of rediscovering her sexually visible self after devoting her adult life to motherhood. Because one of the men who she dates early on in the series is significantly younger than her she is labelled (through the sitcom's title) a 'cougar'; that is, a woman who pursues younger men. Significantly, the rejuvenation of Jules's libido is linked to controlling the consumption of food. Indeed, what is pertinent about the programme is the relationship between her and her best friend and neighbour, Ellie (Christa Miller). Jules and Ellie are in their 40s and their intimacy extends to, and is consolidated through, a mutual sharing of their anxieties over aging. Indeed, aging and body image are two of the main discourses through which the friends relate. Their mining of bawdy humour is a powerful component of their friendship as it demonstrates their empathetic understanding around the tyrannies of beauty. Ellie confides to Jules that when she looks in the mirror 'all I see staring back at me is a big pile of old' (1:4). Jules confesses that she has 'chin whiskers' and 'bingo wings'. Both have issues about consuming food in front of each other. These conversations are excessive and played for laughs as the show satirizes the women's complex and idiosyncratic habits around food and body image. The two friends share an empathetic understanding over the ways that older women are expected to look like girls.

Ellie and Jules' conversations reveal the close bonds that women enjoy, and demonstrate how these bonds are configured through confession, compassion and humour, particularly around the revelations of physical insecurity. The pleasures of women socializing and relating through the revelations of body anxiety are fundamental to girlfriend culture where consumers are sold the experience of being privy to an intimate female social space. Audiences are witness to a homosocial world that privileges the female body as a site of conversation. Talking about women as if they are grotesque is a humorous and intimate discourse that binds friends. Part of the power of representing the female body as monstrous is that the audiences recognize their own inner voices articulated. It is further validated by being communicated within the private pockets of friendship. Ellie and Jules' conversation plays on a tradition of bawdy female humour shared among intimate female networks that is appropriated by other recent 'cougar' films like *Prime* (2005) and *I Could Never Be Your Woman* (2007).

Through this understanding, misogyny becomes a discourse to be mined – a tool with which to mock the male gaze, as well as to pre-empt critique and preserve dignity. We are supposed to laugh at the disjunction between the mediated and the real body as we recognize our own experiences of mirror-horror. The feminine knowledges of Ellie and Jules, as well as the trust garnered through the performance of their friendship, give their representation added emotive value. It also lures us into a sense of trust; that is, they are not being misogynist, they are drawing on a long history of the carnivalesque that offers a critique of normative femininities through its abject humour. Indeed, the expertise and knowledge shared among the women reveal the construction of ideal femininity to be a complex process that can only be understood and admired by other women; the eventual public performance is for the approbation of the girlfriend gaze. Moreover, the best friends' appropriation of the grotesque is a form of self-protection. They are aware of criticisms that can be levelled against them and pre-empt this through an excessive rhetoric.

It is, of course, much more complex than this. Indeed, misogyny becomes legitimated because it is articulated by women for and against other women (Levy, 2003). Ellie and Jules both desire feminine perfection, even if they know that they cannot achieve it. Consequently, a pervasive defensiveness saturates these exchanges. This is evident when they express overt meanness towards women outside their close friendship group such as when Ellie coaches Jules in the joys of experiencing meanness when other women put on weight (1:4). Instead of overtly attacking the technologies of body hatred as summoned by the health and beauty complexes, they retreat into girlfriend-only spaces and find strategies to conform to their dictates. Moreover, because Ellie and Jules are represented on the screen as sexy, flawless women, their obsession with aging is rendered personal, neurotic and distinctively female; there is a disconnect between the characters' self-image and the actors' on screen presence. Their body-hating humour is undercut by the fact that men in the programme – young and old – find them highly desirable. In other words, insecurity and misogyny become the province of women while men are represented as blindly fascinated by the female form. The show does not attempt to satirize the mechanics of girl culture which dictate women should look youthful. Rather, it perpetuates them by portraying the empowered possibilities of older women looking hot and participating in a particularly commodified form of sexual connection, 'dating'. Jules, for example, has the conventional attributes of the glamorous postfeminist girl: flawless skin, glossy hair and a thin body. Consequently, she is an aspirational figure, selling the potentialities of looking young; possibilities which could be partially achieved through the product placement and advertising space that the show promotes.

The figure of the friend in girlfriend culture disguises the technologies of misogynist governance by offering advice and support through a friendly rhetoric. Consequently, the dissemination of body hatred is reconfigured as sentimental and intimate. The rules of patriarchal hegemonic alliances are relayed through the visual and rhetorical signifiers of girlhood. Girlfriend media, like *Heat*, reveal and (superficially) participate in a shared pain – that of having a female body in a culture that obfuscates its relentless (classed and raced) misogyny. Moreover, girlfriend media exploit the fear of unbelonging through offering a mediated experience of friendship; whether this is through the representation of friends and their intimate talk or through the connections cultivated within social networking sites. In addition, they function through the visual representation of normative bodies and behaviours that promise to provide a confirming and comforting gaze when correctly adhered to. Simultaneously, however, they dish out rejection, or at least the possibilities of rejection, if one does not attempt to participate in the consumer practices of girlfriendship. Through these processes, girlfriend media play on and manipulate formative experiences of humiliation, particularly around femininity and the body.

The affect of bestfriendship functions as a powerful form of surveillance and control because belonging to an intimate female group signifies normativity. In the context of the media texts discussed here it also means participating in regimes of fat fear. Girlfriend culture promotes the pleasures of female relationships and their attendant feelings of belonging, security, and identity. Simultaneously, however, it plays on the normative cruelties acted out in the playground. Girlfriend media regulate the body and libido through surveillance networks that garner and maintain their power through provoking feelings of shame and guilt. Moreover, these texts provide solutions to these uncomfortable emotions through selling strategies of body-management and self-promotion. Because girlfriend media circulate primarily through a homosocial world of women it is less easy to be alienated from what is being sold; their power lies in the affect of their intimate social relations.

2
BFF Co-Brands[1]

'Together we are united. Two is more powerful than one.'
(Fearne Cotton)

'We have some fat, gross body parts, too. We're women.'
(*Skinny Bitch*)

How can a girlfriend negotiate the apparent abundance of choice? How is she to choose the right food, the right diet, the right clothes, the right haircut? Which vitamins should she take? When is it OK to eat chocolate? And what type of chocolate? Sales of self-help books are evidence that women are willing to spend more than ever on postfeminist expertise. One niche in the self-help market is books written by girlfriends; authors who market themselves as BBFs and who speak to their female audience within this sphere of belonging. These texts, which include *Backwards in High Heels: The Impossible Art of Being Female* (2009) by Tania Kindersley and Sarah Vine, who define themselves as '[p]roud feminists' (Kindersley and Vine, 2009, 53) and the *New York Times* bestseller *I Know Just What You Mean: The Power of Friendship in Women's Lives* (2001) by Ellen Goodman and Patricia O'Brien, celebrate and sanction female friendship. This chapter looks at two British conduct books written by 'best friends': Trinny Woodall and Susannah Constantine's *What Not to Wear* spin-off books and Fearne Cotton and Holly Willoughby's *Best Friends' Guide to Life* (2010). It also focuses on the American *Skinny Bitch* brand that is written and promoted by Rory Freedman and Kim Barnouin.

As old structures of class and community disintegrate, 'the choosing, deciding, shaping human being who aspires to be the author of his or her own life' becomes 'the central character of our time' (Beck and Beck-Gernsheim, 2002, 23). For those seeking advice about gender normativity and makeover, self-help guides are among the technologies that 'provide the cultural means by which individualisation operates as a social process' (McRobbie, 2009, 19). Women are looking to the lifestyle industries, but also to each other – to girlfriends – for normative performances of femininity, as well as for guidance in negotiating the proliferation of choice that is apparently available. Conduct books such as *What Not to Wear* and Fearne and Holly's *Best Friends' Guide to Life* offer the safety of belonging to a normative set of girlfriends by evoking the affect of bestfriendship. Techniques of examination are employed through insisting that the reader examine her wardrobe, her fridge, her attitudes on life. If they do not conform to the normalizing impulses of the authors, then the reader is punished through shame for being *'all wrong'* (Berlant, 2008, 3). To be included in girlfriendship, women must be discerning consumers who display agency around consumption and a commitment to transformation.

I use the term 'conduct books' because these texts belong to a specific literary tradition rooted in the eighteenth century, whose objective is to govern gendered behaviour as classed. I use *govern* in the Foucauldian sense which defines *government* as the *conduct of conduct*: 'the more or less deliberate attempt to shape the actions of others and of oneself' (Dean, 1999, 198). As a noun, *conduct* refers to behaviour, but as a verb it implies guidance; as a self-reflexive verb – to conduct oneself – it gathers a moral imperative (Dean, 1999, 10). These three uses of the term are pertinent as these textual girlfriends promise to guide the reader into making appropriate and homogeneous choices in the maintenance of an ideal body. In other words, these conduct books advise women on how to behave themselves in a neoliberal society where the self is perceived as an entrepreneurial project.

The very fact of their friendship, as well as their lived experience as women, confers expertise. Girlfriends appropriate and take the place of 'the "natural" knowledges of the family and the mother', which are an essential part of the (non-political) apparatus governing conduct (Rose, 1996, 28). They cultivate a site of feminine intimacy and offer woman-to-woman tried and tested common sense. Expert girlfriends reach out to the reader as a friend, offering her a sense of belonging to a group and, moreover, a group that understands her suffering. From this space, the expert friend is able to manipulate the consumer through declaring a position of authority in makeover culture, as well as exploiting feelings of shame and humiliation incurred in women's experiences of friendships and female relating. Expert girlfriendship appropriates the affect of normative cruelties and consequently veers between bitchiness and identification in its cultivation of normatively distinctive feminine performances.

Misogyny: Trinny and Susannah

Trinny and Susannah met in 1994 and subsequently wrote a column for the *Daily Telegraph* called 'Ready to Wear' which became their first book, *Ready 2 Dress: How to Have Style Without Following Fashion* (2000). This was later picked up by the BBC and converted into the TV series *What Not to Wear* (BBC 2001–2005). Their first book based on the TV series reached the number one slot for Christmas book sales in the UK in December 2002. Trinny and Susannah are represented, both in the books and in the television series, as best friends, supporting and learning from each other. In the books there are photographs of them in the emotional postures of friendship and intimacy, whether this is helping each other dress or put on facemasks. Indeed, in the introduction to *Trinny and Susannah: What You Wear Can Change Your Life* they coin the book 'our beauty biography' (Constantine and Woodall, 2004, 6). This focus on *our* emphasizes their shared image and their coupled brand. In addition, their friendship is portrayed as revolving around, or being significantly involved in, the process and practice of looking good. For example, in its advice over organizing closets, the book states, 'It took Susannah ten years to learn from Trinny the benefits of a more anally organised wardrobe' (Constantine and Woodall, 2004, 187). The importance of maintaining style is a necessary given and friendship is an important factor in sustaining and achieving this.

Although they agree on fashion and beauty, Trinny and Susannah are also depicted as different, particularly in terms of body shape. One of the successful components of their friendship brand is that they can both live out different versions of femininity: Susannah is represented as fat and has 'huge' boobs (Constantine and Woodall, 2004, 16) while Trinny is 'skinny' and has 'non-existent' boobs (Constantine and Woodall, 2004, 17). Trinny has had plastic surgery, while Susannah has not. Like *Sex and the City* or the Fearne and Holly co-brand, which also represent differentiated girlfriends, these varieties of femininity mean that they can appeal to a broader female audience; particularly groups of women who might consume the books and TV series as a way of relating. Indeed, *What Not to Wear* also encourages friendship networks among its consumers for their mutual 'conduct of conduct'. This friendship is written through comparison. For example, comparing body shapes will help define the body's assets and flaws:

> How do you know whether you have saddlebags, if you are an hour-glass or a pear, or if your arms should be hidden at all times? It helps to do this with a good friend because the comparison will make you more aware of the way you are built.
>
> (Constantine and Woodall, 2004, 15)

If money is a problem when it comes to clothes then it is useful for women to swap wardrobes. *What Not to Wear* suggests that friends can network to exchange clothes:

> This is especially good for friends who might have a vast wardrobe that could come winging your way, but it is equally satisfying to help a friend with less money than you without making her feel like a charity case [...] At the end of the day it's about friendship.

It also mentions envy:

> Carrying the weight up top invariably means you have big boobs, fat arms, a wobbly tummy and a shorter neck while your legs, butt and skin will be the envy of all your friends.
>
> (Constantine and Woodall, 2004, 15)

The phrase 'being the envy of' is a manner of speaking, but it is also a telling one. Comparison, envy and competitiveness are recognized to be a useful part of friendship as they encourage women to look after their style and conduct themselves correctly in this image-based culture.

The differences between Trinny and Susannah's personalities and bodies also confer on them the ability to empathize and identify with a broader range of consumers. In their 2005 book, they state that they take a psychological approach to dressing their viewers and readers, and this involves identifying with the women who they address:

> The reason we can so readily recognise the issues we describe in this book is that, between the two of us, we have at some time in our lives manifested *all* of them ourselves.
>
> (Constantine and Woodall, 2005, 7)

Here they create a female space of empathy, encouraging friendship between themselves and their readership:

We want you to feel attractive, happy and proud to be you. When you look different you will act different, and when you act different you will feel different. More than any other book, this is going to be like having us by your side. We really will feel like your ally and confidante because we've been there, so we speak from the heart.

(Constantine and Woodall, 2005, 7)

Friendship and love are written through the effectiveness of being able to control body image. The tough rhetoric of the TV series is still prevalent (and I will discuss this shortly) but it is tempered by the fostering of a nurturing female space. Each section begins with a letter identifying a particular type of sartorially challenged woman. She is addressed as 'Friend' and the letter is signed with the handwritten signatures of Susannah and Trinny. They offer her 'good, practical, woman-to-woman advice that we know works'. They manipulate the reader into believing that the 'fun-loving woman is still in you. We just have to rediscover her. Please trust us when we say that clothes and grooming can dramatically change the way you feel' (Constantine and Woodall, 2005, 19).

The back cover of *What Not to Wear: The Rules* (2003) promises that 'best friends won't tell you the truth . . . but Trinny & Susannah are not your best friends'. This was also the tagline in the TV series. It implies that female friends habitually lie to each other, particularly around body image, and it also points to the flaws in day-to-day friendships as opposed to expert girlfriendships which are more authentic. In addition, because expert girlfriendship is in the service of the beauty complexes it is more trustworthy and advantageous. Like much postfeminist discourse, the tone of *What Not to Wear* veers between castigation and indulgence, bitchiness and belonging. This following excerpt is both sympathetic and damning:

We women have so much piled upon us that it's hardly surprising some of us slowly slide away from stress, upset and advancing years into a muddy puddle of decline.

(Constantine and Woodall, 2005, 18)

This rhetorical mixture of cruelty and identification reaches out to the reader as a friend, offering her inclusion to a normative group and, moreover, a group who understands her suffering. From this space of understanding it delivers the blow, accusing the reader of looking unacceptable and inadvertently humiliating herself.

Sometimes, *What Not to Wear* is more direct in its shaming of the bad dresser. It identifies different categories of women and locates the cause of her inability to change and to look good. Addressing one particular 'type' of woman, it tells her: 'you don't give a damn about yourself' (Constantine and Woodall, 2005, 18). Another category of woman, who is accused of dressing like her teenage daughter, is rewarded with public humiliation for this transgression:

> You are walking down the high street, denim-clad butt swaying, pink sparkly clips holding back your sunlit tresses, Mickey Mouse T-shirt, a tiny bit short, displaying your tummy. You hear a wolf whistle. You spin to smile at the owner of the hard, lean, sweat-gleaming torso, who retorts: 'Ooops, no, not you, grandma, it's the girl behind you I'm after.' How humiliating is THAT? The sexy bricky thought you were dead hot until he saw your true age reflected in the wrinkles of your face.
>
> (Constantine and Woodall, 2005, 234)

This excerpt is extremely problematic in its promotion of street harassment as a means to be more tastefully dressed. Moreover, it introduces the male gaze into the intimate female space; the imagined gaze of the sexy bricky. This fantasy man is conjured up in order to strengthen *What Not to Wear*'s policing gaze.

Men hide in the shadows of the books and are occasionally brought onto the page in order to provide reasons as to why women should transform the way they dress. The archetypal new mother, for example, is not as attractive as she once was and this 'has a huge impact on her physical relationship with her partner which encourages a vicious circle of negative feelings' (Constantine and Woodall, 2004, 7). Or there is 'Mr Commitment', who recoils at the woman's lack of style. Women lack self-esteem and believe they are 'not good enough to be worthy of their prince' (Constantine and Woodall, 2004, 8). *What Not to Wear* offers a pessimistic view of men (as well as a heterosexist view of women) by assuring us that men are only interested in outer image. As Martin Roberts points out in relation to the *What Not to Wear* TV series, men's 'approval at the end of each show validates the transformation project' (Roberts, 2007, 238). *What Not to Wear* adopts a cynical approach to men but simultaneously uses them as a yardstick with which to measure women's self-esteem and empowerment. If the male gaze were eradicated, if these shallow figures did not exist or their opinions were not valued, would *What Not to Wear* have the same power of surveillance?

I want to suggest that men provide an effective fear element in their role as fashion police; the sexy bricky and Mr Commitment are stereotypes representing the arms of the law. However, the real shaming originates from the intimate female space produced on the page. It is a site of identification, empathy, expertise, and support, but it also employs highly emotive strategies to shame the recalcitrant dresser. The goal is not to get the sexy bricky's approval, it is to be a savvy consumer who is empowered to transform herself through making correct choices about the way she looks. If the sexy bricky's disgust will support this, then so much the better.

In the spoof documentary *Trinny and Susannah: What They Did Next* (2004), Susannah is a figure of fun as she dresses in an underwear suit (episode 1). It is played for laughs especially as it camps up her class status. Nevertheless, the self-ridicule gains its humour from a long tradition of disgust at women. *What Not to Wear* encourages the reader to take the same approach to their body in order to identify their 'defects' and their 'assets'. Rather than encouraging weight loss, as in *Skinny Bitch* discussed below, it suggests wearing clothes that support the body's strengths and disguise the flaws. These flaws are written through the language of the female grotesque:

> A naked Susannah is like a fat white maggot, all folds and undulating movement. The breasts have engorged to an E cup, the stomach has emerged like a hernia, open and laid out for inspection above every waistband, and the arms, well, they are worryingly vast and soon to take over my entire body.
>
> (Constantine and Woodall, 2004, 16)

The closeness of Trinny and Susannah's friendship is emphasized through a rhetorical device whereby Susannah moves from the third to the first person in the above citation. This serves to highlight the way in which the friends speak as one within the tight conviviality of bestfriendship, where these insecurities can be revealed. This intimacy is extended to the readership, including them in a network of female self-mockery and knowingness about images of feminine perfection. As in *Cougar Town*, discussed in Chapter 1, we are supposed to laugh at the disjunction between the mediated and the real body as we recognize our own experiences of mirror-horror. The feminine knowledges of these co-authors, as well as the trust garnered through the performance of their friendship, give their co-brand added emotive value. They also lure us into a sense of trust; that is, they are not being misogynist, they are drawing on a long history of the carnivalesque that offers a critique of normative femininities through its abject humour. However, it is hard to reconcile this abusive approach to the body with the promise to make women 'feel good about themselves again' (Constantine and Woodall, 2005, 7).

Health: *Skinny Bitch*

Skinny Bitch, a bestselling diet book in the UK and USA, is written by 'your new smart-mouthed girlfriends', Rory Freedman and Kim Barnouin. Their website promises that they:

> won't mince words and will finally tell you the truth about what you're feeding yourself. And they'll guide you on making intelligent and educated decisions about food. They may be bitches, but they are skinny bitches. And you'll be one too – after you get with the program and start eating right.

Freedman is a former agent for Ford Models, as well as being the primary writer. Barnouin is a former model and the main researcher; the back cover of *Skinny Bitch* states that she 'holds a Master of Science degree in Holistic Nutrition' (although it is from a non-accredited university). The back cover also has a photograph of the two friends standing together, looking thin and glossy. They are experts; icons of transformation; they mirror what we could become if we worked hard enough at the self as reflexive and entrepreneurial project. Their experience in image-based industries, their thinness, their use of 'scientific evidence' (mostly gleaned from websites and newspaper articles), and their friendship, confer them with expertise: *Skinny Bitch* will help the reader become skinny.

Barnouin and Freedman met at a talent agency in 1996, and became 'fast friends'. In their acknowledgements, Barnouin thanks God every day for her 'amazing friend and business partner' (Barnouin and Freedman, 2005, 9), and Freedman thanks her 'for changing the course of my life and enlightening me with your glow' (Barnouin and Freedman, 2005, 8). To date, they have written the international bestselling *Skinny Bitch* (2005), which was also Number 1 in the *New York Times* bestseller list, *Skinny Bitch in the Kitch* (2007), and a book for pregnant women, *Skinny Bitch: Bun in the Oven* (2008). They have also written a motivational journal, presented three workout DVDs and written a diet book for men, *Skinny Bastard* (2009). This chapter focuses primarily on the first *Skinny Bitch* book which did not become a bestseller until

2007 when Victoria Beckham was caught by the paparazzi with a copy in her hand. *Skinny Bitch* is a girlfriend brand that conducts women in the correct consumption of food. The website states:

> We were both completely obsessed with [food]. But we weren't always healthy eaters. So eventually, when we did change our ways, we experienced first hand the difference a healthy diet could make. And the more we learned for ourselves, the more we wanted to share our knowledge and help others.

Skinny Bitch delivers no-nonsense advice in a hyperbolic aggressive-intimate fashion, veering from camped-up abuse to empathy. Mirroring the authentic expert girlfriendship of *What Not to Wear*, it states that the girlfriends 'didn't write this book to make friends. We wrote this book to help women eat right' (Barnouin and Freedman, 2008, 12). In *Bun in the Oven* they aim, 'to give it to you straight. And if you can't take a little rough talk from two Skinny Bitches, then you aren't prepared to be a mother. 'Cause let's face it: kids can be little shits. So toughen up' (Barnouin and Freedman, 2008, 21). For *Skinny Bitch* the correct choices are vegan ones, and ones that eschew alcohol, caffeine, white flour, aspartame and sugar. It criticizes the US Food and Drug Administration (FDA), and the meat and dairy industries. Its tried and tested approach has 226 footnotes citing newspaper articles, books and websites to support its argument.

Skinniness equals cleanliness, purity, health, energy, success and happiness. Fatness (there is nothing in between) means sluggishness, humiliation, co-dependent relationships, self-loathing, being a moron and being 'hindered'. For example: 'Every time you put crap in your body, you are crap', and 'Of course it's easier to socialize after you've had a few drinks. But being a fat pig will hinder you, sober or drunk' (Barnouin and Freedman, 2005, 65 and 12). The body betrays what you eat, and what you eat determines your moral worth. Not surprisingly, food is polarized; it is either a 'vice' or 'healthy'. Fizzy drinks, for example, are 'liquid Satan'. Following this moral framework, the body is written through a religious rhetoric: 'Once you have given up the vice food, then your body will be healthy, clean and pure' (Barnouin and Freedman, 2005, 123). Moreover:

> You shouldn't put garbage in your mouth any sooner than you'd go to church wearing crotchless panties. Now granted, sometimes you wear less than your Sunday best to church, and that's fine – God

loves you, anyway. And sometimes you eat less than your best, and that's okay, too. But you wouldn't make a habit of dressing like crap for church and you shouldn't make a habit of eating crap either.

(Barnouin and Freedman, 2007, 181)

On the one hand, this is the ironic and bitchy language of popular culture. However, linked to its spiritualization of mothers – which I will discuss shortly – and its vegan ethos, this religious rhetoric becomes part of *Skinny Bitch*'s coercing strategy. Truth, health and the correct food choices become the new moral codes, and the fat pig becomes the symbol of bad or criminal choices that harm the earth and the self.

Health is a subjective category that can be understood in a social, rather than bio-medical form; what is considered healthy changes according to social context. In *Skinny Bitch*'s paradigm, health equates to skinniness and looking 'hot'. Because skinniness is popular culture's ideal body image, the reader's failure to be skinny is her failure to be normative. Moreover, *Skinny Bitch* places the responsibility for health on the individual. As Paula Black points out, the 'healthy lifestyle incorporates not only ideas about health or the absence of illness, but also a wider notion of body work and responsibility for health status' (Black, 2004, 164). How to define health is often associated with (middle class) experts. Indeed, health is an unstable marker and this instability renders consumers vulnerable. In other words, if we do not know how to achieve health, or if its parameters are constantly changing, then we are in thrall to the experts who will reveal these secrets. Because health is a cultural ideal, the inability to be healthy (depending on who is demarcating its term) is the failure to be normative. In his discussion of healthism, Rose argues that 'individuals are addressed on the assumption that they *want to be healthy*, and enjoined to freely seek out the ways of living most likely to promote their own health' (Rose, 1999, 86–87). As a consequence of this, they are rendered governable by media that promote health. Because being healthy is coded by the lifestyle industries as essential to acceptable conduct, employing the discourse of *health* is a powerful way to coerce readers into accepting *Skinny Bitch*'s diet choice and celebration of the skinny body.

This focus on self-responsibility, autonomy, crime and punishment reaches extremes in *Skinny Bitch*'s discussion of 'you are what you think'. Citing *Anatomy of the Spirit* by Dr Caroline Myss, *Skinny Bitch* gives the example of 'Julie', who was badly treated by her husband. Julie was diagnosed with breast and ovarian cancer that reflected 'her lack of self-love for her "womanhood" '. However, she did not leave her husband

and consequently died (Barnouin and Freedman, 2005, 189). 'Joanne', on the other hand, was also in an unhappy marriage and '[n]ot surprisingly, she developed breast cancer' (Barnouin and Freedman, 2005, 189). Because she left him, she recovered. Although *Skinny Bitch* tempers its claims, 'Of course, we are not suggesting that everyone suffering from a disease has brought it upon him or herself. We are, however, saying it is entirely possible to do so', there is a clear link here between lifestyle choice and punishment (Barnouin and Freedman, 2005, 189; Eichenbaum, 2010).

Skinny Bitch is described as 'our best-selling manifesto' and it adopts a feminist rhetoric in the fight against the food industries. Readers are assured that it is 'not some dumb, fluffy weight-loss book'. It is 'a well-researched exposé documenting the shady business surrounding what we eat' (Barnouin and Freedman, 2007, 11). Just as *What Not to Wear* recognizes and gains some of its emotive power from acknowledging that women sacrifice themselves for their family, so *Skinny Bitch* encourages women to start looking after number one. It employs the language of solidarity and identification, and invokes the political force of sisterhood to critique the apparatuses that are trying to dupe women into being fat.

What is significant here is that the destabilizing culture that induces us to let go into food and at the same time coerces us into being thin is tackled by *Skinny Bitch*. However, their strategy is to maintain the ideal of skinniness and encourage readers to consume differently in order to achieve this. There is no attempt to critique the regulation of body image. In addition, they construct sisterhood and solidarity as powerful forces that can be harnessed against the food industries in order to become thinner. As well as invoking guilt and punishment, science and health, *Skinny Bitch* promotes unity among women. Women are praised and exhorted, and the website encourages a positive female space: 'We love hearing from you, especially about your success stories!' *Bun in the Oven* is dedicated to 'mothers (especially single mothers), who are the unsung heroes of the world. And for our own mothers, with the deepest love and gratitude.' *Skinny Bitch* harnesses the power of *we*. This is the *we* of Barnouin and Freedman's friendship, but also the *we* of a wider belonging – that of the skinny woman. It is sisterhood in service to makeover.

However, the words *skinny* and *bitch* confer a lack of humanity and a fear of womanliness. Although *Skinny Bitch* admits (in a tone reminiscent of *Cougar Town* and Susannah of *What Not to Wear*), 'we have some fat, gross body parts, too. We're women', this equates womanhood with the grotesque (Barnouin and Freedman, 2005, 177). Fat is female, whereas being skinny – which is more desirable – transcends womanliness in favour of the bitch. Susan Bordo argues that slenderness is attractive because:

> On the one hand, the lean body represents a rejection of the fifties ideal of cuddly, reproductive womanhood, and an assertion of a post-feminist, non-domestic identity. On the other hand, the steadily shrinking space permitted the female body seemed expressive of discomfort with great female power and presence.
>
> (Bordo, 2003, xxi)

Although *Skinny Bitch* is assertive and confident in its message, it expresses a deep anxiety over woman's presence and, I would argue, the female libido. There is a fear over how the female reader conducts herself and whether she is presenting herself along normative lines. The brand insists on the fight to look good. Invoking female networks, they critique the pressures of contemporary society that make women eat bad food, get fat and feel worthless. Nevertheless, rather than fight for social change or expect ideals of body image to implode, they accept and celebrate the situation as it is. In addition, they put the responsibility for coping with stress on the reader, thus reducing what could be potentially political, to something personal. They invoke solidarity, not for cultural change, but to enable women to become 'prettier and prettier, skinnier and skinnier' (Barnouin and Freedman, 2005, 186).

Despite its deification of skinniness, *Skinny Bitch* assures its readers in a postscript that: 'We have a confession to make. We really couldn't care less about being skinny [...] our real hope is for you to become healthy' (Barnouin and Freedman, 2005, 224). However, their last word does not entirely convince as health has been equated with skinniness throughout the book. The readers are assured that '*Skinny Bitch* is the lifestyle we live [...] We devised the *Skinny Bitch* plan so we could have our cake and eat it!' In promoting skinniness and yet protesting that it could not care less, *Skinny Bitch* proves that it wants to have it all: an aspirational body and female self-acceptance; solidarity and misogyny. Freedman and Barnouin coined the title *Skinny Bitch* to market the book because it hooked into a collective anxiety over body image. However, on the last page they relinquish responsibility for this. Their sudden ideological turnaround is typical of postfeminist popular culture where hyperbolic or ironic statements can be detracted with a laugh. Nevertheless, irony gains its rhetorical impetus from a powerful and emotive discourse. In the case of *What Not to Wear* and *Skinny Bitch*, this is misogyny and, specifically, misogyny around the female body. The irony may evoke laughter, but the force of the discourse that underpins it continues to reverberate.

How to be a girl: Fearne and Holly

UK television and radio personalities Fearne Cotton and Holly Willoughby market their conduct book, *The Best Friends' Guide to Life*, across media platforms. In a promotional YouTube clip, they highlight the intimacy of their co-brand. Sitting affectionately on a sofa Holly reveals that the book is 'our perspective on friendship'. Fearne confesses that 'this is what, you know, our friendship is about'. The book is endorsed as an insight into their private lives, as well as delivering guidance in correct girlfriendship conduct. Holly and Fearne extend their intimacy to their consumers, promising that when they read it they will feel 'like you've got your mates around' (Fearne and Holly, YouTube, 2010). On Willoughby's website, Fearne states:

> It's always nice to know that your friends are going through the same thing as you so hopefully girls will read this and really relate to it and get something from it.
>
> (Holly Willoughby: the official website, 2010)

Their performance of friendship bestows their celebrification with the valuable branded attributes of authenticity and coherency. It exposes their humanity and steadfast girliness in an era of liquid love; their togetherness confers a postfeminist credibility. This hand of friendship extends to consumers through their manipulation of a convergence culture where their co-brand is promoted through a proliferation of social media, especially Twitter, Facebook and YouTube, as well as through magazines, and national and cable television. One of the effects of this is that consumers are sold the experience of being in control of the flow of Fearne and Holly's co-brand. Consumers can choose when, what and how they interact with Fearne and Holly, and this heightens how the co-brand is advertised and experienced as a social process.

Fearne and Holly are individual celebrity brands. Apparently ordinary women in their early 30s with high-profile and mainstream careers in media, they have expertise. Holly is a former model and family TV presenter. She has hosted children's shows, as well as *CD:UK*, *Dancing on Ice* (ITV, 2006–2011), *This Morning* (ITV, 2009–) and *The Voice* (BBC, 2012–).

Fearne hosts the late morning slot on BBC Radio 1 and has presented *Top of the Pops* (2004–2006) and *Red Nose Day* (2005–). Her career spans a variety of TV and radio shows, and she has also done high-profile celebrity charity work, including climbing Kilimanjaro and going to Uganda for *Comic Relief*. She has put her name to Boots' cosmetics. The celebrity personas the friends offer are ones of upbeat and girly-laddism. They can banter with the best of the boys, but they also capitalize on their sexuality and their girliness. They are professionals at self-commodifying and creating business models out of femininity. Because they negotiate the postfeminist landscape with apparent ease, they can guide women and girls through the processes of popular culture's normativity. In addition, their bodies are trafficked around a homosocial world of male consumers which means that they can offer advice and strategies for negotiating a mainstream male gaze. They perform apparently different (retro) femininities which give their branded personas normative distinctiveness. Holly is a sexy domestic goddess as she acts out the performativities of wife and mother. Fearne ostensibly refuses girliness by enacting the indie chick in her apparent promotion of non-mainstream music and her narrative of unsuitable boyfriends. This apparent transgression, especially when polarized against Holly, confers their co-brand with tantalizing differences within a normative paradigm.

Fearne and Holly's individual brands merge in the name of friendship and business. As well as co-hosting *Fearne and Holly Go Dating* (2007) and *Celebrity Juice* (2008–), they design clothes in collaboration with the high street fashion brand Very.co.uk. They appear in television advertisements together. For example, they both performed as friends in the 2011 Christmas campaign for Very.co.uk, as well as Imagine, which Holly describes as 'a range of video games for the Nintendo DS especially for young girls that we are the faces for' (*The Mirror* 14 August 2008). The narrative of their friendship is integral to their brand, and consequently photographs of their togetherness appear on their personal websites, on Facebook, Twitter and in interviews with the press. There is a gallery of photographs revealing 'behind the scenes' shots of the filming/photography at Very. *Cosmopolitan* did a photographic feature on their friendship. In an interview in *The Mirror* to promote *Celebrity Juice*, Fearne confesses:

> We clicked from day one and, living two minutes from each other, we spend a lot of time together, drinking tea, playing with our cats and talking non-stop.
>
> (*The Mirror* 14 August 2008)

They are keen to distinguish themselves from celebrities – who they interview – and their intimacy emphasizes the ways in which they are down to earth:

> From the outside both of us appear to have it all, the career, the fun, the glamorous lifestyle, but it doesn't mean we don't have the same worries and fears as everyone else.
>
> (Cotton and Willoughby, 2010, 252)

Their apparent ordinariness is conveyed through the way they tease each other on camera. For example, difference is highlighted in their conflicting dating strategies on *Fearne and Holly Go Dating*. Or in a *Daily Mail* interview, Holly confesses:

> She may be my best friend but when she interviewed Prince William and Prince Harry I have never been more jealous in my life. If it had been me I would've been totally bowled over but she managed to hold it together.
>
> (Taylor, *The Daily Mail*, 17 March 2012)

Their ordinariness is further consolidated through their appropriation of girly markers as Holly states in relation to Fearne's interview with the princes: 'I think as a girl, you can't help but fancy a prince, full stop' (*The Mirror* 14 August 2008).

Fearne and Holly negotiate a complex relationship with their consumers. They have to convey their ordinariness and simultaneously demarcate their branded exclusivity as aspirational and marketable products. They are dependent upon fans' and audiences' co-creation, but the technologies of PR and the socioeconomic status they hold as media icons mean that they hold the power in the co-dependent commercial relation. One of the ways that these unequal strategies of exchange are obfuscated is through the visual and audio signifiers of intimacy that convey emotion work. Arlie Russell Hochschild discusses how the private management of feeling is socially engineered and transformed into emotional labour for a wage (Hochschild, 1983, 2003, x). Heather Nunn and Anita Biressi develop this to explore how emotion work is central to the success of a celebrity and the cultivation of a successful brand. It is essential for public figures to forge relations of trust and emotional intimacy with their publics, and the celebrity is consumed through his or her ability to convey authentic feelings and be connective. Nunn and Biressi examine how an 'ideology of intimacy' is constructed, and argue that the social relationship between the celebrity and their public is considered real through the celebrity's commitment to inner psychological concerns (Nunn and Biressi, 2010, 54). This can be seen, for example, through the celebrity learning their lessons or overcoming a 'dysfunction' in their life narrative (Nunn and Biressi, 2010, 50). Neither Fearne nor Holly have dysfunctional celebrity narratives. Consequently, much of their emotion work is mediated through public displays of friendship. The production of celebrity intimacy is generated through Holly knowing the private thoughts and habits of Fearne, and vice versa. Their friendship is also emotional; it displays their vulnerable selves. Having a best friend provides material evidence of a private and feeling self. The ubiquitous photographs of Fearne and Holly hugging are tantalizing glimpses into a pseudo-private realm where the other is privy to 'the reality' behind the public masks. As Holly writes at the end of the book: 'we are who we are, and love each other truthfully' (Cotton and Willoughby, 2010, 276). A friend reveals a chink of humanity in the glossy armour of the celebrity and the consumer can identify both with the performance of friendship, and with the way in which this performance is central to the friends' public narratives.

Friendship harnesses the emotions that brands draw on: trust and loyalty. These emotions, which have been projected onto and which are absorbed by brands, are then reappropriated by celebrities like Fearne and Holly and reabsorbed as essential and sellable components of their human brand. In addition, celebrities harness social media to confer their mediated selves with added intimacy and to give their brand the qualities of authenticity and coherency. Whereas their Facebook pages and personal websites are polished, with professional photographs, Fearne and Holly's Twitter feeds promise more direct access to their private realms. The co-brands' girliness is sold through their updates as they Tweet photographs of their hair, nails and the cakes that they have baked. But Twitter also gives insights into their private lives. The apparently genuine interaction between the celebrity and her consumers was highlighted, for example, when Holly was criticized for misspelling her Tweets, and she retaliated by revealing to her followers that she was dyslexic.

Fans and consumers are given the impression of participating in their social and familial intimate network, albeit virtually. For example, Fearne follows her mother: Mumatron. In addition, when Holly underwent a two-day labour, fans followed. Phillip Schofield, who co-hosts *This Morning*, announced on air that the baby was on her way: 'First thing this morning I got a phone call from Holly saying she thought she might be in labour.' In order to keep her audience hooked, Holly kept updating: 'We are all like one huge expectant family!' (*Hello!*, April 2011). *Hello!* reported that: 'Holly's close friend, fellow TV presenter Fearne Cotton, added to the drama by posting a photo of herself visiting the hospital.' Once the baby was born, Holly tweeted: 'Thank you for all your support these last few days. Belle Baldwin finally arrived at 5:10pm today weighing 5lb 2oz. She's amazing.' Fearne tweeted: 'So happy for my Holly dolly! A gorgeous baby girl.' Here we can see how friendship and digital media combine to maintain an image of authentic intimacy.

Fearne and Holly's *The Best Friends' Guide to Life* is a re-mediated woman's magazine. It meshes a cultural strategy for promoting girl identity with tantalizing glimpses into the private realm of celebrity. Therapy or self-help merges with the lexicon of feminism, intimacy and girliness. Fearne and Holly are credited as the authors. However, they acknowledge Imogen Edwards-Jones who 'listened to all our endless rambling', and who is presumably the editor and partial ghostwriter (Cotton and Willoughby, 2010, 280). Fearne does most of the illustrations. The book is structured as if the reader is invited to an intimate dialogue. The initials F or H indicate who is speaking and there are non-italicized sentences or paragraphs that highlight the voice of a unified and coherent attachment. The book advises on the performance of girlfriendship through its visual signifiers, as well as its rhetoric. Its format is pink and the style mimics crumpled pages ripped from a school exercise book or diary.

The front cover portrays Fearne and Holly with their heads touching. Their sameness is exaggerated through their lipsticked smiles, big eyes, blue jeans and long dyed blonde hair. They are sitting as if in a teenager's bedroom, backgrounded with pastel blue wallpaper. There is a pervasive nostalgia that themes the text even though Fearne and Holly met as adults. There are photographs of them growing up, as well as portraits of family members. There are also photographs of the friends' togetherness that contribute to the authentic and coherent narrative of their intimacy. The readers are affectively included in the democratization of female aspiration. Fearne and Holly preface the book by stating:

> We are not telling you how to do anything! But we have made many mistakes and learnt quite a few lessons and we hope that by sharing them with you we might help you a bit on your own journey. We also hope that, while being helpful, this book might make you

laugh, entertain you, touch you and most of all that it might become a bit like talking to your very best friend.

(Cotton and Willoughby, 2010, 10)

Their rhetoric of care that reaches out to the reader in the language of inclusiveness harnesses the affect of close adolescent bonds. It is this pink cosiness of friendship that disguises the loving meanness of normativity. Fearne thanks the reader: 'Whether you're looking for advice, a laugh or just a mate, I hope you have found it here' (Cotton and Willoughby, 2010, 279). Holly adds, 'I hope it helps a little, growing up can be a bumpy ride' (Cotton and Willoughby, 2010, 281).

Fearne and Holly explain how to perform the normative but distinctive girlfriend. They obfuscate the language of strategy through using the trope of the cake. Just as self-branding business models break the self down into parts that need strategically managing, so the important components of the girlfriend lifestyle are divided into slices:

Your partner in crime
Your main squeeze
Nine to five
Home sweet home
Me, Myself and I

These denote friendships, boyfriends, work, domestic space and body, respectively. Female friendships come first, and are the most important part of a having-it-all lifestyle. Friends mirror the essential and authentic self, but friends can also be trusted in ways that men cannot. Moreover, friends can get you places and help you achieve ambitions, as Fearne relates: 'Our friendship is ever changing but the foundations remain the same. We have been able to achieve some wonderful things together with our clothing ranges, TV shows and now this book [...] Together we are united. Two is more powerful than one' (Cotton and Willoughby, 2010, 276). Although the book is packaged in doodles and girl talk, there is a rigorous strategic approach structuring the text. The two friends advise on the key to hypervisible success. The private psychological self becomes a performance (Illouz, 2007, 78). Its pink packaging and cupcake icing disguise a hard-nosed approach to postfeminist power.

The spectacular pinkness of the girl is not a return to an essentialized femininity; rather there is a strong performative aspect to this striving to become the embodiment of the teenager. Girlhood is sold as a consumer choice and a form of self-definition that indicates affluence and exclusivity. In an aggressive job market, the perfected girly self leverages a competitive edge. In addition, the girl glosses over an increasingly business-oriented approach to identity, and is effective in covering up what the branded spaces disavow: the strategic ways in which intimacy itself is being reconfigured. The colourful happiness of the girl functions to offset the punishing nature of neoliberal society, which then reconfigures her anxiety as personal. To be critical or to opt out of striving for attractiveness is to be melancholic and old. Indeed, it is no coincidence that the ubiquitous girl embodies the aspirational qualities sold by the pharmaceutical, beauty and wellbeing industries: health and happiness (Ahmed, 2007). These nebulous terms connote a middle class sense of self and an affluent lifestyle. They also contribute to the perception of an apparent erasure of labour. Refusal, rage or insecurity are coded as personal illnesses or pathological failings.

The performance of the girlfriend includes donning the masquerade of niceness. Both Holly and Fearne agree that it is important to be 'nice', to keep 'your head down' and 'be humble [...] no matter what you are feeling, from day one till the end of your days' (Cotton and Willoughby, 2010, 141, 150). In this way they enact the Manhattan Plastic Women's postfeminist masquerade that disguises an illegible rage, as will be discussed in Chapter 3. Fearne and Holly disseminate their expertise through the commercialization of emotion. They advise their readers on appropriate behaviour for the workplace. Holly confides:

> There are days when I feel a bit crap but I would never show that. Even if you are having problems, or there are people you don't get on with, you carry on and you don't let it affect your performance.
> (Cotton and Willoughby, 2010, 140)

They advise on not making enemies, working hard on a reputation, and not bringing personal problems into the workplace. Holly kills with kindness as it is 'very disarming' (Cotton and Willoughby, 2010, 150). Although melancholia, anger or depression are recognized as inevitable, to own up to this in public is prohibited. The attitude they recommend is aspirational and upbeat; it is Naomi Wolf's anti-victim power feminism. Fearne states that: 'I think it is crucial to believe in yourself because no one else is going to do it for you. If I believed all the negative stuff people said to me – that I wouldn't amount to anything, that I should stop dreaming – then I would never have got anywhere' (Cotton and Willoughby, 2010, 161). Entertaining failure is not a possibility.

Holly and Fearne are skilled at advertising their bodies in a commercial world marketed to male consumers. *FHM* calls Holly 'Willoughbooby' and she has appeared every year in *FHM*'s Sexiest Women since 2005. In 2007 she was voted in at 26 and in November 2008 she was on the front cover. The tagline to her photograph is: 'I love boys, I love talking to boys, I love flirting with boys.' The copy on *FHM*'s website admires the fact that she is 'super best friends with fellow early-morning totty Fearne Cotton':

> the former kids TV presenter has the sort of body and flirty character that make her an instant hit with the male of the species. She's even showered in public, stripping down in Trafalgar Square for a water saving initiative. No wonder then, that Holly Willoughby has made it into our World's Sexiest Women poll on three occasions. As if that weren't enough, her breasts have a happy habit of popping out at odd moments.
>
> (www.fhm.com)

Fearne might not aspire to Holly's sex symbol status but she does a turn in appearing in swimming costumes for charity and *FHM* approvingly notes:

> She's more H&M than Hermes, which somehow makes her seem all the more desirable, and the fact that she once told Jonathan Ross that she has 11 tattoos hidden away on her body only adds to the allure. Fun, feisty and just a little bit flirty, Fearne is exactly our kind of girl.
>
> (www.fhm.com)

Fearne and Holly are adept at receiving and playing to this ironic sexualizing banter. On 18 March 2011, as a result of listeners raising over £2 million, Fearne appears in a tiny swimming costume 'for all to see'. The Radio 1 DJ Chris Moyles appreciatively admires her figure and thanks 'that last rush of dirty old men like myself who are standing up for what they believe in. Sure they know it's wrong to stare but it's charity [...] stare away.' Fearne negotiates the performance with aplomb, saying playfully, 'stop looking, what are you looking at?' She feigns embarrassment – 'I don't know what to do with myself' – but hugs Chris and is her professional self as she says her long list of thank yous. She plays up to her sexiness with apparent modesty and acknowledges the importance of charity work (The Official Fearne Cotton Site).

The eroticization of Fearne and Holly's bodies in these media is jocular, self-deprecating and ironic. The male gaze is configured as slightly creepy but harmless. In *Celebrity Juice* Fearne and Holly cooperate in the show's sexual banter and are complicit in Keith Lemon's pseudo-lecherous performances while still maintaining their dignity as girlfriends. Indeed, the very fact of their friendship allows Keith full ironic sexism as the gendered power dynamic is undercut through the representation of two women and one man. Furthermore, the opening credits to *Fearne and Holly Go Dating* mirror a porn aesthetic through shots of clothed crotches, legs, breasts and pseudo-lesbian stares, which mimic the representation of girlfriendship for *FHM*'s male audience. Simultaneously, by portraying them as taller than the buildings that they walk through, the credits copy the 1958 B movie *Attack of the 50 Ft Woman*, which itself has been re-mediated through films, music videos and advertisements. The girlfriends' size highlights their power. Through this meshing of aesthetics, Fearne and Holly appeal to both a male and a female demographic. Indeed, Fearne and Holly are adept at crossing the gender difference of their audience with an apparently unprejudiced attitude. They dispense dating advice and care to both men and women and consequently demonstrate knowledge and expertise around heterosexual relations. Furthermore, by taking a pragmatic approach to their bodies as erotic capital and configuring male sexuality as harmless, they demonstrate to their female viewers how attracting the male gaze can leverage career ambitions. Through the strategic network of girlfriendship, the exploitation of the male gaze is a necessary (and fun) component in the trajectory towards postfeminist success.

'I have been the same weight since I was fourteen'

The girlfriends' bodies are disseminated through narratives of desire. But these narratives are directed at women as well as men. After all, the products they advertise and which are branded with their names are marketed to girls. However, even though their Facebook pages, Twitter and personal websites all offer their fans galleries of airbrushed photo shoots, both Fearne and Holly profess to be acutely aware of the celebrification of desirable bodies and 'how many unattainable, airbrushed, doctored images women get bombarded with' (Cotton and Willoughby, 2010, 236). Furthermore, 'diet and exercise are subjects that both of us feel quite strongly about' as there is such a 'pressure to be a size zero' (Cotton and Willoughby, 2010, 236). They especially blame the magazine industry for this destabilizing understanding of women's bodies. Nevertheless, their attitude to the body is remarkably similar to *Heat's*, as discussed in Chapter 1. That is, they employ morally charged phrases such as 'respecting yourself' and 'letting yourself go' while simultaneously positioning their own perfected bodies as normative and expert. They gloss this contradiction by articulating the postfeminist adage about health and happiness: 'both of us know that it's not about being thin, it is about being healthy' (Cotton and Willoughby, 2010, 236).

The phrase 'to let yourself go' has a moral focus in popular discourse. It implies a lack of self-responsibility and an inability to enact normative behaviours. It suggests the letting go of gendered and classed control, as well as loosening the tight reins of femininity, respectability and taste. One way that *Heat* (and Fearne and Holly) sidesteps the issue of class, sex, misogyny and fat is through the twin discourses of health and happiness. These are ideals that can sometimes trump skinniness. As discussed in Chapter 1, *Heat* celebrates Colleen's weight gain because she 'is looking healthier than ever'. The celebrities' happiness and health mean that their weight gain is acceptable. However, the way that the attributes of health and happiness are measured in contemporary culture, never mind in *Heat* magazine, is unsystematic. These qualities are yoked to a neoliberal market society that uses them as aspirational goals, and yet refuses to signify what they actually are, or consistently changes their parameters. It is a friendly and affective maternalism (or sisterliness) and the arbitrariness of these qualities means that health and happiness are effective policing strategies.

Fearne, in particular, states that she wants to put out a positive message about food. She professes that she is a vegetarian and eats well: 'I don't deny myself things. I eat chocolate and all that. AND I exercise properly. I have been the same weight since I was fourteen. But I have to make an effort to stay that way.' She exercises four to five times a week. Here, healthiness is equated with maintaining an adolescent body at the age of 30 and having the time and money to go to the gym five times a week. Extreme discipline is essential in the maintenance of normativity. Significantly, Fearne's body appears on a pro-anorexia website and is regarded as ideal for young women. Fearne expresses her horror at the use of her body in this way, but the conduct book's chapter on looks is typical of the postfeminist attitude towards beauty and thinness. The authors profess an awareness of the tyranny of skinniness and girlhood, but are complicit in conforming to its conventions. The section on the body is titled 'Me, Myself and I' and is subtitled 'The Inner You, You Time, Me Time, Taking Time Out, Health, Beauty, Space, Looking

After Yourself, Hobbies, Relaxing, Chilling, De-Stressing, Have a Good Lie Down':

> When all is said and done, you've got the bloke, the job, the pad and the pals, you should take a step back and a good look at yourself. You time, or me time, is important in this fast-moving world where we are expected to be all things to all people all the time. When everyone wants, expects, demands an answer to every question right now. So it is crucial to take a step back occasionally.
>
> (Cotton and Willoughby, 2010, 224)

The contradictions that they perpetuate around the ideal body are obfuscated by linking body image with relaxation and time for the self. It mimics the L'Oréal 'you're worth it' marketing campaign where cultivating erotic capital is branded as a selfish pleasure, but is actually a necessary component of postfeminist normativity.

In these conduct books, happiness is achieved through a homogeneous distinction. Consequently, there is no disjunct between appropriating the language of sisterhood and perpetuating body insecurity. Indeed, these processes of female intimacy are intricately bound up with the practices of normative cruelty. The girlfriends' regulation is necessary in conducting consumers into valid gendered identities. These BFF co-brands are high-profile media personalities who are well remunerated for their dissemination of body hatred through the rhetoric of solidarity. They may claim that they do not make the rules and that they are supporting women in achieving their goals. However, *if* they are the experts that they profess to be, then they must also be in a position to challenge the patriarchal normative laws. They hold power and agency as successful women and the fact that their careers are consolidated through the dissemination of misogyny obfuscated as friendship is highly problematic.

These best friend co-brands are the *Mean Girls* of contemporary girlfriend culture. Through denigrating female bodies and dictating the rules of success, they compete with other women. In the context of neoliberal postfeminism, where power is money, visibility and erotic capital, they (with)hold power. Indeed, they leverage it through dictating the conventions of normativity. Their success is based upon the performance of their expertise. Most women do not have the capital to follow up their advice. To go to the gym five times a week like Fearne, to eat *Skinny Bitch*'s bespoke vegan brands, or to shop for a whole new wardrobe like Trinny and Susannah, is for many women prohibitive.

By circulating their knowledge, the girlfriend co-brands extend the hand of friendship. But because these feminine practices are restricted to high-income demographics, they strengthen their power as media experts. In other words, through dictating the rules of neoliberal belonging and making them exclusive, they maintain unequal power structures among women. These self-identified BFFs wield a powerful regulatory force. Their conduct books advise the contemporary woman in performing normative femininities. They do this through framing themselves as girlfriend experts. They extend their bestfriendship to their readers and enjoin them to participate within their affective networks. They intersect the imagery and language of normative cruelties with the tropes of belonging, safety and pleasure associated with female friendship. Through this they participate in the neoliberal networks of control that structure girlfriend media. The girlfriends set up a site of female intimacy, but they do so in the service of the lifestyle industries that prefer women insecure so that they are more likely to buy into the technologies of transformation. The popularity of girlfriend culture demonstrates that consumers do privilege female friendships and feminine spaces. However, through the loving meanness of normative cruelties, which can be a very real and damaging element of women's experiences and relationships, they tap into women's vulnerability: Should I or should I not be a skinny bitch? Are they or are they not my friend? Is their advice to be trusted? Am I or am I not OK? Am I a fat pig? Or a white maggot? Through empathy and identification, through the *we* of friendship, these conduct books convey feminine understanding. Then, in the same spirit of friendliness, they offer the necessity of makeover.

Frenemies

Just as you can choose to eat vegan products that will make you skinny or wear dresses that disguise those monstrous bingo wings, so you can choose your friendship portfolio. And just as food can be devilish and make you fat, so friends can be toxic. Girlfriendship is strategic. Recent conduct books on friendship offer calculated guidance in the maintenance of social networks. They advise on 'decluttering' friends who will interfere negatively with your entrepreneurial self. These conduct books include Florence Isaacs' *Toxic Friends/True Friends: How Your Friendships Can Make or Break Your Health, Happiness, Family, and Career* (2003), Susan Shapiro Barash's *Toxic Friends: The Antidote to Women Stuck in Complicated Friendships* (2009) and Jan Yager's *When Friendship Hurts: How to Deal with Friends Who Betray, Abandon, or Wound You* (2002). There are also overtly strategic guides to sociality like Karen Eng's *Secrets & Confidences: The Complicated Truth About Women's Friendships* (2004) and Clea Hantman's *30 Days to Finding and Keeping Sassy Sidekicks and BFFs: A Friendship Field Guide* (2009).

Hantman's book is marketed to teenage girls but, like *Fearne and Holly: The Best Friend's Guide to Life*, it is intergenerational. It follows a business model through being practical, time-bound and outlining clear aims and objectives:

> Have you ever noticed that when you study with people who really get the material, you understand it better? The same goes for friends. When you are with people who are good at being friends, you become a better friend. Lousy friends drag you down, drain your soul, wear you out. You have the ability to choose which sorts you surround yourself with.

Friendship is allied with choice. The fact that you can be discerning about which friends you select is empowering:

> These choices make up our world and our experiences. You have the power to make good choices; you just need to be informed. What are you looking for in a friend? What means the most to you? What won't you put up with? What shouldn't you put up with?
>
> (Hantman, 2009, 2)

This is an overt example of the commercialization of friendship. It promotes a strategic accrual of social capital through the language of consumerism, and outlines a business-minded approach to managing intimacy.

Conduct books that address female friendship intersect the language of body makeover with emotional transformation. They commodify the experience of intimacy and offer expertise in women's friendships. Just as looks can be worked on, so can female sociality. Like clothes, friends can be de-cluttered, and this tidying up of emotional messiness can have an effect on the way you look. Andrea Lavinthal and Jessica Rozler's book *Friend or Frenemy: A Guide to the Friends You Need and the Ones You Don't* (2008) is a useful index of the mediated girlfriend culture that I am working with, both in the landscape that it identifies and in its sphere of address. The figure of the toxic friend or 'frenemy' is pervasive in girlfriend culture. She is 'part friend and part enemy, part passive and part aggressive. She's a shape-shifter, going from sweet to sour in the matter of a happy hour and she often leaves you with the same headache you get after having one too many two-for-one apple martinis' (Lavinthal and Rozler, 2008, 92). Lavinthal and Rozler advise that:

> Once you realize that you've flushed some toxins from your system, you'll redirect the guilt, learn how to be more positive, and focus some much-needed attention on the good people in your life.
>
> (Lavinthal and Rozler, 2008, 203)

Just as Samantha's belly is the grotesque consequence of a failing relationship in *Sex and the City 1*, so correcting your friendships can make you look better. Moreover, in a culture that values personal branding and strategic planning, the approach to friendships can mirror that of the consumer. You can be discerning about which women are in your life and can choose those who will visibly consolidate social capital. A girlfriend's friendship portfolio is her key to success.

Friend or Frenemy playfully extols the joys of female friends in a woman's life and bemoans the lack of 'rules' in making, keeping and ditching friends in an age of relocation and social media. Lavinthal and Rozler insist on the importance of creating a 'Framily' to counteract women's increasing isolation because, although it 'requires a lot more effort to stay in touch with your friends and keep those relationships alive than it used to', friends are more necessary than ever (Lavinthal and Rozler, 2008, xviii). The authors identify a contemporary 'friendship crisis'. They claim that people are more in touch on a global scale, and yet have become more personally detached. Maintaining that Facebook and 'the Crackberry' have created a new set of rules, regulations, norms and expectations around friendship, they advise on 'friendship maintenance', and offer guidance on making and breaking friendships.

The book is marketed to a cross section of women and girls, and the authors reference the pleasures of New York and American popular culture including, of course, *Sex and the City* (which they are keen to emphasize is not real). The girlfriends they celebrate range from celebrity duos like Paris Hilton and Nicole Richie, through to *The Hills* and The Spice Girls, particularly the track 'Wannabe'. They blur the line between real and virtual friendships by including Margaret Thatcher and Hillary Clinton in their 'Top Celeb Girl Crushes' list. The strategic advice they dispense is both practical and tongue in cheek; it promotes a reflexive (neoliberal) girlfriendship. Appropriating the format of conventional conduct books that advise on normative feminine behaviours in relation to men, they define problems in girl-on-girl relating, and give practical advice on 'How to Deal'. There are quizzes and an agony aunt called 'Ms Friendship Manners'. Interspersed with their irreverent postfeminist wisecracks, they outline strategies on 'diversifying your friend portfolio' to make you 'a more well-rounded person' (Lavinthal and Rozler, 2008, 138). They also suggest ways to balance friendship and coupledom; how to get back with friends after you have ditched them for a boyfriend; and how to negotiate three-way friendships.

Even the authors of *Skinny Bitch* advise on how to relate to women, particularly how to transform negative emotions into entrepreneurial success. They suggest using the energy of envy as a means to get skinnier:

> You know how you feel when a tall, thin, pretty woman walks by and something inside you wants to say, 'That skinny bitch!'? The book takes that envy and anger and gives you a new place to put it.
>
> (*New York Times*, 2 January 2008)

They also recommend, 'Don't be insecure or competitive or feel threatened by women who are thinner or prettier than you. Be happy for them; it will make you look better' (Barnouin and Freedman, 2005, 186). Participating in their co-brand means that envy (and its attendant shame) will be transmogrified into the desire and inspiration to become skinnier and skinnier (and bitchier and bitchier?). A so-called toxic emotion becomes a value that will make you prettier. Indeed, this may have been the inspiration behind *Thinspiration*, which celebrates *Skinny Bitch* as a guide and mentor. The affects of envy are often evoked in celebrity culture in order to generate aspirational forms of consumption, particularly around the body (Holmes and Redmond, 2006, 122). We can see this played out, for example, on the pro-anorexia site that uses Fearne's 30-going-on-14-year-old body as desirable. As Apter observes, there 'is a thin line between admiration ('I think she's wonderful') and envy ('I want to be like her, but I'm not'). As we admire someone, we compare ourselves to her – and that comparison can hurt' (Apter, 1999, 213). The combination of the democratization of celebrity with the intimate rhetoric of friendship, as well as the commercialization of these relations, means that girls are compelled to identify with figures like Fearne and Holly.

Much of the advice generated in these co-branded self-help conduct books is about relating with women in work. Indeed, as more and more women enter the market place, it seems that they are looking for guidance on to how to engage with women in power as well as how to hold power themselves. If we are experiencing 'The End of Men' as Hannah Rosin (2012) argues, then we need to know how to relate to women in the workplace. Women are learning how to interact with other women and how to find *themselves* (as well as to consolidate their careers) through watching and experiencing how other women relate. Friendship or female sociality is being reassessed in contemporary neoliberal global North economies, and the proliferation of self-help books around friendship is a response to this niche market. In an article in *Businessweek*, Liz Ryan discusses the prevalence of frenemies at work due to increasingly informal environments and 'the abundance of very close, intertwined relationships that bridge professional and personal lives' (Ryan, 2007). According to Ryan, people have less inclination to develop friendships outside work. Indeed, it is indicative of 'the merge' as identified by Rosin and which I discuss further in Chapter 3.

Both Fearne and Holly, and Lavinthal and Rozler, examine women in the workplace and advise on how to cope with its feminization. Work relationships between women are conceived as fraught. The site of women's paid labour proliferates with 'Worker Bee-otches' (Lavinthal and Rozler, 2008, 78). Fearne and Holly ask, rather flippantly and unhelpfully, 'WORKING WITH OTHER WOMEN – DOES THE SISTERHOOD EXIST?' Situating the contemporary workplace in a feminist context, Fearne and Holly admit that 'the [feminist] battle has been long and hard' and that they are the privileged inheritors of their foremothers:

> Men still earn more than women even when they are in exactly the same jobs. And given the jobs that both of us do, on-screen female talent isn't treated the same, doesn't get paid the same and also doesn't last as long (it gets traded in for a younger, firmer model).

They gloss over this by retreating into the language of choice. Holly chirps: 'The choices are all there for us if we want them' (Cotton and Willoughby, 2010, 153).

Holly and Fearne both testify to experiences of women stepping on other women on their way up: 'we know that for some women, their worst enemy can be their fellow sister just across the table' (Cotton and Willoughby, 2010, 153). Fearne argues that women compare themselves at work more than men do, but warns that you shouldn't take the bait.

Although she states that men in a work context can be 'difficult and unpleasant', it is women who are constructed through the language of power, whether this is positive or cruel. Holly likes 'a big powerful woman boss. I am very happy to play second fiddle to her. I get on well with women. I am not a pushover. I am just a bit more silent at getting my own way'. Nevertheless, she relates the time when a female colleague was 'getting at me because of my weight' (Cotton and Willoughby, 2010, 154). What is interesting here is the way in which they reveal competition between women to be rife and yet, through their strategic BFF sisterhood, they appear to opt out of this power struggle.

According to Fearne and Holly, women make more complex and competitive colleagues, whereas men 'don't care so much'. Holly reveals:

> You can use your femininity to your advantage as well. You can keep your cards close to your chest and take a while to play them because men always underestimate you. Sometimes men can be quite stupid.
>
> (Cotton and Willoughby, 2010, 154)

Underneath Holly's feminine masquerade is a disdain towards men. What is intriguing about Holly and Fearne's assessment of sisterhood in the workplace is how they attribute power to women, and configure men as 'quite stupid'. Despite exposing gender inequalities along the lines of pay and promotion, they perceive women as wielding a complex emotional dominance. Through presenting men as a bit dim and women as influential (and sometimes cruel) they embody an illegible rage. They veil their own anger about sexism in the workplace through infantilizing their male colleagues while simultaneously demonizing women through highlighting the dynamic of female competition. Knowing that she is treated as a lesser citizen in relation to her male work colleagues, Holly refuses to critique political realities. Instead, she harnesses her erotic capital through adopting the masquerade of girliness, and consequently using femininity to her 'advantage'. In this way she disempowers other women as access to this masquerade is exclusive. Men in girlfriend culture are a foil to women's own lack of power. In addition, indignation over the tyranny of body image and unequal pay is rerouted as patronizing contempt towards 'stupid' men. Holly and Fearne retreat into the sphere of girlfriendship, where discontent over injustice and male power is redirected towards their bodies and the bodies of other women. The next chapter takes this identification of an illegible rage further to examine the strategic sisterhoods of US television.

3
Strategic Sisterhoods

The new power babe wanted to be around other powerful women. They wanted women to be ruling the world, not men.

(Bushnell, *Lipstick Jungle*, 2005, 333)

In a 2009 *Guardian* feature showcasing ten 'Icons of the Decade', Naomi Wolf celebrates *Sex and the City*'s Carrie Bradshaw, asking whether she 'did as much to shift the culture around certain women's issues as real-life feminist groundbreakers?'

I stepped into a restaurant in New York – and in brushed a woman in big sunglasses and crazy boots, who warmly greeted the staff in a manner so familiar to me I smiled instinctively. I thought it must be a friend of mine. Well, I wasn't completely wrong. Actually, it was Sarah Jessica Parker, a stranger. Yet every woman in the room reacted with a similar happy, gut familiarity.

Why? Not because of the actor – because of the character. Because we had all heard Carrie's stories from our own girlfriends, and recognised in her something of our best selves. Hey girlfriend!

(Wolf, 2009)

Wolf positions Carrie as a feminist icon, and the show as strikingly progressive. Her response to Sarah Jessica Parker is one of affect; the celebrity provokes a visceral and emotional reaction, a 'gut familiarity', which unites women. Their personal investment in the figure of Carrie, a character who is scripted as defining her friends as essential to her subjectivity, inspires trust, connectivity and the quasi-spiritual 'best selves'.

In her *Guardian* article, Wolf politicizes Carrie because the character legitimates female sociality through her hyperglamorous representations. The pleasures of women talking about their sexual and emotional lives were, at one time, relegated to sites of invisibility and therefore lacked legitimacy. However, as the market constantly seeks new spaces and new markets in which 'to extend its lines of flight' (Deleuze and Guattari, [1980] 2004), so female friendships have been deemed valuable and worthy of representation. HBO's spectacle of intimate female relationships in *Sex and the City* (HBO, 1998–2004) was a particularly successful business venture. What previously might have been imagined as shameful – women's intimacy – has now been commodified, reproduced and celebrated. Wolf locates herself, the women in the room, and the figure of Carrie who could be 'a friend of mine' in a restaurant in New York. It is presumably a high-end establishment frequented by celebrities. Commercial space here, like the shows discussed in this chapter, become troped through liberal feminist rhetoric, female sociality and affluence.

Sex and the City, Lipstick Jungle (NBC, Living TV, 2008–2009) and *Cashmere Mafia* (ABC, 2008) are Manhattan dramedies. Part comedy, part drama, they are located within the branded cultures of Manhattan. In the final section of this chapter, I look at *The L Word* (Showtime, Living TV, 2004–2009) which I argue repurposes and relocates the heteronormativity of the straight white strategic sisterhoods in the commercial spaces of LA. In these shows the corporate world is reproduced, not only as women-friendly, but as explicitly female. The offices, boardrooms, shops, restaurants, gyms, cafes, clubs, bars and sidewalks are represented through networks of women as they socialize through a branded commodity culture. The commercial structures are the mise-en-scène; they enable, enact and legitimate sociality. Moreover, it is a segregated landscape that prefigures Hanna Rosin's survey of the American workforce in *End of Men*. It is a topography where men are desperate and women hold the power. As Rosin argues, 'In 2009, for the first time in American history, the balance of the workforce tipped toward women, who continue to occupy half the nation's jobs' (Rosin, 2012, 4). It is a workforce that has the power to spend. The fetishized and segregated landscape is portrayed as hedonistic and spiritual: shopping for shoes becomes, as one of the characters from *Lipstick Jungle* notes ironically, 'a religious experience' ('Pink Poison' 1:3).

Girlfriendships are constructed as social capital, and the feminine self is produced as a self-brand. Although men appear as lovers, husbands, colleagues, bosses, waiters, it is the female interactions – predominantly cooperative and sociable – that are the visual and emotive focus. These girlfriendships are strategic as the women support each other in the mutual maintenance of hypervisible and affluent postfeminist identities. The women evidence the super breed of 'Plastic Women' identified by Rosin:

> Studies that track women after they get their MBAs have even uncovered a superbreed of Plastic Women: They earn more than single women and just as much as the men. They are the women who have children but choose to take no time off work. They are the mutant creature our society now rewards the most – the one who can simultaneously handle the old male and female responsibilities without missing a beat.
>
> (Rosin, 2012, 8)

In a world where men are represented as emotionally and professionally incompetent, loyal friends are crucial in having it all: the high-powered corporate career, Fendi, Valentino, luminous skin, showcase apartments, personal offices with swivel leather chairs – and children. Girlfriends are necessary in the successful merge of public and private, career and emotions; they ensure that the self as competitive project is running successfully in all spheres. Moreover, the representation of their friendship is the emotional insight needed to penetrate the plasticity of the corporate world's 'mutant creatures' (Rosin, 2012, 8). And, as I argue below, prohibition of homosexual desire is key to their girlfriend reflexivity.

Girlfriend reflexivity: *Sex and the City*

Sex and the City is a television series (with two feature films) that focuses on four girlfriends in their 30s and 40s: Charlotte York (Kristin Davis), Miranda Hobbes (Cynthia Nixon), Carrie Bradshaw and Samantha Jones (Kim Cattrall). We know the characters through their processes of social consumption, whether this is talking about sex over lattes in the Union Square Coffee Shop, shopping in Jimmy Choo, or having beauty treatments in the Helena Rubenstein Beauty Gallery. We are attuned to the girlfriends' conversations and Carrie's voiceover in order to follow the plot. It is through their sociality that the narrative is revealed: who is having sex with whom and how. Together they relate their mistakes, weigh them up, and make sense of their emotions, relationships and aspirations. They validate each other's lives and identities through what Miranda calls 'girl talk' ('Pick-a-Little, Talk-a-Little' 6:4).

In the first episode of the second season, 'Take Me Out to the Ballgame', the four girlfriends discuss sex over breakfast. Carrie has just ended a year-long relationship with 'Mr Big' and she is confessing her broken heart. Miranda tries to steer the conversation away from men: 'Why are we still talking about him? He hurt her. He's out of the picture. Let's talk about something else.' She is interrupted by Charlotte who reveals that 'there's something wrong with my boyfriend', and then relates how her new date keeps touching his testicles. Carrie and Samantha humorously speculate that this is because they are too long. Miranda is outraged:

> That's it. I'm out of here. All we talk about anymore is Big or balls or small dicks. How does it happen that four such smart women have nothing to talk about but boyfriends [...] it's like seventh grade with bank accounts. What about us? What we think, we feel, we know. Christ! Does it always have to be about them? [...] Give me a call when you're ready to talk about something else besides men for a change.
>
> ('Take Me Out to the Ballgame' 2:1)

Leaving the restaurant, she dons a bright blue hat that matches her big blue puffa jacket. For the rest of the episode – and to complement her belief that 'she was the only person in New York with any real perspective on men' – she is depicted like a pre-pubescent boy wearing dungarees and white trainers.

Later that evening, Carrie sees Mr Big in a bar and breaks down in front of a new date. She makes an emotional phone call, sobbing, 'I know that things aren't good', and asking to meet at 'our place'. We are provoked into believing that she has phoned a man. However, it transpires that she has arranged to meet Miranda, and the episode ends with the girlfriends talking about sex and men over French fries. Miranda confesses that she bumped into an ex-boyfriend with his new wife. She confides how she was struck with panic, remembering the pain that she suffered when they broke up. She tells Carrie to take all the time that she needs to get over Mr Big. To coincide with her reassimilation into girl talk, Miranda has capitulated her dungarees for a more feminine purple top and is back in the convivial atmosphere of a restaurant. It is only once she acknowledges that discussing men is central to her emotional life, that she is able to regain her heterosexual visibility.

Postfeminist identities are difficult to enable, but they are represented as lucrative. *Sex and the City* reveals how it is impossible to succeed without one's girlfriends. At the end of the same episode, Carrie's voiceover asserts that the most important break-up rule is to remember that 'you'll never get through it without your friends'. Girlfriends are essential in negotiating the emotional difficulties generated when relating with men; difficulties that might make a girlfriend lose her visibility. She might become too emotional and cry in front of her date, just as Carrie does, or she might make bad fashion choices like Miranda. Significantly, as I argue below, repeatedly talking about men is necessary to the construction and preservation of heterosexual subjectivities. Despite the most consistent and loving relationships throughout the series being between girlfriends, conversations about men are central to their sociality. Indeed, it is through these conversations that they are able to contain and manage their emotions, and consequently maintain their poise and femininity. Because incoherency and rage are indicators of victimhood, and serenity is an essential component of the ideal postfeminist woman (Negra, 2009), so girlfriends need to support each other in working through and controlling any potential abjection. As Carrie tells Samantha: 'angry women are scary' ('The Post-It Always Sticks Twice' 6:7).

Monitoring emotions is part of the girlfriends' management of their entrepreneurial and feminine selves. These selves are produced through girl talk but also through the wider practices of 'girlfriend reflexivity'. Anthony Giddens and Nikolas Rose identify the contemporary self as a project. According to Giddens (1991), the self is 'made'; it is an undertaking that is continuously worked and reflected upon. The made self is produced through a reflexive understanding of one's biography that is created, monitored and revised through sets of narratives that explain one to oneself as well as to others. Rose develops this understanding of the self as a project through a Foucauldian framework. He argues that shifts in modes of governance mean that citizens are made accountable for their own regulation. In particular, subjects are expected to assume a reflexive selfhood through which they must constantly invent themselves in response to the labour market. As traditional institutions are erased, so the focus is on the self as an entrepreneurial subject (Rose, 1996). In *Sex and the City*, the four girlfriends confess their intimate lives to each other. They communally reflect, work on, revise and monitor each other's life narratives. It is through their girl talk that they understand each other and themselves as successful postfeminist subjects.

Girlfriends control each other's emotions. Lisa Blackman, in her discussion of self-help media, identifies the importance of correctly processing feelings in postfeminist culture. She argues that women are encouraged 'to engage in emotional practices that produce them as feminine subjects who are capable of emotional detachment from others'. However, they are simultaneously expected to remain open to heterosexual relationships (Blackman, 2004, 228). In girlfriend media women strategically manage feelings among themselves through girl talk, which provides a site for venting. This renders girlfriends low maintenance and unthreatening to men because they can handle and work through their emotions elsewhere. It is through the practices of girl talk that they learn to be composed, open and nurturing, while simultaneously maintaining self-sufficiency. Controlling emotions through female sociality renders the girlfriends capable of successfully negotiating heterosexual attachments.

Social capital

Carrie has the right kind of friends. They constitute her social capital. According to Bourdieu, cultural capital is relational and cannot be understood without the other forms, particularly social capital. Social capital is made up of developed (or inherited) social networks that can increase an individual's status and power within society (Bourdieu, 1984). In the context of the Manhattan dramedies this is 'the sum of the resources' that accrue to each girlfriend 'by virtue of possessing a durable network of more or less institutionalized relationships of mutual acquaintance and recognition' (Bourdieu and Wacquant, 1992, 119). Girlfriends are invested in the strategic sisterhood and this means that at its heart lies a network of exchange. Charlotte gives Carrie the money for a down payment when Carrie is forced to move out of her rent-controlled apartment after a break-up. For the price of 'two martinis', Samantha becomes Carrie's publicist for the promotion of her book launch and transforms it into a glamorous, celebrity event. Miranda gives her girlfriends free and essential legal advice. They all maintain and police each other's postfeminist visibility, as well as developing each other's social networks. The girlfriends' togetherness intersects with promotional strategies as they ensure each other's distinctiveness within the normative paradigm of their friendship.

This is particularly evident in the way the girlfriends cultivate each other's entrepreneurial selves through the monitoring of emotion. Illouz (1997) maintains that as capital enters more private domains, the ability to talk about one's emotions becomes a value statement about one's capacity to function successfully in a neoliberal society. She argues that the 1900s saw new forms of intimacy emerging that were based on talking about love within the context of a marriage. This talk was a means for middle class women to manage their sexuality and economic status, as well as being a vehicle through which to reveal themselves to the male other. Illouz argues that emotions were consequently extracted from the inner life and commodified for use as a therapeutic self-reflexive tool (Illouz, 2007, 26). We can see these practices of extraction and commodification taking place through the girlfriends' conviviality as they confess their intimacies to each other. Significantly, Illouz maintains that the correct management of emotions became overtly linked to systems of exchange and business as this model of emotion talk was appropriated by corporations through new systems of management that tapped into and mobilized the emotional resources of service workers. To evidence the ability to speak about emotions in the prevalent language of psychology became a marker of social mobility. The ability to commodify one's experiences of heterosexual intimacy and to speak of them through a therapeutic model became evidence of correct sociality.

The *Sex and the City* girlfriends know how to be emotional. Or rather, they know how to commodify their emotions in the correct conduct of affluent heterosexual subjectivities. In an image-based popular culture, to be seen is to be valorized and so Miranda's questionable sartorial choices (discussed above) reveal how talking about men is explicitly linked to being hypervisible. As soon as Miranda gives up conversing about heterosexual sex with her girlfriends, she surrenders her feminine representability. It is not so much talking about sex that is abject in this television series; rather it is *not* talking about sex that reveals a girlfriend's victimhood. Refusing to put men at the centre of one's social discourse exposes the failure to reproduce sexual desire as erotic capital. It exposes a girlfriend's inability to navigate a social landscape where her entrepreneurial success is manifest in the self-brand.

Carrie Bradshaw as self-brand

Girlfriend reflexivity is intricately bound up with where and how the girlfriends socialize. This could be the Magnolia bakery where Miranda and Carrie share cupcakes, or it could be the designer labels like Gucci which they covet together. Brands and branded spaces confer wholeness on the girlfriends in contrast to men, who are destabilizing. They are linked to the powers of healing and, significantly, Carrie often makes the links between therapy and buying shoes. Indeed, the girlfriends relate through appropriating the myths associated with successful brands. Their reflexivity is produced through what Ellis Cashmore (2006) terms 'brand integration' in a franchise that is notorious for its product placement: Manolo Blahnik, Dolce and Gabbana, Prada, Perrier water, as well as other high-end goods. This includes the site of Manhattan that is landscaped as the global centre of fashion. Indeed, certain brands such as Stella McCartney and Vogue connote the signifiers of postfeminist success such as enablement, empowerment and entitlement. By interacting with and through these brands the girlfriends are healed and contained by such meanings.

The healing power of brands extends to the self-brands that the girlfriends create through their reflexivity. Self-branding resolves anxieties around being a fragmented and incoherent feminine self, and glosses over divisions created through uncontrolled emotions or abject bodies. The processes of self-branding are particularly manifest in the character of Carrie, whose private life merges with her professional life. Carrie's visibility is intricately tied up with brands, whether this is the branded spheres through which she is made visible or those that she consumes, but she also produces herself (through her girlfriends) as a visible celebrity brand. Alison Hearn maintains that self-branding 'involves the construction of a meta-narrative and meta-image of the self through the use of cultural meanings and images drawn from the narrative and visual codes of the mainstream cultural industries' (Hearn, 2008, 194). The character of Carrie vacuums up cultural signifiers as part of her self-narrative. She is constituted through ideologies of girl power, 'boho chic', as well as the myths surrounding the intellectual position of the writer (Arthurs, 2004). A connoisseur of promoting a normatively distinctive and quirky sartorial look, she is a cultural sign denoting feminine success, glamour and authenticity. Carrie also successfully cultivates youth as a sign of her affluence. She is frequently represented in her bedroom in the postfeminist masquerade of an adolescent girl writing in her diary and sharing her most intimate thoughts about her girlfriends and romance. The recurring image of Carrie at her window mirrors a princess in a fairytale castle.

Carrie skilfully and coherently commodifies her assets – sexuality, body, emotions, girlfriendships – for consumption in a newspaper column for the fictional *New York Star*. She makes a living out of girlfriend reflexivity. Although the series occasionally pokes fun at her minor celebrity status, Carrie is a figure of entrepreneurial aspiration both within the TV series and for viewers. Her intimacy (and that of her girlfriends) is her asset. She successfully manages her emotions by objectifying them and turning them into capital. Indeed, she is highly effective at constructing and profiting from 'the therapeutic narrative of self-realization' (Illouz, 2007, 48). Carrie's column is intricately tied up with her private life and her public self-brand – both of which merge. In the episode 'Unoriginal Sin' she experiences a dating dry spell and therefore has nothing to write about in her column; she is unable to turn 'pain into gold' ('Unoriginal Sin' 5:2). Her image is plastered on the sides of buses to promote her column, and her body also appears in *Vogue* and on the front cover of the book that she eventually publishes in season 6. Through this merging of the public and the private, through professionalizing her intimacy, Carrie's sexuality is freed from its traditional feminine dependency on the marriage market. Consequently, she is paid and accumulates celebrity status through her ability to speak in a particularly aspirational discourse about sex. Her success in commodifying and analysing her emotions according to prevalent models of therapy, and her ability to turn them into a lucrative form of communication, reveals her empowerment in a market economy.

Carrie's consistent self-brand is constituted through a group of women friends who maintain her normativity through their networks of surveillance. They also render her distinctive. Having a friendship group of diverse women means that each girlfriend can have a coherent identity. Each girlfriend acts out a sexual identity that is reflected in their different hair colour: brunette Charlotte is a romanticist, blonde Samantha only wants sex; red-haired Miranda is ambitious. Indeed, they all act out parts of Carrie, who is the most well rounded of the four. They police each other to make sure that each retains their different personality but they always locate this difference within a normative paradigm. In the episode 'Frenemies' Charlotte and Samantha fall out as Charlotte is offended by Samantha's approach to sex: 'You can't just sleep with any guy!' she cries ('Frenemies' 3:16). Through the course of the episode, each character explores her distinctive self-brand. Samantha spends time with a woman who is more sexually open than her and Charlotte rekindles her friendship with prudish women. However, face to face with exaggerated versions of themselves, they realize that they have transgressed too far. It is only when they retreat back to the normative boundaries of their friendship group (and sexual conduct) that they can reunite as girlfriends.

Carrie's success as an entrepreneurial project in a homosocial world of women provokes Wolf into declaring a fictional character a feminist icon. Wolf divides Parker (who leaves little impression on her) from Carrie, and this privileging of a fictionalized femininity over an embodied woman reveals much about the centrality of the branded and coherent self in Wolf's construction of 'power feminism' (which I discuss below). After all, the character of Carrie is the output of a collaboration between writers, makeup artists, designers, directors, producers, brands and the actor herself. In a popular culture that seeks a coherent life narrative, real people can be too inconsistent. One of the inconveniences of being a celebrity is that the myths that are constructed around the human brand can be erratic and Parker's lack of coherency makes her a problematic feminist icon. Whereas Carrie is a knowable figure, the various characters that Parker plays, as well as her advertising contracts and public interviews (not to speak of the way that she is over-identified with Carrie), means that she is difficult to fix.

Moreover, Parker is mother of three. In interviews, she disassociates herself from Carrie's sexual play. The self that Parker performs highlights her private domestic life, which is tightly bound up with her husband. Her public persona is not consolidated through a friendship cohort in the same way as, for example, Courtney Cox and Jennifer Aniston, or Fearne Cotton and Holly Willoughby. The October 2000 issue of *People* describes Parker as 'nothing like Carrie', and as 'squeaky clean, happily married, and ready for kids'. In a June 2000 interview for *The Los Angeles Times*, Parker admits, 'I don't think I could live the way she lives'. She states in *Vogue* that 'as a mother – and as somebody whose schedule isn't always my own – I don't shop a lot, or think about clothes a lot' (14 September 2011). Although Parker echoes some of Carrie's bourgeois bohemian gestures in *Failure to Launch* (2006), in *I Don't Know How She Does It* (2011) she is a powerful (if ditzy) lawyer, and in *The Family Stone* (2005) she is a neurotic bigot.

Because she summons the values of trust and girlfriend expertise in consumers, the figure of Carrie as performed by Parker is harnessed to give other brands added value. The character's success at girlification and self-branding is yoked, through Parker, to other brands. For example, she was the face of Gap from 2004–2005. Gap's campaign, with the strapline 'How do you wear it?', portrayed differently attired versions of Parker. This marketing strategy referenced Carrie's frequent fashion reinventions, as well as pointing up the slippages between the celebrity and the character. The spring campaign represented her singing 'I like being a girl' and wearing Gap's 'pretty khaki'. Here, Parker overtly performs the girl-woman Carrie. However, Gap soon replaced her with the more distinctively girly body of the British 17-year old singer, Joss Stone.

Parker had outgrown the (post)feminist icon she performed, and which consolidated her career.

Plastic women: *Lipstick Jungle*

In *Fire with Fire: New Female Power and How it Will Change the Twenty-First Century* (1993) Wolf maintains that women should reconfigure the way they relate. She argues that they should support each other in pooling resources and creating possibilities in the market. Her feminism is enabled through crossing women's challenges to patriarchy with the logic of business in order to form 'power feminism'. In particular, she addresses the 'psychological problems women have about getting and using power' (Wolf, 1993, 300). To overcome women's habits of self-sacrifice – or hoarding power – she privileges networking groups where women can share resources and contacts. The impetus behind this is to encourage women to mobilize female networks in finding and accumulating capital; it is feminism driven by a desire for economic equality between the sexes. Wolf suggests that these resource groups would be modelled on old boys' networks, and the possibilities of success therein. However, these networks would also have the feminine attributes of fun and sociability. Consequently, feminism could generate wealth, while still maintaining feminine cultures and the quality of friendship.

Girlfriendships are a business investment and intimate connections are created in order to cultivate and consolidate a feminine power cohort in Manhattan. Girlfriends relate through an exaggerated and neoliberal version of Wolf's power feminism. They combine her reconfiguration of the old boy's network with branding cultures, and the power of erotic capital and its attendant hypervisibility. They are examples of pooling resources, creating possibilities, challenging patriarchy, networking and sharing contacts. Wolf suggests that feminists should reconfigure the technologies of power through the framework of friendship. This would ease women's anxieties over managing power as it would be shared. In addition, it would enable women to retain their feminine skills set within the traditionally masculine world of business. They would be able to maintain the attributes of care, fun and pleasure that are conventionally associated with femininity. Moreover, Wolf advises that the rhetoric among women should be less 'Troubles' and more 'Possibility talk'. Instead of complaining about their inferior status in relation to men, women should converse through the language of aspiration. This shift, according to Wolf, will change the way that women behave in groups (Wolf, 1993, 300). The move from discourses of victimhood into possibility in relation to market logics will, ideally, encourage women to perceive each other differently. Women will interact and view each other more as 'resources and repositories of power' or 'comrades in strategy', than 'threatening competitors (or sentimentalized "sisters")' (Wolf, 1993, 301).

Candace Bushnell, author of *Lipstick Jungle* (2005), was also executive producer of the TV series *Lipstick Jungle* for NBC. Her website describes the show as 'what the ladies on *Sex and the City* might have been like, had they been married characters rather than New York singletons' (www.candacebushnell.com). *Lipstick Jungle* centres on three glamorous girlfriends dressed in Jimmy Choo and Dior: Nico O'Neilly (Kim Raver), Wendy Healy (Brooke Shields) and Victory Ford (Lindsay Price). Nico and Wendy are married and Wendy has children, which means that much of *Lipstick Jungle* eschews the hopeful narrative of the heterosexual romantic dream. Although men, intimacy and sex are core themes, they are primarily situated within the context of an ongoing relationship or marriage. The characters are struggling to negotiate their happy ever after. Although love affairs proliferate, it is the stress of doing it all (and potentially losing it all) in a corporate world that drives the plot. Indeed, much of the series is about puncturing the romantic dream and relying on friends to support them in their inevitable disappointment.

The first episode opens with a montage of the three girlfriends dressing, which is typical of romantic comedies and chick flicks, where the designer labels are just as central as the women wearing them. Set against the women walking to work, a newsreader announces *Wall Street* magazine's list of New York's 50 most powerful women:

Wendy Healy, the president of Parador Pictures, is number 12 on the list. And moving up from 25 on last year's list, is Nico O'Neilly, the editor-in-chief of *Bonfire* magazine. At the bottom of the list is fashion designer Victory Ford, who barely made the cut after stumbling at last year's Fashion Week.

Wendy drops her crocodile skin purse, the contents fall out, she catches her hair in her mouth. Like the opening credits of *Sex and the City*, this reveals the vulnerable woman behind the projected image in order to incite recognition between the viewer and the character. This puncturing of the aestheticized image was crucial in the creation of a fan base in *Sex and the City*; it appealed to women who struggle in an image-conscious society, and consequently identify with – and are canny about – the reality behind the glamour (Arthurs, 2004).

Fiercely loyal and committed, the corporate sisters frequently support each other in the cut-throat world of business. They share contacts and build up each other's reputations. In *Lipstick Jungle* women's domestic worlds are just as privileged as the world of work, and this is one of the ways that the home/work divide is resolved. Indeed, according to Rosin, the super breed of Plastic Women is not so much experiencing a work/life balance as enduring 'the *merge*' (Rosin, 2012, 195). The girlfriends bring their children to media events, and discuss work in the bedroom. In the first episode Wendy is on the phone in the bathroom at home while arguing with her boss about starring Leonardo DiCaprio in a new movie. She is simultaneously discussing private schools with her husband, while her son is covered in vomit and her daughter wanders around the bedroom. In season 2, Victory employs Wendy's teenage daughter and acts as an emotional intermediary between her and her mother.

Friends offer essential mutual support in this maintenance of the home/work and motherhood/career merges. Sociality is overtly strategic and linked to career success. Nico and Wendy work for the same corporation, and they are also integral in supporting Victory in setting up her fashion designer label. Wendy gives Victory the opportunity to design a dress for the red carpet at the premiere of one of her films ('Bombay Highway' 1:4). Victory initially rejects her billionaire lover because he does not understand the significance of her friends: 'Wendy and Nico were there for me. They introduced me to everyone, took me under their wing, and they are... Well, they're a hell of a lot more than fine. They're more than great, Joe! They're my family' ('Pink Poison' 1:3). Victory conflates the emotional, familial and social with the logic of business through celebrating how they increased her social capital by introducing her to 'everyone'. When Victory discovers her clothing designs have been stolen by her former assistant, she calls Nico and Wendy and they mobilize emotional and professional strategies to help her.

Because they work in media and fashion, their image is central to their self-brand. Highly visible in niche sections of the Manhattan gossip industry, the girlfriends' power and consequent minor celebrity status means that their private lives attract as much public attention as their professional lives. Women's bodies must conform to an ideal, but their faces and demeanours must appear to be untrammelled by labour. This erasure is essential to their femininity. Because their branded image is integral to their professional success, girlfriends are necessary in the mutual maintenance of a serene, competent and flawless mask. In the celebrified brand that is New York, looking flawless is not narcissistic, it is an essential business strategy. This is evident in an aspirational sense as these women literally embody their wealth in terms of labels and cosmetics, but also because it is their livelihood. Girlfriends go to the gym or shop together, and they direct each other's image – 'you can't wear green', Victory tells Wendy. Sensing that Nico's married life is flagging, Wendy tells Victory: 'Buy her that massage oil' ('Pilot' 1:1).

Much of the plot pivots on the characters' ability to brand the products (magazines, fashion lines, films) that they market, but also their mediated image. The mechanics of self-branding are much more overt than in *Sex and the City*. As fashion designers, publishers and media icons, their identities, public image and their products conflate. Nico and the magazine she works for are seen as being 'one and the same' ('The Lyin', The Bitch, and the Wardrobe' 2:6). Because Victory is a fashion designer, she is 'way too close to my product' ('Pilot' 1:1). She spends the early episodes of the second season with a female strategic brand manager, trying to 'brand my name'. This extends to the men she dates and consequently with whom she will appear on Page 6 of the *New York Post* ('Let It Be' 2:3). Nico and Wendy encourage Victory to pose naked in her advertising campaign as it will 'tie your image to your brand' and when people get into the sheets that Victory has designed and posed for, they will be 'closer to being Victory Ford' ('The F Word' 2:4). Whereas the male characters seem free of needing to cultivate their image and, interestingly, are usually loners without friends, the women are dependent upon each other for supporting their public profile.

'I'm hiding testicles under my skirt!': The masquerade

Men are at the centre of the girlfriends' discourse, but they also inspire rage and fragmentation. Consequently, segregated space becomes a safe site for the girlfriends to negotiate and manage the emotions that they cannot share with men. When a girlfriend faces a difficult situation with her lover, the scene cuts immediately to an instance of girl talk. In *Sex and the City*, Miranda is horrified by a lover who kisses her straight after having oral sex and thus forces her to eat 'me' ('Cover Girl' 5:4). Through talking about this with her girlfriends Miranda diffuses her disgust while still maintaining her relationship with him. Indeed, when she eventually explains to him how she feels, he dumps her, evidencing how men do not have the capacity for girl talk and cannot handle women's emotions. In *Lipstick Jungle*, Wendy's husband is a stay-at-home dad, but he is threatened and emasculated by her success. Wendy tells him:

> You want me to apologize for who I am? For being able to give my family some of the perks that come from working my ass off to get to this place? It's not like you haven't had opportunities.

He replies: 'What opportunities? Every dream I've had has been put on hold. My ambitions, they have to be squeezed into an hour of your schedule.' Exasperated, Wendy tells her friends: 'I thought that marriage was the one thing I didn't have to manage' ('Pilot' 1:1).

Segregated space is also a contained site for explicit liberal feminist rhetoric. *Lipstick Jungle* repeatedly addresses discrimination in the workplace. When Victory is crushed by the bad reviews of her collection, Nico tells her:

> I find it offensive that women always feel that we have to apologize for our success. There are no flukes. There is no luck. There's just talent, and hard work, and the ability to bounce back when you're knocked down. No more, no less.
>
> ('Pilot' 1:1)

Nico often puts the spotlight on sexism. When one of her male colleagues betrays her and accuses her of having 'a little fit', she replies: 'You know, when a woman expresses her concern that an important business matter be dealt with correctly, she's not throwing a fit. She's just doing her job.' When she is told by her male boss that he doesn't want to promote her because she, as a woman, is 'hardwired differently', she tells her friends:

> He fired that shot hoping I would get all flustered and emotional, and then he'd have support for his sexist argument. It's a lose-lose situation in the corporate world. If you want to start a family then you're distracted, and if you don't, then there's something wrong with you. You're unnatural. You hate men. You're hiding testicles under your skirt!
>
> ('Pilot' 1:1)

The girlfriends are intellectually and creatively equal to men, often surpassing them because of their intimate knowledge of what women want and consequently what drives the market. They do not question their entitlement to power and have no desire to sacrifice their career for children. They perceive themselves as deserving of success, having made it due to their creative talent, integrity and hard work.

If men are such a problem then why does the narrative drive of the Manhattan dramedies, in Miranda's words, 'always have to be about them'? Persistently talking about men is one of the main ways that these women produce and perform their heterosexual identities. Joan Riviere maintains that 'womanliness' is a 'mask' that hides 'the possession of masculinity' and averts 'the reprisals expected if she was found to possess it'. Moreover, there is no line between 'genuine womanliness' and the 'masquerade': 'they are the same thing' (Riviere, 1986, 38). This recognition of femininity as a mask is developed by Judith Butler to argue against a fixed gender identity located within the female body. Rather than there being a 'doer behind the deed', Butler argues that the 'doer' is 'constructed in and through the deed' (Butler, [1990] 1999, 181). Identity is therefore understood as a practice or an act of repetition and gender itself 'becomes a free-floating artifice' (Butler, [1990] 1999, 10). The segregated spaces of the Manhattan dramedies enable the performativities of a hypervisible femininity. The girlfriends' shared heterofemininity is spectacular as they are depicted as spatially polarized from 'them', the men. This visual polarity makes them attractive to men and is necessary to their feminine self-brand. The girlfriends' gynaeoptic surveillance networks ensure that the women are 'doing' heterosexuality through centring men in their conversations. We can see how they police 'gender norms' in 'the service of shoring up heterosexual hegemony' (Butler, [1990] 1999, xii).

McRobbie argues that the 'post feminist masquerade' constitutes feminine totality (McRobbie, 2009, 66). Using Riviere's theories of womanly masquerade she argues that this apparently freely chosen and overtly performative femininity deflects from anxieties about retribution from men. It veils women's competitive status in the workplace and disguises their fear of losing feminine desirability within the heterosexual matrix. McRobbie argues that underneath the masquerade is an illegible rage. In these Manhattan dramedies, girlfriends are essential in managing and containing this rage. Indeed, the girlfriends' sociality is a powerful component of the masquerade itself. Like Fearne and Holly, discussed in the previous chapter, they support each other in keeping their emotions under control and by performing girliness. They are able to meet for lunch during work time and immediately launch into cheery banter as if they are in an impeccably dressed school canteen. This is a nostalgic fantasy where women, free of responsibility and crushing time schedules, congregate with ease at short notice. Negra identifies a '(re)gendering of retreatism' in 'a turbulent and highly unsettled economic and social moment' (Negra, 2009, 15). The girlfriends retreat into female friendship which, when correctly performed, is a place of heteronormative safety. Women who do not have friends are pathologized, both because they evidence 'let go' and because they lack the feminine nurturing qualities that girlfriendship delivers. In *Lipstick Jungle* the monstrous Janice Lasher is about to publish the confessions of Wendy's former nanny that will expose Wendy as a bad mother. Nico takes revenge by hiring Lasher's personal assistant to write scandalous stories about her boss. The nanny's confessions are subsequently left unpublished and Nico tells Lasher: 'That's what friends do for each other. You'd know that if you had any' ('Pink Poison' 1.3). Despite the women in *Lipstick Jungle* being ruthless working women themselves, the protagonists are saved from being figures of pathos because they have friends. Although the women have high-profile and eye-poppingly affluent lives, the core of their friendship is centralized and consequently viewers are assured of the women's ethics of care.

Even though the girlfriends have enormous amounts of power and do not need men, they cling on to the masquerade. This is partly because the masquerade functions as a prohibition against the girlfriends desiring each other. Power is maintained and manifest through hypervisible heteronormativity as well as strategic relating. Girlfriends police each other's libidinal energies and complex feelings, ensuring that they are correctly channelled into erotic capital. If these libidinal energies were released among the girlfriends, the structures of control would be threatened and they would be in danger of losing it all (their capital is, after all, dependent upon their heterosexual spectacle). Libidinal energies include sexual desire but also competition and envy. The girlfriends do not compete with each other, and there is an unspoken consensus that envy is destructive and unfeminine. Competition is meted out towards men and other women, but within their intimate togetherness they reinforce the rules of feminine loyalty. It is prohibited (and inconceivable) that they will date each other's lovers. When Wendy and Victory find out about Nico's steamy affair with a younger man they are horrified. Enacting the policing gaze of the slut-shamer their main concern is that her sex drive will devalue her self-brand: Victory worries that Nico 'stands to lose everything. Everything' ('Bombay Highway' 1:4).

Sex and the City has been praised for self-consciously exploring the instability of feminine identity as well as radically queering performativity. Jane Gerhard celebrates its 'queer postfeminism': the show's main characters create a social world of passionate same-sex bonds that 'supplements the heterosexual world of men in which they also live' (Gerhard, 2005, 44). However, whereas the girlfriends manifest a sophisticated level of speak in relation to emotions, their sexual subjectivities are actually girlish. Because they mock and infantilize men, sex becomes de-libidinized and unthreatening. As David Greven argues, '*Sex and the City* is a museum of unnatural history, with its innumerable exhibits of the varieties of pathological male freakishness' (Greven, 2004, 33). Men in the act of sex are depicted as hilarious. They are all attractive but embody apparent sexual deficiencies (apart from Mr Big). Charlotte's lovers have bestially hairy backs, are impotent, or scream 'bitch whore' on orgasm. Miranda's boyfriends are covered in her vaginal fluids or have one testicle. Carrie's lovers live with their parents, want to piss on her, or get married. Furthermore, the girlfriends' sexualities could not be ridiculed in the same way as the men's (this is saved for the films, which I explore in chapters 4 and 5), because the history of misogyny would render this representation violent rather than funny. This is especially the case as the girlfriend identities in *Sex and the City* are consolidated through their flawlessness. To be captured in a state of sexual abjection would be highly incongruent with the portrayal of postfeminist woman as perfection.

The girlfriends in *Sex and the City* (with the exception of Samantha, whose subversive sexual approach comes from its frequency rather than who she chooses to have sex with and in what configuration) are conventional in their attitudes to sex and cultural difference. Their sexual performances take place within a normative and heterosexual frame – and it is their friendships that set the parameters of their normativity. When Carrie dates a bisexual man she worries with her girlfriends: 'When did all the sexes get confused? [...] I'm not even sure bisexuality even exists. I think it's just a layover on the way to Gaytown.' Miranda calls it 'greedy' and Charlotte maintains, 'I'm really into labels: gay, straight. Pick a side and stay there' ('Boy, Girl, Boy, Girl...' 3:4). Even Samantha's forays into lesbianism with Maria Diega Reyes (Sônia Braga) kills two birds with one stone: the representation of a woman of colour and the consumption of female on female sex. However, this is quickly discarded as non-serious by the end of the three episodes which span the duration of their relationship. As Melissa M. M. Hidalgo argues, 'lesbianism is coded in racialized terms in order to exoticize it'. Maria's race is aligned with a taboo, an 'other-than-white, other-than-norm characterization that maintains distinct and separate spheres of existence'. In addition, friendships have to be 'maintained and contained within a heteronormative framework, and sexual relationships between women become a commodity to be used and discarded, excluded altogether from the narrative economy' (Hidalgo, 2008, 132). Indeed, these forays into dating lesbians and bisexual men only serve to reinforce and police the strategic straightness of the sisterhood.

Exclusive sisterhoods: *Cashmere Mafia*

Simultaneous to the production of *Lipstick Jungle*, Bushnell's friend and the original executive producer, creator and writer of *Sex and the City*, Darren Star, produced *Cashmere Mafia* (the programmes also share the same costume designer, Patricia Field, evidencing the centrality of branded cultures). Because it is centred on a powerful group of corporate women, the series is very similar to *Lipstick Jungle*; only there are four girlfriends instead of three: Zoe Burden (Frances O'Connor), an investment banker, Juliet Draper (Miranda Otto), the COO of a hotel chain, Mia Mason (Lucy Liu), a publisher, and Caitlin Dowd (Bonnie Somerville), the vice-president of marketing for a cosmetics company. Like *Lipstick Jungle*, two of the characters, Juliet and Zoe, are married with children. The four girlfriends met in business school and have high-profile jobs in the corporate world. The fear of losing it all, the feminist rhetoric, the sense of entitlement and the merging of the private/public divide are all represented in a similar context to *Lipstick Jungle*. *Cashmere Mafia* is slightly more irreverent, sexually ironic and daring (although the second season of *Lipstick Jungle* upped its sexual comedy with Nico's botoxed vagina). For example, Caitlin has a brief sexual relationship with a woman of colour (like Samantha in *Sex and the City*), and Mia dates Zoe's 'manny'. Ultimately, however, both forays are a means to shore up the boundaries of heteronormative sex with wealthy white men.

In the first episode, Mia competes with her fiancé over the position of publisher at a high-profile magazine. When she wins the contract he breaks off their engagement, complaining, 'I'm going to want someone to come home to' ('Pilot' 1:1). His desire for a conventional wife develops into a magazine cover with the strapline, 'Women chow down on men', followed by an article describing corporate women as cannibals ('Dangerous Liaisons' 1:3). In response, and in an attempt to heal the rift, Mia runs an editorial titled, 'A modern man needs a modern woman'. Men threaten the girlfriends' emotional stability, as well as their career success. Heterosexual men are never friends; they are figures of ridicule, anxiety, antagonism and disdain. Their envy of women's success, as well as their propensity to affairs, renders them untrustworthy. Whereas these women are 'Plastic', the men are 'Cardboard'; they are yet to evolve into the new gender roles (Rosin, 2012). These Plastic Women are having, doing, managing and merging it all. When Zoe in *Cashmere Mafia* is in an important business meeting she receives a call from her nanny, who resigns. Zoe finishes the meeting via a conference call while her children wreak havoc around her. Later that day she meets her friends to support Juliet who is hosting an important benefit event. Before the event the girlfriends have to tell Juliet that her husband is having an affair. They gather round, provide emotional support, and open up a space so that she can confess her pain. Then they style her in a red dress and act as her emotional bodyguards throughout the night. This includes asking Juliet's daughter to be supportive, as well as being frosty to Juliet's husband. During the speeches Zoe runs out to attend her daughter's recital. The next day the girlfriends meet in a restaurant to pool their resources and 'review options' ('Pilot' 1:1). They draft 'a revenge sex spreadsheet' of single male friends to enable Juliet to have an affair ('Conference Call' 1:2). Caitlin arranges for a makeover and then fixes a date as a way to make Juliet feel empowered. Professional, emotional and familial lives merge and it is the network of girlfriends that makes this merge possible.

Like the sisterhoods of *Sex and the City* and *Lipstick Jungle*, not all women are accepted into the tight network of power babes. Women who date other women's husbands are demonized. Indeed, women outside the closed friendship group are threatening. A 'stay-at-home-mom' is revealed to be 'a monster' as she attempts to seduce Zoe's husband and 'hit on' her kids through subverting her authority ('Conference Call' 1:2). When Zoe catches Juliet's husband cheating, the girlfriends make sure that the mistress is excluded from all the top restaurants. Juliet meets 'the other woman' to arrange an armistice and her priority is to keep her friends free from the cruelty of her enemy's much-read blog: 'It's one thing to screw my husband, and quite another to screw with my friends' ('Dangerous Liaisons' 1:3). Friends pull together to make sure that private crises remain out of the public eye, but also to ensure they are all coping.

Rosin argues that 'the US economy is in some ways becoming a kind of traveling sisterhood: Professional women leave home and enter the workforce, creating domestic jobs for other women to fill' (Rosin, 2012, 5). This class division is evident as the Plastic Women rigidly demarcate themselves from the female domestic help who are essential in managing 'the second shift' of housework. Indeed, women who will not contribute to the girlfriends' cultural and economic capital are excluded from their strategic friendship networks. Zoe's nannies, neighbours and childcare are all unreliable or malicious. As she tells her husband, 'We're being held hostage by our help' ('Pilot' 1:1). Zoe's young research analyst (who is demonized through an unwise affair with her boss) is also a threat to her power. Secretaries, assistants and au pairs are major players in the women's success, but they are situated outside the celebration of female sociality. The fact that women outside the privileged space of the immediate family and friendship circle have such close proximity to the face behind the image is threatening. Moreover, demonizing the domestic help masks the inequalities among women by giving an emotive or moral force to what is, in fact, symbolic violence. The relationships between the wealthy, usually white, women and their employees are complex and based on an insurmountable mutual suspicion. Sisterhood only extends to the immediate friendship and there is a distinct lack of trust between women.

In these Manhattan dramedies, socializing in an intimate and exclusive group of straight women is crucial to success in the workplace, which itself is intricately bound up with the self as entrepreneurial project. Illouz, Berlant and Skeggs have, in different ways, identified how private life is increasingly experienced through exchange value. As the self is approached as a life plan, project or brand, 'intimate relationships increasingly put at their center a political and economic model of bargaining and exchange' (Illouz, 2007, 37). Andrew Wernick identifies that self-presentation and promotion accompany the 'mate/companion/friendship market' (Wernick, 1991, 188).

Significantly the glamorous mise-en-scène and the high-end brands obfuscate these strategic relationships. Girlfriendship, like heterosexual dating, is sentimentalized in order to mystify the networks of exchange that take place through women's attempts to accrue social capital. It blurs the commercially driven strategies at the heart of the strategic sisterhoods' relating. When Carrie meets Miranda for the late-night girlfriend date in 'Take Me Out to the Ballgame', discussed above, the scene is shot to suggest that she is attempting to reignite her affair with Mr Big; it is suffused with the affect of the heterosexual date. Sex between the friends is foreclosed, but the sphere of consumption is eroticized. Illouz examines how heterosexual dating is an intense consumer activity and consequently it is 'the very act of consumption that constitutes and creates the romantic moment' (Illouz, 1997, 76). In addition, romantic love is associated with 'forms of "positional" consumption, aimed at displaying status in a competitive system of social stratification' (Illouz, 1997, 71). The corporate sisters participate in positional consumption.

On what and where they spend their money enacts and creates their 'womantic' moment or girlfriend reflexivity.

Both *Lipstick Jungle* and *Cashmere Mafia* take on the relentless whiteness of *Sex and the City* by casting Asian-American actors for the characters of Victory and Mia. The ethnicity of these characters is rarely alluded to and it is not an issue when they are relating with their girlfriends. It only becomes a knotty subject in their relationships with men. Victory and Mia are both represented as interacting with their parents in at least one episode, thus highlighting their heritage. When Mia dates an Asian-American surgeon she is briefly offended when he tells her 'I don't date Chinese', due to the pressure that he experiences from his family. In *Cashmere Mafia* Caitlin falls for Alicia Lawson (Lourdes Benedicto), a lesbian who is also a woman of colour. Their difference is highlighted in a work meeting when one of the men complains that makeup is mainly marketed to white women. Alicia puts him down by stating that 'white women wear make-up too' and smiles at Caitlin. Later, alluding to the name that they have given to this makeup for white women, she complements Caitlin on her 'blush without blush' ('Pilot' 1:1). When the gossip bloggers find out about Alicia and Caitlin they brand Alicia 'hot chocolate' ('Dangerous Liaisons' 1:3).

This crass labelling of racial difference is the only allusion to their relating through intersectional identities in the whole show. Rather than constituting part of their erotic connection, race is reified, static and something to be laughed at. Their relationship never deepens and any energy that might arise through their difference is glossed over. Although they date for about a month, we don't hear about or see them have sex; their relationship lacks overt desire or passion. Indeed, while on a date with Alicia, Caitlin gives a number to a man who she meets in the bathroom ('The Deciders' 1:4). Again, we see how 'lesbianism is coded in racialized terms in order to exoticize it' and how 'sexual relationships between women become a commodity to be used and discarded' (Hidalgo, 2008, 132). Like Samantha and Maria in *Sex and the City*, this relationship serves to reveal Caitlin's experimental self-brand rather than being a vehicle to address heteronormative identities in any meaningful way.

'Friendship is just another word for foreplay': *The L Word*

The L Word repurposes *Sex and the City* in a strikingly different way from *Lipstick Jungle* and *Cashmere Mafia*. It is an example of a media text that attempts to explore the productive complexities of race in lesbian relationships, as well as friendship. *The L Word* represents the lives and loves of a lesbian friendship group. Contextualized within the repurposed genealogy of the straight *Sex and the City*, the show is ground breaking. It tackles coming out, the abuse of women, gay marriage, addiction and childbearing. There is no central protagonist but Alice Pieszecki (Leisha Hailey) sometimes presents the conduit for narrative. This is exemplified, for example, in the final episode of season 3, when she speaks for the entire friendship group as Shane McCutcheon (Katherine Moennig) prepares for marriage. She says, 'You are our best friend' and 'we love you very much':

> You are the most loyal friend, and I can speak for the group, that we have ever met. And you have never left our side when things have become dark.
>
> ('Left-Hand of the Goddess' 3:12)

Although it references *Sex and the City* through its strapline – 'Same Sex, Different City' – and its ongoing narrative focuses on the same friendship group, there are significant differences. It replicates *Sex and the City's* homosocial girlfriend conviviality but incorporates a woman's libido as a vital, loving and embodied component of lesbian, bisexual and transgendered subjectivities, rather than merely as erotic capital. As Alice quips, 'Lesbians think that friendship is just another word for foreplay' ('Pilot' 1:1). Indeed, the on-off friendship/sexual relationship between Alice and Dana Fairbanks (Erin Daniels) is one of the most touching of the show. Because desire between women is not foreclosed, so friendship has a depth that reaches beyond the strategies of exchange. Whereas sexuality is a means for straight girlfriends to exercise control and power over and against men, same-sex sex is central to the girlfriends' political and personal identities. Although it is also a tool of control between the characters (and they also monitor each other's hypervisibility) the affective boundaries of friendship, sex and desire are constantly – and pleasurably – being breached. Their relating is messier, knottier, less strategic and more ambivalent than the Manhattan power babes.

The L Word also represents women relating with and through intersectional subjectivities, and the writer, Ilene Chaiken, responded to critiques over the lack of women of colour by casting Carmen de la Pica Morales (Sarah Shahi) in the second season. The knottiness of loving through difference is particularly evident in the relationship between Bette Porter (Jennifer Beals) and her lover Tina Kennard (Laurel Holloman). Bette is 'out' on the show as biracial. Her racial identity is not glossed over in the same way as Alicia in *Cashmere Mafia*. Bette's identity is pointed up in the first episode of the series, when she and Tina discuss having a black sperm donor:

Tina: How could you not tell me that Marcus Allenwood [Mark Gibson] is black?

Bette: God, I...I don't know. I guess I should have. I just didn't think it would be a problem for you to use a black donor.

Tina: I didn't say I didn't want a black donor. I just think we should have discussed it.

Bette: We absolutely discussed it, Tina. Right at the very beginning. We said that if you were going to be the birth mother, that we should consider finding an African American donor. That way the child would be more like our child.

Tina: But I wasn't prepared.

Bette: I don't understand. Other than being committed to spending the rest of your life with me, what more do you need to do to prepare?

Tina: Look at me, Bette. I don't feel qualified to be the mother of a child who's half African American. I don't know what it means to be black.

Bette: I think that I can make a contribution in that department.

Tina: And don't you think, on top of everything else, to also have two moms, that is a lot of otherness to put on one child? ('Pilot' 1:1)

In the same episode, Bette's identity is questioned by her older, black half-sister Kit Porter (Pam Grier), who implies that Bette masks her blackness. Kit states, 'maybe what's worked best for you all these years, you know, getting all your pretty things and, you know, putting together your pretty life, is that you let people see what they want to see' ('Pilot' 1:1). This questioning of Bette's authenticity is repeated by Yolanda (Kimberly Hawthorne), who is an African American member of Bette and Tina's therapy group: 'you never once refer to yourself as an African-American woman [...] they didn't even know you were a black woman. I think before you have a child, you need to reflect on what it is you're saying to the world while hiding so behind the lightness of your skin' ('Listen Up' 1:8). As Warn argues, these complex plotlines are not developed, which 'is typical of the show's hit-and-run approach to messy topics' that blunts its 'impact on biracial visibility' (Warn, 2006b, 194, 196). Nevertheless, as Warn also contends, this does not mean that the representation of a biracial identity is totally negated. These instances are exciting and knotty examples of women connecting across difficult political and personal issues; ones which are not explored in the other TV series discussed in this chapter.

Fandom and co-producing media brands

A key component of *Sex and the City*'s success was the way in which HBO made effective use of social media through its interactive bulletin board and rigorous systems of brand promotion and consumption. Consequently, *Sex and the City* developed and mined a market through evoking female sociality at the level of plot, but also by employing a cooperative community in order to co-produce its brand. *Sex and the City* was so popular because it was able to cross over from the TV screen and penetrate the friendship groups of its viewers. Indeed, referring back to the *Guardian* article that opened this chapter, Woolf assumes that the female audiences of *Sex and the City* saw 'a secret set of their own dramas spring into art' (Wolf, 2009). Astrid Henry and Deborah Jermyn also make links between the TV show *Sex and the City* and female sociality. Jermyn argues that the show opened up a site that 'evoke[d] the spirit of female support and exchange networks described in Adrienne Rich's "lesbian continuum"' (Jermyn, 2006, 202). The representation of a strong and fun friendship reached out and appealed to groups of friends, creating the appearance of an interdependent female intimacy; or a 'thoughtful, complex and instructive' fandom (Jermyn, 2006, 216). Examining the interaction between female networks (including herself and her students) Jermyn argues that the show privileged 'shared televisual experience and social interaction among female fans' so that '[t]alk about the show has become a valued and enjoyable component of [the students'] own friendships' (Jermyn, 2006, 202).[1]

Neither *Lipstick Jungle* nor *Cashmere Mafia* were as popular as *Sex and the City*, and *Cashmere Mafia* was never aired in the UK. This is partly because *Cashmere Mafia* and *Lipstick Jungle* aired just before the financial crisis and did not portray the glamorous economic optimism of *Sex and the City*. There is a pervasive fear of losing it all which underpins both shows; the anxiety of the women (and presumably the television networks) is palpable. ABC delayed the premiere of *Cashmere Mafia* because of concerns about programming and promotions, and it was cancelled after the first season. *Lipstick Jungle* experienced reduced episodes due to the 2007–2008 Writers Guild of America strike, and ended after its second season, although there was a petition among fans to reinstate it. In addition, because *Lipstick Jungle* and *Cashmere Mafia* were broadcast through network television, this affected their sexual content and dialogue. They were torn between the puritanism of the networks and the wish to capitalize on the irreverent and ironic *Sex and the City*.

Following the 2008 financial crash, viewers did not want to watch women flaunting and fussing over their wealth. Perhaps the sisterhoods' strategic relating in *Cashmere Mafia* and *Lipstick Jungle* was too overt and the women were too much like the Plastic Women as identified by Rosin. In addition, ABC and NBC lack the powerful branded clout of cable networks like HBO, as well as the niche markets of the other networks (Lotz, 2006). *Lipstick Jungle* and *Cashmere Mafia* were never rewarded with the same loyal female fan base. Although *Lipstick Jungle* attempted to create interactive fashion and community groups, it did not succeed in promoting *Sex and the City's* mass culture and thrift store cross-over elements. Furthermore, despite having the TV/movie cross-over actresses Brooke Shields and Lucy Liu, they were not able to replicate the star personality of Parker. Although Liu starred in the girlfriendship movie, *Charlie's Angels* (2000), she does not have Parker's woman-friendly star persona which has enabled her to reach out to female friends as an audience. (Jermyn, 2006a, 78).

Significantly, *The L Word's* 'true legacy' was its ability to 'elucidate connections' successfully, 'to ignite and create a sense of community among lesbians around the world' (Warn, 2006a, 8). *The L Word* succeeded in fostering a devoted and engaged fan base that became involved in the co-production of the narrative through their overt and vocal desire to see queer lives and bodies at the centre of a TV programme. *The L Word's* fan communities and the ways in which they interacted with the show through such sites as www.l-word.com and www.thelwordonline.com were crucial to the show's success (Pratt, 2008). The viewers were active in creating editorials, reviews, petitions and blogs, and the virtual sites were a means for fans themselves to develop friendships, share coming out stories, trade fan fiction and communicate 'advice and support for each other' (Pratt, 2008, 140). The show's official website, www.sho.com encouraged these discussions by using the same type of material as fan-based sites, and there was a web-based contest in 2006 for fans to create their own episode. The writer and director, Chaiken, as well as members of the cast, made it clear through interviews that they wanted to hear from their audience. Because of these marketing strategies, consuming the programme was as much 'about discussing, analysing and re-enacting the series with friends and other viewers as it is actually watching the episodes' (Warn, 2006a, 7). This was also the case for *Sex and the City*. However, what is pertinent about *The L Word* is its politicization, precisely because it was representing – and actively engaging with – a marginalized and previously unseen community. The programme was critiqued by fans for the normatively beautiful 'femme' cast which did not reflect the reality of queer communities (Kosofsky Sedgwick, 2004). Even the butch character, Shane, embodies the postfeminist signifiers of femininity through her thinness. Indeed, the strapline suggests that the network hoped to capture the straight demographic. Robert Greenblatt, President for Entertainment for Showtime, who decides the final casting decisions, aimed to attract broad audiences, including straight women (Goodridge, 2003, 48). Greenblatt asserted:

> ultimately, we want people everywhere to buy it. So yes, the women are all attractive and we make no apologies about that. It's television. Who wants to watch unattractive people, gay, straight or whatever?
>
> (cited in Glock, 2005, 38)

As Faye Davies argues, although the plurality of the market allows for the representation of lesbian relationships, 'the range of discursive practice is defined by the need for a broad audience (within narrowcasting context) and the resultant range of advertisers'. Consequently, these 'representational selections may enable alternative discourses, but not necessarily ideologically resistive discourses in terms of political identity and power relations' (Davies, 2008, 193). Creating and performing femininity drives the market; it is a commercial enterprise. To represent women letting go of the reins of control and embodying masculine signifiers is not good business in a neoliberal economy. It is for this reason that a character like Ivan Aycock (Kelly Lynch), a drag king, is more comfortably positioned as a man within the show, rather than a butch woman. Female masculinity is erased, as Kit states, 'if you were a man, you would be the *perfect* man' ('Limb from Limb' 1:13).

Baumgardner and Richards assert that 'whenever women are gathered together there is great potential for the individual women, and even the location itself, to become radicalized' (Baumgardner and Richards, 2010, 14–15). However, this affect of empowerment is extended and purloined by the brands that dominate these spaces. Michelle M Lazar notes, in relation to advertising in public space, that '[t]he emancipated woman today not only has access to the public sphere', she also 'has female-only spaces reserved for her use in the public, as seen in the lexical and phrasal expressions in the ads: "exclusive/exclusivity", "private", "ladies/women only", "reserved for ladies" and "just for ladies" '. In her discussion of L'Oréal's famous strapline 'because you're worth it', Lazar argues that even when it is presented in the body of an advertisement, 'there is still no explanation in the copy as to why women are worthy; the reason "because you're worth it" is reason enough'. The strapline draws on the affectivities of feminism, intimate publics, self-help and the free market, but is vague enough not to alienate any potential consumers (Lazar, 2009, 377).

Although the Manhattan dramedies draw on liberal feminist rhetoric and configure their sociality through entitlement, this is the commercialized language of neoliberal postfeminism. Friendship in this context is intricately bound up with corporate success. This has implications for the viewers, fans and audiences who are affectively drawn into the sociality of these television programmes. The blurring between the mediated and the real becomes problematic when it is so strategically bound up with the advertising industry and product placement. Brands are keen to associate themselves with the affect of friendship in order to cultivate loyal and engaged consumers. However, because brands function through commercial sense they link into representations of straight, white hypervisibility in order to evoke aspirational desires for femininity as erotic capital. Consequently, as evidenced above, working class women are subject to ridicule. Problems also arise when this affective engagement becomes an engagement with exclusive friendships that discriminate against sexual and racial identities.

Adam Arvidsson argues that a good brand is one where consumers 'are invited to actively co-perform the themed experience' (Arvidsson, 2006, 79). Consequently – in theory at least – the processes of co-participation (evidenced by fandom) mean that viewers can influence how television producers cast, write and create representations of female sociality. In *The L Word*, for example, the politicization of the programmes' consumers meant that transgendered bodies, through the character of Max, were given substantial (if problematic) plotlines, and the show itself evolved in response to the engagement of its fans to include women of colour. I develop this focus on race in Chapter 5, but first I extend my examination of the girlfriend flick's strategic 'womances' in an economic climate where men apparently hold less power in the workplace.

4
Womance

We can handle anything. We'll be each other's wives.

(The Women)

The wedding aisle is a sign of completion in the romantic comedy. It is where the lovers achieve their resolution. This chapter explores how female sociality in girlfriend media is played out against the backdrop of a straight, white wedding. Whereas the romcom typically portrays boy meets girl, boy loses girl, boy gets girl, movies configured through 'a womance' relate the ups and downs of girlfriendship. Rather than being desirable ends in themselves, the emotional signifiers of a heterosexual marriage or motherhood are employed to heighten the affect of womancing girlfriends. Increasingly, the traditional feminine fantasy of the perfect man providing financial security and a happy ever after ending is no longer wanted or tenable in a precarious economic climate where women hold more power in the workplace. Instead, the focus is on the loyalty of girlfriends. The male love interest is marginalized or rendered benign, and it is women's ability to shine for and with their girlfriends that drives the narrative. In the womance, the aisle is a highly sentimentalized locus of friendship and reconciliation between women: the two white-gowned sisters in *In Her Shoes* (2005) express their sibling love in the aisle while the grooms stand by. Similarly, in *Bridesmaids* (2011), it is the relationship between the girlfriends that delivers the climax of the film.

The aisle can also be a site of violence and melodrama in the conventional romcom. In *Sweet Home Alabama* (2002), girly Melanie (Reese Witherspoon) dumps the groom, and floors his career-driven mother-in-law so that she can retreat to her hometown with her childhood sweetheart. In *Made of Honor* (2008) Tom (Patrick Dempsey) punches the groom of his female best friend when he realizes that she is the love of his life. The womances that I look at in this chapter also depict the aisle as a space of conflict, but this time it is between women. For example, in *Bride Wars* (2009) the two girlfriends catfight in the aisle in a spectacular display of fury over being unable to achieve their perfect day. Like the lovers in the romcom, in the womance, girlfriends experience betrayal and heartbreak before they reconcile at the end of the film. Nevertheless, in the womance this betrayal centres on the sabotaging of each other's body image, wedding day or pregnancy. Significantly, mothers are absent, either because they are dead, incompetent, eccentric or simply marginalized at the level of plot. Consequently, the girlfriends are dependent upon each other in order to acquire the correct and normative feminine skill set that will guarantee them success in the postfeminist lifecycle. Postfeminist success is measured through competition: a girlfriend must be more visible than her friend in order to mark her distinctiveness. In addition, if a girlfriend achieves marriage or pregnancy before another then this evokes envy. Indeed, because the girlfriends' success in a postfeminist culture is measured through comparison, this becomes problematic if they are reliant on the same girlfriends to provide support, stability and success.

The girlfriend flick

In *The Independent* on 8 June 2008, Guy Adams heralds the arrival of the 'girlfriend flick'. Mentioning *Baby Mama* and *The Women*, he reports how groups of women are consuming films about female friendship. He cites Ray Richmond, TV critic and entertainment columnist for *The Hollywood Reporter*:

> Women are attending films differently to men...They are going in groups, as a sort of sisterhood, and want to see something that appeals to 'us.' It's a spiritual pilgrimage, and there's a feeling with these sorts of films now that it's more than just a movie: it's a cultural imperative to attend.

Richmond and Adams both highlight a contemporary trend for films about female friendship. However, they also note how these films are received and consumed by groups of women. Adams' lexicon of 'sisterhood' suggests a politically motivated consumption practice. It resonates with Wolf's configuration of Carrie as a feminist icon, as discussed in the previous chapter.

The 'girlfriend flick' is a useful term as it points up the films' status as a sub genre of the 'chick flick'. Moreover, it highlights the significance of the girly components of the postfeminist girlfriend. Suzanne Ferriss and Mallory Young situate the chick flick within 'chick culture', which is 'productively viewed as a group of mostly American and British popular culture media forms focused primarily on twenty-to-thirty something middle-class women'; a demographic that is a huge force in an economy based on consumption (Ferriss and Young, 2008, 1). The chick flick also celebrates female sociality and consumption, both on and off the screen. As Ferriss and Young note, going to the movies, like shopping, is an experience that women prefer to share, and they suggest that an important part of chick flicks' appeal comes from their consumption as a communal experience (Ferriss and Young, 2008, 15). The girlfriend flick is distinguished from the chick flick because it explicitly employs the tropes of the womance. That is, the visual signifiers of womancing girls provide the plot and the primary relationship in the film. In addition, a girlfriend replaces the traditional male position, whether this is in the wedding aisle, through pregnancy, or on a honeymoon. Girlfriend flicks, like the chick flick, fetishize the glamour of boutiques, bars, clubs, restaurants and upscale apartments. However, these signifiers primarily deliver the mise-en-scène of the girlfriends' entitled togetherness. These hedonistic pleasures – whether they take place in the opulence of Manhattan, Mexico or the camped-up Orientalism of Abu Dhabi – produce girlfriend sociality. Entitlement and sisterhood are intricately bound together through the viewing of the womance.

I prefer to use the term 'womance', as opposed to 'girlfriend flick' to describe these films because the female friendships are configured through the tropes of romance. That is, the glamorous consumer spaces that girlfriends socialize in emulate the mystificatory pleasures of dating. Moreover, the primary emotional relationship is between two women who love each other ferociously but without having sexual relations. To some extent, this replicates or mimics the tropes of the bromance. However, as I argue below, the ways in which the girlfriends womance through the practices of consumption and hypervisibility differentiates their togetherness from the buddies of the bromance. The term 'womance' points up the romantic tropes that enable the girlfriends' togetherness while also signifying their delibinized relating. These girlfriends do not have sex with each other and, because they enact the slut-shaming and body policing of the strategic girlfriend gaze as described in Chapter 1, so same-sex desire is foreclosed. I argue in the final section of this chapter that because *Bridesmaids* and *Your Sister's*

Sister disrupt these normative aspirations, they offer more polysemic spectatorial positions.

The womance can be distinguished from earlier friendship films because of its focus on the female self as entrepreneurial self-project. In her seminal study of female friendship films of the 1980s and 1990s, Karen Hollinger outlines different genres of friendship films, including the sentimental film that depicts a nurturing group of women who help each other integrate into the mainstream. According to Hollinger, these films fail 'to offer any serious confrontation with women's issues', which are 'typically rendered on such a personal level or the solutions proposed are so simplistic and unrealistic that the significance of women's problems is minimized rather than accentuated' (Hollinger, 1998, 237). Nevertheless, according to Hollinger, they contrast with mainstream films because they offer a female spectatorial position and, moreover, the films' mixture of retrogressive and progressive elements 'makes them particularly open to multiple reading possibilities' (Hollinger, 1998, 237). In other words, they may have a predominantly conservative message and fail to alter the subject position of the female spectator, but they do dramatize female characters' making of self and reach out to the audience in order to implicate them in the female quest for self-development (Hollinger, 1998, 244).

Hollinger compares these earlier friendship films with the chick flick in her 'Afterword' to *Chick Flicks*. She remarks that the chick flick promises female viewers that they, 'can be whatever they want to be and have whatever they want to have' while simultaneously showing 'a renewed acceptance of traditional notions of femininity that were largely rejected by second-wave feminism' (Hollinger, 2008, 225). What is significant here is that Hollinger's 1990s' feminist desire for 'self-development' comes to fruition in the neoliberal economy of the womance. Moreover, these films have a pedagogical aspect in that they advocate and contribute to the development of the self as entrepreneurial project, particularly around the tropes of the body, femininity and authenticity. They advocate a female sociality that collaborates in the promotion of the individual self.

Hollinger's 'Afterword' was written before the spate of girlfriend flicks in 2008 and she consequently notes that 'the almost exclusive focus on female bonding seemed to have run out of energy'. The entry of women into directorial and managerial roles changed the contours of women's films, opening up the possibilities of the chick flick. However, feminist notions of sisterhood remained 'anathema to mainstream filmmaking' (Hollinger, 2008, 223). Hollinger blames the increasingly conservative climate in the US. Why the womance, then, if the political climate is still conservative? I suggest that girlfriend media are, in part, a response to a growing lack of trust in men's ability to provide stability. A market opened up for female solidarity in the face of precarity. In addition, the representation of networks of women can be harnessed to induce lucrative practices of consumption in branded cultures. The films that I look at in this chapter are directed by men (although both men and women are credited as writers) with the exception of *The Women* (Diane English) and *Your Sister's Sister* (Lynn Shelton). English's experience in getting funding for the film may reflect other women's attempts. English had a 12-year struggle to get the finance to back the production and it was eventually funded by Mick Jagger. According to Jane Fleming, the Los Angeles president of *Women in Film*, the difficulties experienced by English in making her film are typical for female filmmakers, especially those who want to make films about female friendship; of the top 250 films in 2007 only 7 per cent were directed by women (Adams, 2008; Hollinger, 2008).

Competition: *In Her Shoes* and *Baby Mama*

The (upper) middle class women represented in these films are economically independent and so men no longer represent the financially happy ever after. Men wield less power and consequently women's conflicts are not overtly about them. Nor do women display the pathologically jealous femininities of the 1990s' friendship films such as *Poison Ivy* (Katt Shea Ruben, 1992), *The Hand that Rocks the Cradle* (Curtis Hanson, 1992) or *Single White Female* (Barbet Schroeder, 1992). These are comedies after all. Nevertheless, these womances still express a deep anxiety over trusting girlfriends. Indeed, the rifts between the women replicate and reinforce the archetype of the duplicitous woman who lies at the heart of misogynist understandings of femininity. Like the corporate sisterhoods of Chapter 3, celluloid best friends do not compete over men. However, they do compete for visibility and recognition – from other women. I discussed in Chapter 3 how the 'Plastic Women' manage to achieve a delicate balance between recognition and attachment through their strategic relating. In other words, envy, competition, and sexual transgression were prohibited in order to maintain the visibility of each other's branded profile. In contrast, the narrative drive of these womances depends upon crisis and resolution, and the traumas that the girlfriends experience together are produced through their competitive and envious emotions.[1]

Discussing the concept of 'time panic' within the life stages of the postfeminist female subject, Negra states:

> Crisis and fulfillment in virtually all these life stages center upon the discovery of personal destiny, the securing of a romantic partner and motherhood, and the negotiation of the problem of paid work (seldom its rewards). Those women who cannot be recuperated into one of these life-stage paradigms generally lose representability within a popular culture landscape dominated by postfeminist definitions of femininity.
>
> (Negra, 2009, 47)

The dyadic girlfriend flicks which feature two female leads (*In Her Shoes*, *Bride Wars*, *Baby Mama*) depict girlfriends becoming hysterical over their position in the lifecycle – whether this visibility and its consequent validation are achieved through marriage or motherhood. Difference is signified through hair colour, representability and money. Dowdy brunettes are polarized from sexier blondes, and remunerated girlfriends support their unemployed or low-income girlfriends; that is, until the films' resolution, when the brunettes have it all and the low-income girlfriends gain capital. By the end of each film, their hair colour remains the same but the girlfriends have achieved postfeminist normativity through the heterosexual completion of marriage or pregnancy or both. These films set up the relationship between the two female leads as one of womance but also of competition.

In Her Shoes used the tagline 'She's your best friend, your worst enemy and the one person you can't live without!' It centres on the tumultuous and competitive relationship between two sisters, blonde Maggie (Cameron Diaz) and brunette Rose (Toni Collette). Since the death of their manic depressive mother, Rose has taken care of Maggie, reluctantly bailing her out when she is in trouble or needs money. Collette put on 25 pounds to play the workaholic and frumpy lawyer who owns a closet of unworn shoes. Her voiceover at the beginning of the film compares herself to her sexy, slender sister: 'There are women – thinner women – who have lace bras, silk thongs... things designed to excite a man. A thong would look ridiculous on me. I wear cotton briefs. My life is about working long hours.' When Rose is asked by a date, 'You eat everything?' she looks down at her body and replies, 'What do you think?' In contrast, Maggie is slutty, unemployed and an undiagnosed dyslexic. She is always filmed with mirrors, as if reflecting her self-absorption and preoccupation with image.

Maggie betrays her sister by having sex with Rose's date. Rose is devastated and throws her out of the house. Mimicking the separation between heterosexual lovers, the two sisters must struggle with their life lessons alone. Rose leaves her job to become a dog walker. She loses weight. She also starts dating a former colleague, who will later become her husband. Maggie, on the other hand, discovers her grandmother living in Florida, and she learns to read. Whereas Rose is learning the art of image and femininity, Maggie is earning money through advising the women in her grandmother's retirement community on their wardrobes. She has relinquished sex for self-development. Both characters are represented as blossoming, but also as desperately missing each other: Maggie laments, 'without her I don't make sense'.[2] The sisters are eventually reunited at their grandmother's instigation. At first, Rose is wary of trusting Maggie, but their friendship is cemented once Maggie has proved her trustworthiness in giving Rose a splendid makeover and choosing the perfect wedding dress. Thanks to Maggie, a thinner, unbespectacled Rose walks down the aisle, neatly packaged in a 1950s' white dress, lace, flowers, and pearls; Maggie has proved herself to be a true girlfriend through assisting Rose in being the spectacle of a perfect bride.

At Rose's wedding, Maggie also wears a white dress and it is *her* vows to Rose that we see as she recites 'i carry your heart' by e.e. cummings. (She learns to read through Elizabeth Bishop's 'One Art', which was originally written for Bishop's female lover.) The groom is largely ignored. Rather than the wedding scene being one of homoeroticism, however, it is a scene of sameness. Both sisters are feminized through their white dresses, reflecting Rose's repudiation of melancholia and Maggie's relinquishing of indiscriminate sex. Deprived of a mother to teach them how to be feminine, they have had to learn the art of appropriate – but distinct – femininity themselves. By the end of the film, Rose has lost weight, her lonely spinsterhood and her job. But she has been remunerated with normative beauty, a husband and happiness. Maggie has learnt to read and to rein in her sexuality. No longer shot with mirrors, Maggie has *become* the image, a perfect model of girly femininity with her cheerful smile and white dress. The two sisters learn to recognize the necessity of supporting each other's bid for normativity – whether this is through image or marriage. They learn to be girlfriends.

It is not just body image and the perfect bridal spectacle that is desirable. Female-only spaces are celebrated in prioritizing and panicking over the intimate sphere of career, pregnancy and motherhood. *Baby Mama* (2008) is a pertinent illustration of this. Eschewing New York glamour for a more downbeat setting in Philadelphia (like *In Her Shoes*),

Kate (Tina Fey) is a successful businesswoman who is refreshingly friendly, professional and liked by her colleagues. Kate wants it all. Following a successful professional career, she now wants a baby. Self-consciously and knowingly addressing women-centred concern, she tells us: 'I still aspire to meet someone, and fall in love, and get married, but that's a very high-risk scenario. And I want a baby now. I'm 37.'

Although we are encouraged to see Kate as controlling – the lesson she learns in the course of the film is to accept the messiness of relating – she is not a demonized powerful woman. Recounting her career trajectory, she confesses: 'I didn't cry in meetings. I didn't wear short skirts.' And then asks, 'Is it fair that to be the youngest VP in my company I will be the oldest mom at preschool? I made a choice. Some women got pregnant and I got promotions.' Kate has fertility problems and the film traces her attempts to become a mother through adoption, IVF and surrogacy. Along the way it critiques powerful men, including her boss, and numerous doctors who are shown to be unsympathetic and insensitive (unlike her) when dealing with people in a professional capacity. One doctor, while drinking coffee out of a mug shaped like a pregnant woman, keeps repeating, 'I just don't like your uterus.'

Kate's desire for motherhood is also a bid for representability and it is a girlfriend, Angie (Amy Poehler) – the surrogate mother whom she employs – who aids her. The film centres on Kate's growing relationship with the unemployed and working class Angie. Tropes of womance mystify the business transaction at the heart of their relating. For example, they are shown sharing vows through a pastiche of a heterosexual romance. Against the backdrop of a sunset, Kate tells Angie 'I hope you like me...I need you'. Angie replies lovingly, 'I want you to put your baby inside me', which leads to a soft-focus artificial insemination scene where the two women gaze at one another as the doctor inseminates Angie – all to the sound of 'My Endless Love'. *Baby Mama* is a departure within girlfriend media as it represents women relating successfully across the difference of class. Although they stereotypically adhere to their classed clichés, they also puncture one another's pretensions and learn from each other. This is both a bid for girlfriend sameness and a positive portrayal of connecting across difference, however superficial: Kate teaches Angie healthy eating and Angie gives Kate a makeover when they go clubbing. Angie also ruptures Kate's affluent and aspirational outlook. Kate tells Angie, 'You know, studies show that babies can learn a second language in the womb.' Angie replies, 'You know, you should play an English tape, so it can come out talking, and it can be in commercials, and you'll make a lot of money.' Angie amusingly defines organic food as 'crap' 'for rich people who hate themselves'. *Baby Mama*, to some extent, politicizes the difficulties women face with insensitive and unreliable men. However, the actual conflict is between women. Kate is envious of Angie's ability to conceive, and she literally polices her body through monitoring what she eats. This control comes to a head when Kate discovers Angie dying her roots and drags her to the bathroom, violently showering her while Angie cries, 'I'm clean, I'm clean'. The two friends work through their antagonism when Angie remarks that 'I can have a baby and you can't and that drives you crazy.' Kate apologizes: 'I'm sorry I may have over-reacted [...] I might be a little bit jealous and I'm sorry I called you stupid.' However, the ultimate betrayal is by Angie. Angie is dependent upon Kate for money and this unequal power relation highlights how their relationship is based on commercialism. Angie lies about being pregnant with Kate's baby; it is *her* eggs that have been impregnated by *her* husband. Moreover, she wants what Kate has bought – her foetus. Once Kate learns this she withdraws support and friendship, publicly calling her 'white trash'.

The two friends separate. Through this separation, they achieve normativity and sameness. Kate is miraculously able to conceive and the closing credits show her flashing an engagement ring on her finger. Angie changes her eating habits, swapping Dr Pepper for water, and she tells Kate, 'You ended up teaching me how to be a mother.' The film ends with Kate and Angie watching *Tom and Jerry* (a symbol of their tumultuous friendship) while holding their babies. Although there is an attempt to look outwards in the portrayal of problems affecting women, we can see Kate's professional success and issues of fertility being 'normalized' or resolved through her naturally conceived pregnancy. Although the girlfriends' friendship is romanticized, this is sanctioned through a heterosexual wedding and/or pregnancy. The primary intimate relationship between two women is rerouted as a heterosexual one between a man and a woman, and libido is, in Chris Holmlund's terms, 'strait-jacketed' (Holmlund, 2002). In addition, the class conflict, which attended this relationship structured through a business transaction, is obfuscated through the romantic resolution of sameness.

Reliable and trustworthy girlfriends are needed to support their transition into an appropriate feminine identity. Nevertheless, because girlfriends are dependent on one another to monitor and survey each other's self-government, there is a pervasive anxiety that the girlfriend will sabotage this. Because representability and the body as brand have superseded men or the marriage market as signifiers of resolution and completion, the ultimate betrayal is to destroy a girlfriend's visibility. In these girlfriend flicks, betrayal leads to anger, confrontation and eventual separation. However, as with all romantic comedies, this estrangement is essential as it means that the films culminate in the characters producing individual and distinctive identities within the normative paradigm of the postfeminist political economy.

Bridezillas: *Bride Wars* and *Sex and the City 1*

Competition, betrayal and reconciliation in the wedding aisle are central to the womance plot of *Bride Wars*. Like *In Her Shoes*, *Bride Wars* nostalgically references the intimacy of childhood friendship. This is either through photographs or flashbacks. The opening credits of *Bride Wars*, for example, reveal a wedding ceremony performed by the girlfriends when they were children (the most conventionally feminine of the two playing the groom). Unlike *In Her Shoes*, which depicts the sisters competing over men, *Bride Wars* represents two friends fighting over the perfect wedding day. Blonde, ambitious Liv (Kate Hudson) and sweet brunette Emma (Anne Hathaway) have been best friends since childhood. They both covet the fantasy of a June wedding at the Plaza. Despite being in long-term relationships, having careers – Liv is a lawyer and Emma is a schoolteacher (the ultimate sweet profession in Hollywood) – they are hysterical in their pursuit of the ideal wedding; Emma, the poorer of the two, has been saving up since she was 16.

Girlfriend consumption is constructed through the luminosities of sentimental dating, and the girlfriends exercise together, shop, lend clothes, dispense advice and champion one another's appearance. Liv's parents are dead, and Emma consequently plays a primary supporting role in her life. Liv lends her clothes to Emma, 'See? I told you those jeans would look great on you.' Or, 'Emma, yellow. Not your colour.' Liv even buys Emma designer clothes. At a friend's wedding, when the bride is publicly humiliating Emma for wearing the same dress 'like, a bazillion years ago', Liv protects her: 'What's your point? Because it's a classic. If a dress works, you work it hard.' The bride replies, 'See, that is sweet. And loyal. Girlfriends sticking up for each other.'

Both their boyfriends propose and the plot pivots around a mix-up over wedding dates, with neither Liv nor Emma willing to relinquish their dream of the June wedding. Because the wedding is, as one of their girlfriends says, 'The best day of a girl's life', neither of them wants to share it with the other. Previous gestures of mutual support over body image are turned into sabotage, and the film attempts to gain much of its humour through the bridezillas physically and verbally abusing each other's body. Emma produces a shocked gasp from the audience of watching girlfriends when she tells Liv, 'Your wedding will be huge...just like your ass at prom.' Emma turns Liv's hair blue by switching preparations at a salon. In retaliation, Liv replaces a light tan with a heavy orange one in Emma's tanning cubicle. Emma attacks Liv's body by sending expensive chocolates and cookies to her workplace, pretending that they are from Liv's fiancé. From this point on, Liv is constantly eating high-fat food – a symptom of her being victim to melancholia and an uncontrolled appetite. As in *Mean Girls*, the normative cruelties of adolescent friendships spill into violence. The girls sabotage what they know will hurt each other the most – the way they look.

At work, Liv furiously exercises on her walking machine while simultaneously eating and planning her wedding. This leads to humiliation as, having put on five pounds, she is unable to wear her Vera Wang wedding dress; we have already been told, 'You don't alter Vera Wang to fit you, you alter yourself to fit Vera Wang.' Finally, Liv is humiliated in a crucial male-only meeting with an important client. Her blue hair is wrapped in her shirt, her bra is exposed, and she breaks down under the pressure of her weight, her imminent wedding, and her best friend's betrayal. She is publicly demoted. Significantly, it is after this demotion that Liv discovers, 'I am awake'. Her separation from Emma has allowed her to discover a more domesticated and passive femininity that can be enacted outside the rigour of a mixed working environment.

Despite this mutual abuse, however, the two friends are also portrayed as missing each other. It isn't until their eventual marriages (they are both to be married on the same day in separate rooms at the Plaza) that they reconcile. Liv has swapped Emma's DVD wedding montage for one that captures her drunk on spring break. Furious, Emma runs into Liv's ceremony, flooring her. The women catfight on the aisle in their bridal gowns until they are exhausted. They are shot from above lying on the aisle like postcoital lovers in bed, declaring their mutual love. Like *In Her Shoes*, this is a declaration of sameness: Liv has become more feminine, 'I cry all the time', and Emma has ditched her victim acquiescence. Emma and her fiancé decide to split up, and she eventually marries Liv's wealthier brother. This is significant as it means that she can buy her own designer clothes; it is part of her trajectory to having it all and consequently becoming normatively distinctive. The final scene finds both friends pregnant and their adolescent cruelties are resolved.

In *In Her Shoes*, *Baby Mama* and *Bride Wars*, 'strait-jacketing' glosses over and resolves the violence of their mutual sabotage. Straight and benign men provide the emotional stability that the women need.

Themes of representability and time panic are also foregrounded in *Sex and the City 1*, where the girlfriends support each other in successfully achieving (and sabotaging) their visibility. Both *Sex and the City* films have tenuous narratives and plots. They are explicitly set up as continuations of the TV series, and follow its advice mode, which was structured through Carrie's sex column. The first film includes flashbacks to previous events. Carrie tells us: 'Year after year, my single girlfriends were my salvation.' Throughout both films, Carrie's voiceover addresses key postfeminist issues: How to keep a relationship dynamic after marriage? How to reconcile motherhood with identity? How to age sexily? How to be monogamous? These problems are set in a fantasy land of walk-in closets, *Vogue* shoots and private butlers.

In *Sex and the City 1*, Carrie and Mr Big decide to marry. This sets in motion a photo shoot with Carrie camping up the fetish of the white bride in a plethora of designer gowns. However, Carrie lets her wedding 'get bigger than Big'. In her fantasy-come-true makeover sequence, Carrie is shot in a cornucopia of white lace, with her girlfriends looking on. After the shoot, Vivienne Westwood sends Carrie the dress she was photographed in, and the wedding subsequently becomes more glamorous. Mr Big likens the preparations to a circus and feels he doesn't know her anymore – she has become akin to the commodities that she fetishizes – and he gets cold feet. Carrie is stood up. She must learn her lessons – the importance of love over spectacle, of reason over image – and then she will achieve her man. In addition, Carrie's girlfriends have encouraged her pursuit of the perfect and abundant wedding; they have led her astray with their feminine love of spectacular public consumption. Following Mr Big's no-show, Carrie goes on honeymoon with her girlfriends – another instance of womancing. Five months later, Miranda confesses to Carrie that she advised Big not to marry: 'I was really upset. And I bumped into Big and I said that you two were crazy to get married.' Carrie feels that her route to representability through the wedding has been sabotaged by her friend. Betrayed, she cries, 'you ruined my marriage'. The friends eventually reunite and, in doing so, learn the value of forgiveness – forgiving each other but also their beloveds. The film ends with Carrie and Mr Big married, Miranda and her husband reunited, the birth of Charlotte's child, and Samantha back to her sexy and slim self, after her deteriorating relationship. They have all achieved their representable status.

Romantic comedies – and the girlfriend flick – address and condemn the commercialization of intimacy, usually by focusing on the bride as needing to learn restraint before she is successfully wed. Indeed, the pursuit of perfection as an attainable component of the wedding has inspired the figure of bridezilla – popular culture's image of the narcissistic bride. The postfeminist bridezilla has a monstrous desire for her own spectacle at the expense of her groom and girlfriends. Because women are often scapegoated as getting lost in consumption ('women love to shop'), *Sex and City 1* and *Bride Wars* suggest that women have an innate propensity to lose their reason in the face of retail. This irrationality is increased when it comes to weddings. As one groom in *Bride Wars* says to the other: 'What is it about weddings that makes girls go crazy?'

Rebecca Mead discusses how the image of bridezilla has gained common currency in US culture, arguing that the bridezilla's vilification is evidence 'that weddings themselves were out of control, and that a sense of proportion had been lost, not just individually but in the culture at large' (Mead, 2007, 3). She argues that the breakdown in traditional authorities has left people vulnerable 'to the pressures and persuasions' of the wedding industry. Nevertheless, to blame a female stereotype for society's excessive consumption has its roots in a misogynist discourse which scapegoats women for anxieties over the dehumanizing practices of the market. Bridezilla reincarnates for a twenty-first-century urban milieu the potent and emotive archetype of the irrational woman, who has had a long and successful literary history. In *Bride Wars* and *Sex and the City 1*, anxieties over the amorality of the market intersect with traditional configurations of women as avaricious. We have seen her in Juvenal's Roman satires and Alexander Pope's *Rape of the Lock* (1716). Just as Jonathan Swift undressed the coquette in 'The Lady's Dressing Room' (1732) to reveal a stinking and monstrous whore whose investment in commodities has turned her into one herself, so bridezilla metamorphoses a desirable and supportive girlfriend into a narcissistic harridan of appetite and hubris. Moreover, the bridezilla embodies contemporary anxieties over self-branding. Just as women in the imaginations of Pope and Swift were repulsive because they commodified themselves into sexual objects, the bride has lost her humanity in the empty pursuit of perfection. The wedding ceremony is a sanctioned binge. However, the bridezilla holds the responsibility – and sometimes blame – for this excess. Significantly, the girlfriend flick is a response to the recklessness that fuelled the financial crisis, and it holds women responsible for the excesses of deregulation.

Although girlfriend flicks gesture towards love over labels, much of the viewing pleasure is generated through the glamour of the women and their milieu: the affective pounding of the soundtrack and the dizzy spectacle of fashion and perfection. This paradox is resolved through a system of reward and punishment, so the marriage takes place once the bride has learnt her lessons about love, labels and image. In contrast, the women who are still lost in excess fail at the aisle. The bride's worthiness is measured through her ability to negotiate consumer culture and the self as project. The films offer the spectacle of the bride as perfection, but only once her moral framework is shown to be flawless. These films are glossy product placements, a paean to shopping, boozing and doing lunch. They entice us to let go and simultaneously remind us – at first insidiously and later through the narrative of reward and punishment – that we must exert control and discipline at all times: excess, coded through fat or obsession with image, is bad and lazy and will make us lose our jobs, boyfriends and girlfriends.

In addition, women are represented as vulnerable to competition and envy, especially over representability and image. There is still a pathology attached to their portrayal, revealing how women 'go crazy' when they are left on their own together. *In Her Shoes*, *Bride Wars*, *Sex and the City 1*, and *Baby Mama* resolve women's mutual hysteria through the straight closure of a heterosexual relationship with a man and the achievement of normative distinctiveness. Moreover, girlfriend romance serves to veil the violence that has been inflicted between friends. The girlfriend flick addresses the complexities of competition, envy and bullying that can be evident and deeply painful – in different configurations – in women's relationships. However, because they gloss over this through a romantic girlfriend sentimentality or womance, these issues are not convincingly explored and function merely at the level of affect.

Intergenerational: *The Devil Wears Prada* and *The Women*

In her book, *Not My Mother's Sister*, Astrid Henry identifies 'how the mother-daughter relationship is *the* central trope in depicting the relationship between the so-called second and third waves of U.S. feminism'. Perceiving herself as the dutiful daughter of feminism, she notes how 'writers of all ages, feminists and non-feminists alike, were describing feminist intergenerational relationships in familial terms' (Henry, 2004, 2). She argues that this 'matrophor' has far-reaching implications for contemporary feminism. Ferriss and Young state that the appropriation of *chick* by third-wave or 'post' feminists mirrors the use of *queer* by gay activists:

> the word *chick*, like *girl* (and even *bitch*), has been wielded knowingly to convey solidarity and signal empowerment. [...] Part of third-wavers' response to feminism has been the deliberate re-appropriation and re-visioning of terms that make second-wave feminists cringe [...] Much as homosexual activists transformed the disparaging term *queer* into a slogan to proclaim solidarity and increase their cultural visibility – 'We're here. We're queer. Get used to it' – so the women of the third wave seek to reclaim and refashion their identity through terms considered unacceptable by the previous generation.
>
> (Ferriss and Young, 2008, 3)

The equation of *chick* or *girl* with *queer* is problematic. *Queer* signified (and signifies) hate; it is an overt form of abuse. On the other hand, *chick* had (and has) very different connotations. It can be understood as demeaning by many women, but not all. Indeed, because it signifies normativity and belonging, it can be inclusive and complementary – an identity to strive for. In addition, it was not used as an overt form of violence in the same way as *queer*. Conflating *chick* or *girl* with *queer* exposes how much authority is projected onto the second-wave feminist movement.

Indeed, the portrayal of intergenerational interaction in the womance is fraught and sometimes violent, reflecting the relationship between second-wave feminism and contemporary postfeminist popular culture. With the exception of *The Women*, all the womances have absent or dead mothers, or women fighting across differences of generation. This is the conflict between feminism and the girl: the lifestyle-oriented power of the postfeminist chick who is in thrall to having it all, against the politicized (or ignorant) feminine performance of the previous generation who might puncture the dream. In *The Devil Wears Prada*, the heroine and her boss share an unspoken mutual admiration, but their differences are clearly marked as insurmountable. In the chick flick *Sweet Home Alabama*, the post-50s older woman is a bully in the guise of the Mayor of New York played by Candice Bergen. Bergen also plays the despotic wedding planner in *Bride Wars*. Kate's mother in *Baby Mama* is an insensitive embarrassment who is played for laughs. Unlike the cougars and Samanthas of US television, her characters refuse to 'do girl' or to interact with other women through the sentimental commercialization of girlfriendship. The supplanting of mothers by girlfriends or sisters is also a structural and didactic device. Rather than being disciplined into a feminine identity by her mother, the girlfriend is perpetually in training with and through her friends. The girlfriends are always striving to become better and more perfect versions of themselves. If the girlfriend self is an entrepreneurial project then she is 'never finished with anything' (Deleuze, 1992, 5). In a gendered framework, and in the context of girlfriend culture, this means that femininity is continually being made new and more innovative. No longer is it something learnt from mothers and previous generations. Instead, feminine performativity is learnt through girlfriends and marketed to their audiences though the womance. In these films, as well as in chick flicks such as *Coyote Ugly* (2000), *Mean Girls* and *Clueless* (1995), the heroine must learn the skill sets of the most marketable femininities.

Based on the 2003 book of the same name by Lauren Weisberger, *The Devil Wears Prada* is a satirical look at the world of *Vogue* and its editor, Anna Wintour. Set in the offices of a top fashion magazine, unstylish Andy Sachs (Anne Hathaway) lands a job as co-assistant to Miranda Priestly (Meryl Streep), a bullying boss. The film traces Andy's journey from fresh-faced, idealistic graduate to savvy, glamorous PA. This transformation takes place through the dual manoeuvre of being abused by her bitchy colleagues and being seduced by the 'visual treat' of fashion (Ferriss, 2008, 54). Andy's mother is absent throughout the film. Like *Bride Wars*, it also stars Hathaway, whose large, innocent facial features mean that she is often cast as guileless or unsophisticated. Indeed, in both *Bride Wars* and *The Devil Wears Prada*, Hathaway transforms herself from being bullied by women, into a woman who can stand up for herself. This film is not a dyadic friendship film like *Baby Mama* or *In Her Shoes*, neither is it a group friendship film like *Sex and the City 1* or *The Women*. In fact, there is no celebration of female friendship, the women being primarily devilish. Ferriss (2008) classifies it as a 'make over flick'. Nevertheless, it depicts female sociality in the workplace, where the relationship between women mirrors the performance of normative cruelties, as well as the animosity meted out between battling girlfriends. It is relevant in its depiction of a female-controlled workplace and female networks, as well as its representation of women policing one another's bodies through the girlfriend gaze. It is an excellent example of women (and a gay man) enacting and generating the affect of normative cruelties.

In the opening credits, a shot of a woman's hand counting almonds into a bowl is juxtaposed with the image of Andy walking out of a bakery with her face in an onion bagel. That she is eating this type of food (or food at all) distinguishes her as an outsider from the fashion world. Although she professes that she is happy with her size six, by the end of the film she has managed to go down to a size four. In the crucial turning point before the stock trope of the makeover sequence, Andy complains to her gay male colleague, Nigel (Stanley Tucci), that she is being maltreated by Miranda. Nigel's reaction is to turn the focus back onto Andy and chastise *her* for acting like a victim. Calling her by her (barely acceptable) dress size he snaps, 'You are not trying, you are whining. Wake up six!' In response, Andy ostensibly takes control of her life and becomes the perfect assistant, working until 2 am at the expense of her family, relationship and friends. For the rest of the film she is immaculate, alluringly dressed, made up and seductively shot in designer clothes. The film's tone becomes heroic as Andy proves her worth and her ability as a professional, sexy woman. She also drops a dress size. Andy's transformation is primarily enacted through fashion (and through her masochistic surrender to Miranda's every whim), but success is also partly linked to food – knowing *how* to have it all. Before Andy's makeover, Miranda calls her 'the smart, fat girl' and Andy herself admits, 'I'm not skinny'. Nigel insists, 'there's nothing in this whole closet that will fit a size six I can guarantee you'. Although he is wrong, he continues to make snide comments about her weight until she loses it. The scene between Andy and Nigel is significant because it acts out the postfeminist insistence on not being a victim. However, the film inadvertently exposes it as an insistence on embracing one's victim status to the point where it feels like empowerment.

Nevertheless, it is Andy's co-worker and primary rival for Miranda's approval, Emily (Emily Blunt), who suffers the most for her body. The queen of discipline, she tells Andy: 'Well, I'm on this new diet. It's very effective. I don't eat anything and when I feel like I'm about to faint I eat a cube of cheese.' After she is run over, and subsequently upstaged by Andy, Emily's emotional trauma is acted out through eating chocolate mousse and bread; she has let go into the emotional appetite of the victim. Like the bridezillas and the queen of The Plastics in *Mean Girls*, Emily's suffering is played for laughs as she has coveted power over a more nurturing femininity and consequently deserves punishment. The film eventually critiques Andy's adoption of the fashion magazine lifestyle by having her walk out of the job. Nevertheless, she decides to leave through fear of ending up like the divorced and lonely Miranda, not because she rejects the way she looks or her success. Ultimately, the film is a celebration of the changes she has undergone in this cut-throat and predominantly female environment.[3]

By the end of the film, Andy is set to reap the joys of the corporate world while maintaining her integrity and femininity. Significantly, her career trajectory will now be under the saner eye of a heterosexual male boss. Indeed, in contrast to the girlfriends', the straight male's gaze is a friendly one, insisting that the women are perfect just the way they are. In all these womances, despite the heterosexual romantic plot, the man's objectifying gaze is remarkably absent. The men accept their beloveds, solidly reining in any hysterical preoccupation with image. In *Bride Wars*, Liv's fiancé tells her 'I want a human wife' as opposed to the image of perfection that she attempts to project to her girlfriends. Whereas the girlfriends sustain the postfeminist dream of representability and help each other realize it, heterosexual men provide relief from the control networks of the girlfriend gaze. These films represent what happens when strategic sisterhoods go awry. Unleashed in an unregulated free market of hyper-consumption, girlfriends become monstrous. With their characters metamorphosing into bridezillas and sacrificing their friends and lovers for fashion, these films reveal contemporary anxieties over promotional culture. Prevalent concerns over economic deregulation, a financial system out of control, and brand engagement is reconfigured as a personal relationship between women.

The Women disposes of men altogether. There are no male actors in the film. In addition, it aims to fissure the controlling girlfriend gaze that dominates these womances through depicting more friendly female networks who relate across generations. The film represents four thin society Manhattan socialites including (on the edges of the plot) an African American lesbian played by Jada Pinkett Smith. Because it is a group friendship film, it allows more possibilities of identification for the female spectator – however limited these roles actually are. The plot centres on the girlfriends' solidarity as Mary (Meg Ryan) discovers that her husband is having an affair with the spritzer girl (Eva Mendes) at Saks Fifth Avenue. Mendes plays to Latina cultural stereotype – an unprivileged, catty, gold digging man-eater. In addition, Mary and the spritzer girl are in competition. Nevertheless, Candice Bergen manages to escape her typecasting and plays a sympathetic mother. The youngest generation, particularly Mary's daughter Molly (India Ennenga), innocently rupture their mothers' obsession with acquisition. One of the children shouts in Saks, 'I hate this store!' and her mother replies, 'I want you to listen to me. I'm going to say something very important, and

I want you to remember it for the rest of your life. Nobody hates Saks.'
Indeed, Saks plays an important role in the film as providing the entitled
(if ironized) consumer backdrop to female sociality.

The film addresses issues relating to women's bodies and sexual desirability. Mary's daughter, Molly, has a painful relationship with her
femininity and burns tampons in protest against becoming a woman.
Mary's best friend, Sylvia (Annette Bening) is the editor of a fashion
magazine and Molly questions her use of skinny women:

> Molly: I hate my body. I want to look like the models in your
> magazine.
> Sylvia: Nobody looks like those girls, okay? Not even them. They're
> all airbrushed and retouched.
> Molly: Then why don't you just put regular people in there?
> Sylvia: I know it's hypocritical. Life is complicated.

It *is* complicated. Not least because the women in this film span three
generations, but they look roughly the same age (Bergen has a painful
face lift in the film). It is a complication that runs throughout girlfriend media which, to some extent, address the suffering involved in
attaining a perfect body image and yet reinforce it through fetishiz-
ing girliness. Girlfriend media attempt to depict the complex relations
women have with their bodies. However, because these media are by
their very nature commercial and dependent upon corporate sponsorship, they are also complicit in inspiring body insecurity. These texts are
therefore highly destabilizing. The actors' screen presence and the producers' drive to deliver audiences to the advertisers mean that questions
relating to misogyny and the punishing nature of postfeminist popular
culture struggle to be effective.

The Women portrays many of the stock tropes of the girlfriend flick.
There are gestures of 'emotionally eating': when Mary discovers that her
husband is having an affair she binges on butter and sweets. She also
has a makeover as it is implied that her husband left because she let
herself go. She competes with her husband's girlfriend. After some self-
help courses and a new haircut, Mary is able to get her entrepreneurial
life back together. Betrayal is enacted as Sylvia sells the details of Mary's
divorce to a journalist in order to secure her job. When Mary and Sylvia
fall out, Mary confesses that 'this is so much worse' than being betrayed
by a man; losing Sylvia is like having a phantom limb. There is also the
ambitious hardworking woman in the character of Sylvia, who states
that 'I am the man I want to marry', but who eventually discovers her

femininity, a man, and starts to relax her hair, thus signifying a return to femininity. Throughout the film there are no men on screen whatsoever and this absence serves to politicize *The Women*. Their nonexistence highlights the film's artificial segregation so that the men become more present in their exclusion. This is particularly notable in the power that they wield and which evokes the women's illegible rage (McRobbie, 2009). Mary is sacked by her father and Sylvia is almost fired by her male boss, eventually walking out of her job in order to preserve her integrity. Both Mary and her mother have unfaithful husbands, and Molly is distressed by her father's abandonment. The final credits imply that Sylvia sets up her own glossy magazine featuring the four girlfriends on the cover. This demonstrates that she has taken to heart Molly's earlier complaint, and that she is going some way to making women's intimate publics and the magazine industry less 'complicated'. The film ends with Sylvia and Mary reconciled after Sylvia's betrayal. Sylvia praises Mary's fashion show:

Sylvia: Your daughter looked at you today in a new way. You gave her a mother who got something for herself. That's important. Remember when they said we couldn't have it all?

Mary: We can have it all. The question is, do we want it?

Sylvia: I don't want it all. I just want a nice piece of it.

Mary: I don't want it all either, because it's exhausting.

Sylvia: We can handle anything. We'll be each other's wives.

Mary: Do you know how loveable you are, Sylvie Fowler?

The climax of the film is open-ended. Perhaps Mary will pursue her career, or maybe she will put her energies into supporting her daughter. Rather than being issues that include the support of men, or address a wider political arena, her choices become purely female and individual.

Imperfect: *Bridesmaids* and *Your Sister's Sister*

In some ways, the womance mimics the brotherly love of the bromance such as *The Hangover* (2009), *Superbad* (2007) and *Knocked Up* (2007) where imperfect masculinities are celebrated. However, there are significant disparities. Karen Boyle and Susan Berridge argue, in the context of *Baby Mama*, that 'the denial of the possibility of same-sex desire between the two women', which is achieved through comedy, conflict and betrayal, 'also works to dilute the intensity of their friendship and to render the leads curiously asexual in the contexts of their hetero-romances'. This is persuasive, as I have been arguing that girl-friend reflexivity is fundamentally strategic. In other words, sexual desire is prohibited or redundant because these friendships are struc-tured through a business logic, where women are striving for repre-sentability. In contrast, as Boyle and Berridge maintain, male friendship films, 'openly admit and, indeed, celebrate, men's fascinations with one another in a context where the line between the homosocial and homo-sexual may at times be rendered visible, but is more rigidly policed' (Boyle and Berridge, 2012, 7). In the womance, girls' friendships are rep-resented as enhancing each others' achievements within a postfeminist consumer landscape. Friendship is rerouted as tactical, calculated and planned. Whereas bromance movies represent men relating through the sexual desire for a woman, in the womance the women do not seem interested in men or in sex – only the commodification of their own libido as visible erotic capital.

Traditionally, heterosexual male homosocial bonding is constructed through the traffic of the bodies of women. Consequently, anxieties over sexuality and the body are projected onto women and it is women who bear the burden of to-be-looked-at-ness (Mulvey, 1975). This is exac-erbated in postfeminist culture where women are expected to adhere to the dictates of perfection. Because male subjectivities can be con-stituted through power, intellect, humour and other forms of cultural capital, men are represented as having a different relationship to their body. The performance of heterosexual masculinity in the bromance is not overtly constructed through the body's commodification as a per-fect 'guy' spectacle. Indeed, much of the humour of the bromance is garnered through laughing at the male body and sexuality; at exposing the body's abjection rather than reining it in through normative cruel-ties. Buddies appear to be careless about their bodies. Moreover, because male bodies are not produced through a misogynist tradition of the grotesque sexual appetite, these portrayals have a different affect. This is still corporeal violence, of course, as masculinity is just as regulated as femininity and it also holds its own skill set. However, the disci-plining regime through which the buddies structure their friendships with and through their bodies coheres differently.[4] In the economy of the bromance, it is the women who embody and signify sex as an ideal spectacle or overt erotic capital. In the final two films discussed in this chapter, however, women's aspirations for flawlessness are punc-tured for more libidinous and loving friendships, and it is to these that I now turn.

Bridesmaids received high critical acclaim and good box office ratings. It is produced by Judd Apatow who also produced *Girls* (discussed in the next chapter) as well as the bromances *Knocked Up*, *Superbad* and *The 40 Year Old Virgin* (2005). The central womance is between girlfriends, and planning a wedding drives the plot. In addition, the two main girlfriends, Annie (Kristen Wiig) and Lillian (Maya Rudolph), have been best friends since childhood. However, they live in Milwaukee and the film eschews the glamour of Manhattan. Wiig does not have the glamorous youthful luminosities of Hathaway or Hudson, or the same association with branded culture as Sarah Jessica Parker. She does not have a glamorous star persona and, because she has starred in texts portraying male friendships such as *Knocked Up* or the television show *Bored to Death* (HBO 2009–), she brings to her character a personality that is more akin to what Rosin defines as 'the omega male':

> This often-unemployed, romantically challenged loser can show up as a perpetual adolescent [...] He can be sweet, bitter, nostalgic, or cynical, but he cannot figure out how to be a man. 'We call each other "man," says Ben Stiller's character in *Greenberg*, 'but it's a joke. It's like imitating other people'.
>
> (Rosin, 2012, 56)

Like the omega male – and unlike the postfeminist girlfriends discussed above – Annie is represented as working out how to be a woman. She is unemployed and without a coherent life strategy or business plan. Her lack of entrepreneurialism is both permitted and heightened through the film's clear demarcation from other girlfriend flicks' overreliance on product placement. High-end commodities and brands are not as fetishized and consequently there is space for girlfriend engagement outside the ubiquitous control of a promotional culture. The film punctures the dream of perfection and represents the girlfriends as flawed but loving each other. Significantly, because the characters are not perfect, the humour functions as a natural extension of their identities, rather than a punishment.[5]

Annie and Lillian's bestfriendship is tenderly portrayed, particularly in a coffee shop scene where they laugh together as Annie rubs chocolate in her teeth. It is a scene of imperfect pleasure outside the frame of cultivating sex and emotion talk, as humour and tenderness are the dominant modes of communication as opposed to competition for visibility. Near the beginning of the film, Lillian asks Annie to be her Maid of Honour, which means that Annie must create the perfect bachelorette party, the perfect dress fitting, the perfect shower and the perfect wedding. Nevertheless, the film keeps puncturing these ideals. The bridesmaids get acute food poisoning when they are fitting dresses and this fissures the stock makeover sequence. This scene takes huge scatological pleasure in depicting the bridesmaids going to the toilet in the sink. It ends with the bride-to-be defecating in the street. Although the humour is directed at the women's bodies, it does not replicate the mutual sabotage of other girlfriend flicks, nor the misogyny of *Sex and the City 2* (as I discuss in the next chapter). This is because there is less of a focus on the self as a coherent and competitive brand. The food poisoning is accidental and, consequently, the scene is saturated with pathos rather than bitchiness.

The friends are not competing for visibility. Rather, the rift occurs because Annie is jealous of Lillian's new friend – the perfect Helen – and competes with her for Lillian's affections. Annie and Lillian eventually fall out when they are on an aeroplane going to Las Vegas for the bachelorette party and Annie (high on sedatives and alcohol) instigates a forced landing in Wyoming. Helen takes over as wedding planner and, in true womance fashion, Lillian and Annie split up and then miss each other. They are eventually reunited at the wedding and the sentimental focus is on them singing together, rather than the bride and groom; the groom, typically, is almost non-existent throughout the film. Annie's drug-fuelled and drunken acting out, as well as the cynicism and anger that she performs throughout the film, is refreshing in a postfeminist branded culture that relentlessly promotes either the happy or bitchy archetypal girl. In addition, rather than working in media or fashion, Annie is single and works in a jeweller's shop selling (or failing to sell) engagement rings. She does not have it all, and neither does she strive for this. She does not express her rage on the body of her friend (like in *Bride Wars, Mean Girls,* or *In Her Shoes*), and neither does she express it through 'emotionally eating' like Mary in *The Women,* or through the cold isolation of Carrie in *Sex and the City 1*. Instead, she enjoys a full and libidinal catharsis. Annie destroys Lillian's perfect shower in a scene of slapstick raw anger. This is not due to jealousy of Lillian's situation in the postfeminist lifecycle. Rather, Annie seems to be genuinely angry at commercialized fakery of the shower, as well as experiencing and expressing pain at missing Lillian.

Because the girlfriends, with the exception of Helen, do not strive for perfection, they are not punished within the moral framework of the girlfriend flick. The girlfriends in *Bride Wars* and *Sex and the City 1* have to learn their lessons around consumption and appetite before they can achieve resolution. Carrie, Liv and Emma are trapped in the glossy paen to affluence that is the womance and they are scapegoats in its fetishization of commercial culture. Lillian and Annie, however, are situated in the mediocre drabness of Milwaukee and they do not strive for hypervisibility (although Lillian does have a big wedding). Consequently, they do not have to be humiliated within the ethical framework of the film. In fact motherhood, marriage and all the coveted life stages on the postfeminist lifecycle are unidealized. One of the bridesmaids, for example, shouts at her children: 'Hey! Shut your filthy fucking mouth!' and bemoans that she is, 'surrounded by savages'. The characters do have to learn lessons of friendship, however. They can only reconcile once they have articulated how much they miss each other, and once Annie has overcome her depression, signified by postfeminist symbols of empowerment: male desire and the revitalization of her entrepreneurial self through her cupcake business (...of course).

We are encouraged to have empathy for Annie's character. She is heteronormatively beautiful – thin and blonde – but she is represented as tired and rough around the edges. She is not afraid to puncture her image. There is less fetishization of her flawless girl-beauty. In addition, these are girlfriends relating across difference as Lillian is a woman of colour. However, her race is not reified in the same way as it is in the films discussed in the following chapter. Lillian is not a secretary or subservient to Annie, neither is she a marker of racial authenticity signified through a retreat to her hometown. Instead, Lillian and Annie are girlfriends relating equally and with a loving friendship across difference. This is a rare occurrence in girlfriend media texts, even if it is never a point of productive complexity during the course of the film. Because *Bridesmaids* punctures the neoliberal dream of perfection, women's bodies are (relative to the texts of popular culture) freed from the punishing girlfriend gaze. Whereas most girlfriend media sell the pleasures of a female homosocial bonding through the bodies of women in order to regulate normatively distinctive femininities, this text partly subverts this regulation through the celebration of imperfection and humour.

Your Sister's Sister, like *The Women*, is directed by a woman (Lynn Shelton). It differs from the previous films because it includes a man, Jack (Mark Duplass), in the already existing friendship between two sisters, Hannah (Rosemarie DeWitt) and Iris (Emily Blunt). This in turn complicates the homosocial structure of the womance. In addition, he is an emotionally and economically precarious male, more akin to the characters in the bromance. Like *In Her Shoes*, *Your Sister's Sister* is a sibling film where the ultimate betrayal is sleeping with a sister's date. However, this film does something different with that stock trope. Hannah is a lesbian and Iris is recovering from the death of her ex-boyfriend (who was also Jack's brother) some years previously. Hannah's sexuality means that the sisters are not overtly competing over men or over postfeminist hypervisibility.

At the beginning of the film, Jack is in a state of grief over his brother's death. In order to help Jack take stock of his life, Iris invites him to spend time alone in her father's lake house. She hopes that this solitude will help him get his life back in order. Unbeknownst to Iris, her sister Hannah is also staying there to recover from a recent break-up. On their first night there, after their surprise encounter, Hannah and Jack have sex. The following day, Iris unexpectedly turns up. It transpires that Hannah had sex with Jack in order to get pregnant. Moreover, she did not know that Jack and Iris had the potential to be in a relationship. Indeed, at the beginning of the film Iris and Jack have not admitted these feelings to themselves or each other.

Like the womances, Hannah and Iris are represented through the tropes of lovers. They sleep in the same bed and are shot from above as if in postcoital intimacy. The film is set in the literal retreat of their childhood – their father's lake house – on an island outside the city of Seattle. What binds the sisters is conversation. Most of the film is cen-tred on their convivial speech; they are constantly talking about feelings and experiences. Consequently, the real betrayal is that Hannah did not tell Iris that she had sex with Jack; it is her secrecy which is painful for Iris. Hannah eventually confesses to Iris because she believes that this is information that Iris needs in order to make informed decisions about her future. Significantly, there is no competition for sexual power between the sisters. Moreover, they do not have desires for representabil-ity that supersede their loyalty to one another. Although Hannah wants a baby, this is configured differently from conventional chick flicks as she is gay and her love for Iris supplants wanting to be a mother.

Unlike the womances, they do not split up for the stock melancholic montage sequence. They both stay in the lake house. Although they do not speak to each other and there is a degree of animosity, the prox-imity of their relating means that there is an attempt to understand each other through engagement. The lesson they must learn is not to become more similar. Rather, they are learning and flexing trust in order to deepen their love. Significantly, their womance betrayal is triangu-lated by Jack, who opens out the female space while simultaneously not foreclosing friendship between the women. Jack leaves Hannah and Iris in order to confront his unexpressed grief over his brother's death. His emotional journey is reflected through long and arduous bike rides up hills. In fact, it is Jack who has to learn the most lessons in the course of the film before he is able to achieve resolution through winning the love of Iris. That is, he must overcome the omega male performance that he has been identified with and this is primarily done through becoming responsible and also through participating in the sisters' conversational capital. In addition, the film does not end with marriage and babies in the conventional sense. Hannah believes she might be pregnant with Jack's baby and the three of them agree to participate in the baby's upbringing. Although the film ends on a cliffhanger as we do not know the result of Hannah's pregnancy test, it does go some way to celebrating a queerer family paradigm and puncturing the dream of postfeminist representability. Significantly, Hannah and Iris are able to be creative and compassionate in their negotiation of anger. The love between the sisters is primarily expressed through their conversations, making their friendship one where it is possible to 'speak out' and to work through the knots of (sexual) difference and betrayal.

Bridesmaids and *Your Sister's Sister* consciously depart from the glossy perfections of the womances discussed above. The feelings of betrayal and anger that the girlfriends experience together are not produced through anxieties over representability. Consequently, friendship is not competitive. Rather, the qualities of trust, loyalty and humour are represented as ontologically valuable in themselves. Instead of representing strategic friendships, these films portray women who value intimacy as sacred in its own right, rather than a route to postfeminist visibility. These films deconstruct the technologies behind self-branding, as well as the heterosexual 'wedding imaginary' which provides the backdrop or trope of girlfriend representability (Sgroi, 2006, 114). Importantly, these two films depict girlfriends relating across racial and sexual difference. In both cases, these differences are glossed over and are not a means to explore the potentially fruitful complexities generated from relating across and through intersectional identities. Nevertheless, they are useful portrayals of girlfriends disengaged from the narrative polarities of niche and mainstream media platforms, and communicating together.

Bridesmaids mimics the gestures and signifiers of bromance by relishing in the bawdiness that the celebration of imperfection can offer. Because it punctures the ideals of consumer perfection, the girlfriends are not hostage to self-spectacle in the same way as the pre-crash girlfriends. Consequently, they are able to play with the scatological references which deliver much of the humour in buddy movies. *Your Sister's Sister* represents two beautiful women, and Iris evidences the perfect postfeminist life. Moreover, the film potentially ends with the traditional trope of babies. Similarly, *Bridesmaids* has its conventional drawbacks as it plays on the stereotypes of foolish women. Nevertheless, in the context of the branded cultures that saturate a straight white girlfriend media, they are both welcome departures. These texts represent 'imperfect' girlfriends or girlfriends who do not fit into the typical normatively distinctive paradigm. In addition, they represent them struggling together for feminine subjectivities in a world that no longer promises that they can have it all. It makes for a different kind of reflexive girlfriendship.

5
Making White Lives Better?

The veil across the mouth, it freaks me out. It's like they don't want them to have a voice.

Sex and the City 2

The Mammy: *The Help* and *Sex and the City 1*

From the white nostalgia of *Mad Men* (AMC 2007–) to the new Oscar-winning *The Help*, there has been a resurgence in media representations of black women cast as maids and servants. The assumption of a post-racial society has opened up a site for old stereotypes. This racism is implicitly justified because these portrayals are claiming to be authentic representations of the past.[1] In *The Help*, the stereotype of the Mammy – the archetype of the black female servant – is resurrected in the name of authenticity. The plot centres on Skeeter Phelan (Emma Stone), a college graduate who accepts a job at the local paper in her home-town of Jacksonville as the house-cleaning agony aunt. As part of her research she interviews her friend's 'Help', Aibileen Clark (Viola Davis). Through these interviews, Skeeter realizes that she can further her career by writing a book from the perspective of the Helps. This is a subversive project in 1960s Mississippi, and Skeeter is cast as the girl-heroine who innocently sees through the retro racism of her peers. Although she should represent the generation of second-wave feminists, she is troped through the signifiers of postfeminism: she is girly, happy, thin and relentlessly entrepreneurial. The two main Helps, Aibileen and Minny Jackson (Octavia Spencer), have prominent speaking parts which are eloquent and, within the context of the film, have depth. However, they are scripted through the tropes of self-effacement and martyrdom. Minny, for example, sacrifices herself for her children by getting beaten by her husband (she will eventually leave him to work for a white couple). The black men are either humbly obedient, cowardly or abusive. They do not have much to say. The marginalization of men is typical of girlfriend media. However, set against the (obfuscated) backdrop of the civil rights movement this representation is further problematized.

It is the new generation located in the girl-thin body of Skeeter that will provide the courage to cross the race barrier. She has the freshness that we are expected to admire. She has the guts to quest for truth. 'Courage skipped a generation', her mother tells her. The white women (with the exception of Skeeter's mother) are thin, normatively distinctive and, like the women in *Mad Men*, spectacular in their retro 1960s fashion: ski pants and pinched waists visually accentuate their thinness. This is especially true for Skeeter, who is cast as a tomboy (although she will achieve her prince once she realizes that she is beautiful enough). In contrast, Aibileen and Minny are big and wear the hideous grey clothes of the hired Help. They roll their eyes and are played for laughs. However, because they are on the side of good we are expected to laugh with them rather than at them. They are older than the colourfully dressed white girls, and they are asexual. The film achieves this stereotyping through its bid for historical authenticity: these are the bodies and sartorial styles of the past. While the white women are troped through the signifiers of twenty-first-century girlfriends, Aibileen and Minny are denied style, romance, love and sex. In this way, the film purposefully obscures the past as although the clothes might be historically accurate, the (mis)recognition of black women as subservient mammies without sexuality was and is a white fantasy.

In a mawkish display of historical revisionism, the civil rights movement is erased. It is replaced by a sentimental relationship between a white girl and her black servants; politics is subsumed under the radical possibilities of the girl reaching out with friendship. Black men and women are depicted as so deeply frightened that they become dependent on Skeeter to tell their stories. Skeeter moves to New York on the backs of the black servants but she sends each of the Helps some of her royalties. In the climactic feel-good moment, these adult black women are portrayed as overjoyed and grateful towards their benefactress. In addition, institutionalized racism is glossed over through the image of white innocence. This white innocence is not just evident in the girly naivety of Skeeter, but also in the purity of the white children who are under the charge of the Helps. Aibileen repeats to her white child: 'you is smart, you is kind, you is important'. Although there is a hint that it is difficult for Aibileen to look after white children at the expense of her son, she never actually states this. Instead, she is depicted as a better and more authentic mother than the white women, as she offers a genuine love that rises above racial difference. The film suggests that it only when white girls grow up and are indoctrinated by a racist society do problems between white and black women arise. The insinuation or implication is that racism is superficial and therefore can easily be unlearnt. It reinforces the post-racial ideal.

In the featurette which accompanies the film on the IMDB website, the actresses who play Minny and Aibileen insist that the film transcends the cultural moment – including the civil rights movement – and they speak through the language of therapy and self-help. They transmogrify racial segregation into a contemporary issue of inner struggle and overcoming obstacles. Significantly, they configure the film as a means to unite women. Davis states, 'these women enter each other's lives and they all suffer with each other' and, 'these characters give each other permission to dream. Something about that makes people feel that it is possible.' Spencer concurs: 'everyone can see themselves in any one of these characters' (IMDB). This is typical of the discourse of intimate publics as identified by Berlant who argues that embedded within the

> solidaristic activity of the intimate public of femininity is a white universalist paternalism, sometimes dressed as maternalism [...] bourgeois white women writers have mobilized fantasies of what black and working-class interiority based on suffering must feel like in order to find a language for their own more privileged suffering.
>
> (Berlant, 2008, 6)

We see the discourses of privileged suffering – coded here through the language of self-empowerment – being mapped onto the civil rights era. Berlant identifies the universalizing of human suffering where, 'romantic conventions of individual historical acts of compassion and transcendence are adapted to imagine a nonhierarchical social world that is postracist and "at heart" democratic because good intentions and love flourish in it' (Berlant, 2008, 6).

Despite this universalizing of suffering, *The Help* represents black and white female bodies as insurmountably different; a barrier that can never be crossed. This difference is signified through change and transformation. Whereas the white girls achieve makeovers and makeunders, the black women are represented as static and authentic. Because white girls need to learn the lessons of vanity, appetite and consumption (signifiers of the ambivalence of a branded culture as discussed in

Chapter 4), the villain of the film – Hilly (Bryce Dallas Howard) – is punished through inadvertently consuming the wrong kinds of food. Minny makes her a chocolate pie partly made of faeces, which the unknowing Hilly eats voraciously. Like the queen of The Plastics in *Mean Girls* and Emily in *The Devil Wears Prada*, Hilly receives the just deserts of the postfeminist Mean Girl in being publicly humiliated by the disfigurement of her flawless looks. Hilly's girly healthiness is punctured through the faecal dessert. The Helps, however, are denied any kind of transformation. In addition, any weaknesses or flaws in their physical appearance – Aibileen falls in the mud as she is running for safety from a white attack – are sentimentalized and represented in such a way as to provoke pity. Whereas Hilly's imperfections are coded through punishment, black women's lack of normative style is configured through victimhood – which is itself a postfeminist sin. Moreover, they are reliant on the white women to ventriloquize their lives.

But it is not just period nostalgia that positions black and white women as benefactress and maid. We see this relationship updated for a millennial Manhattan in *Sex and the City 1*, where Carrie plays the benefactress to her African American personal assistant, Louise (Jennifer Hudson). On Carrie's return from her womancing honeymoon she hires Louise to help her cope with her public humiliation (after all, the wedding was announced in *Vogue*). Louise is in her 20s and from St Louis. She shares a one-bedroom apartment with two others, has six siblings and a degree in computer science. She has come to New York to 'fall in love' and to enjoy fashion. For her, this means renting designer handbags, and she and Carrie bond over her rented Louis Vuitton. Louise is hardworking, reliable and genuine. Carrie states, 'I began to think of her as Saint Louise from St Louis.' She is also romantic. When Louise and Carrie go out for a drink (Carrie is buying), Louise explains how her hometown boyfriend broke up with her, but she is firm: 'I'm not gonna give up on love. Love is the thing, you know. You see that? [pointing to her key ring] That's love. And I'm bringing it to me all day long.' Louise's refusal to give up is rewarded as she eventually marries him.

In the television series there were very few African Americans represented, so the character of Louise is an attempt to puncture the overwhelming whiteness of the female landscape. Louise is on a different trajectory and in a different place on the postfeminist lifecycle from Carrie. We have been told that Carrie and Samantha came to New York with nothing, and when Carrie was in her 20s she forwent food for *Vogue*. When Carrie buys Louise a drink she tells her that the

20s are for enjoying yourself: 'Your 30s are to learn the lessons. Your 40s are to pay for the drinks.' Although Louise is distanced from the core gaze through her curves, which attest, like the characters played by Marcia DeBonis in *Lipstick Jungle* and *Bride Wars*, to a low income and disposable status, she does become a bride. Her curves therefore could be a positive mark of her difference (Smith-Shomade, 2002). Rather than relinquishing 'almost all signifiers of racial difference' and subsuming 'ethnicity into the dominant repertoire of normative white femininity', Louise refuses to be as skinny as the white woman she works for (McRobbie, 2009).

Nevertheless, Louise is not a protagonist and consequently her primary role in the film seems to be true to racial stereotype; that is, 'to make white lives better' (Springer, 2008, 84). Carrie's leaving present to Louise is a Louis Vuitton handbag: 'It was the best money I'd ever spent' she confesses. This gift is partly represented as an older woman helping a younger version of herself. However, contextualized within the racial politics of the *Sex and the City* franchise, this is actually a charitable and patronizing gesture. Kimberly Springer argues that postfeminism assumes a universal category of women, and that 'racial and gender stereotypes are the commodity and the discourse that make difference legible in popular culture' (Springer, 2008, 78). This commodification is written at the level of the body and in the possibilities of consumption. Louise is not overtly stereotyped like the Helps. She evidences style and has a consciousness of fashion (even if she does not have the capital to fully participate in its practices). She is also found to be attractive by her (black) fiancé and eventually marries him. She has her own romance narrative and, moreover, she is located in the (domestic) spaces of Manhattan. However, her race is commodified within the film as she plays PA to the primary character and she is never hypervisible in the same way as the core girlfriends.

Patricia Hill Collins identifies the modern Mammy in contemporary popular culture:

> The image of Mammy, the loyal female servant created under chattel slavery, has been resurrected and modernized as template for middle-class Black womanhood. Maneuvering through this image of the modern mammy requires a delicate balance between being appropriately subordinate to White and/or male authority yet maintaining a level of ambition and aggressiveness needed for achievement in middle-class occupations.
>
> (Hill Collins, 2004, 140)

Louise is ambitious, which is evidenced by her degree in computer science. Nevertheless, her career trajectory is such that she does not encroach on the entrepreneurial territories of the girlfriends. Moreover, because she ends the film retreating to the community of her hometown with a ring that 'ain't rented', she never will compete with the white girlfriends in their high-profile careers. Eschewing the glamour of New York, Louise is not, like the girlfriends, in awe of its commerciality and branded spaces. She is scripted through authenticity, through never giving up on love, and also through retreat. In this way, she is demarcated from the consumer apparatus and appetites of the skinny white girlfriends. She does not belong in their policing networks and cannot participate in girlfriend reflexivity.

Springer discusses how the black woman in *Waiting to Exhale* (1995), *Down in the Delta* (1998) and *Beauty Shop* (2005), 'either returns to her family and black community who she has neglected or she turns to a tight network of sister-friends' (Springer, 2008, 86). As Springer notes, 'the retreat to family or sister-friends is actually a coming back to blackness – the implication being that when a black female protagonist has it all, she becomes a snob and is in danger of no longer being authentically black' (Springer, 2008, 87). Springer's invocation of a tight network of sister-friends is a pertinent one in relation to retreat and the girlfriend flick. For Springer this focus on the sister-friends is part of the depoliticization of the status of black women in contemporary culture. Rather than addressing wider political issues, women retreat back into the safety of an authentic, nurturing sameness. Springer warns against the retreatist narrative when it is applied to black women:

> Given black women's presence and success in the workplace, what does it mean for postfeminism to re-domesticate them with the assistance of racial stereotyping and a sexual double standard?
>
> (Springer, 2008, 86)

Louise's retreat, her authenticity, her curves, but also her place in the film's hierarchy of consumption – she is employed by Carrie – mean that retreat for her is a particularly conservative gesture. She may be permitted part of the narrative of representability but read against Springer's theoretical frame (and within the context of *Sex and the City 1* where the girlfriends are firmly placed in the urban setting of New York), she must know her place in the racial and gender power structure. Love and labels provide the bridge across the racial and cultural divide for women in the postfeminist girlfriend flick, but these places are fixed.

Orientalism: *Sex and the City 2*

Samantha runs a successful PR company and in *Sex and the City* 2 she is invited by a wealthy businessman to experience his hotel in Abu Dhabi. The four girlfriends are flown there in his private jet and are assigned a private butler on their arrival. Every fantasy – as long as it's not sexual – is catered for in the opulence of this Orientalized topography. In a bafflingly crude depiction of the United Arab Emirates, the backwardness and restricted freedoms of the culture are contrasted with the freedom of the American women. The film's Orientalism is overt in its depiction of the 'exotic' and 'inscrutable' Orient deviants, who are juxtaposed with the (white) transparency of the honest girlfriends (Said, 1978, 38–41). Said defines Orientalism as an 'epistemological and ontological distinction between the West and the East'. This distinction is achieved by marking the East as lacking 'civil society or individuality' – the properties that the West is naturally assumed to have. Non-Western societies are, therefore, pushed back in time and constructed as primitive and backward, but authentically so (Yeğenoğlu, 1998, 6). This is evident throughout the film through the portrayal of souks, the emphasis on 'traditions', as well as the fantasy landscape. Compared with, for example, Mr Big, Muslim and Arab masculinity are conflated with irrationality, barbarism and violence.

The film sets up a contrast between the high visibility of the girlfriends and the women of Abu Dhabi who wear the veil, niqab or burqa. It appears to evidence McRobbie's process of disarticulation which 'displaces possible solidarities, with a re-instated hierarchy of civilisation and modernity', as well as participating in 'a discourse which celebrates the freedoms of fashion-conscious "thong-wearing" Western girls in contrast to those young women who, for example, wear the veil' (McRobbie, 2009, 27). As the four girlfriends sit outside their luxury hotel, Carrie observes two women in niqabs and states, 'the veil across the mouth, it freaks me out. It's like they don't want them to have a voice.' One of the women orders food, and Carrie tells her friends, 'French fries for the lady with the veil. How is she going to do that? A lift for every fry. That is a major commitment to fried food.' Within the context of *Sex and the City*'s camp irony, where everyone is subject to ridicule, this should be a harmless quip. However, understood through McRobbie's process of disarticulation and Said's Orientalist framework, we see the girlfriends laughing at an inferior, feminized and objectified culture. The conservative and neo-imperialist gesture is startling, and it firmly implicates the film within a discourse of distancing and objectifying the Arab world.

The four girlfriends find themselves in trouble when an inappropriately dressed Samantha drops condoms on the floor and a crowd of stereotypes gather round to abuse her. The friends are eventually rescued by four women in niqabs who take them into a dried flower shop for safety. It is there that the women discover their connectivity. The Arab women are reading the same book on the menopause as Samantha, evidencing a global desire to maintain sexual desire and youthful looks. But what really unites them is fashion. As the women take off their niqabs, Carrie's voice-over tells us, 'And there, in a dried-flower shop, halfway across the world... underneath hundreds of years of tradition... was this year's spring collection.' It is a moment of unity and recognition. Just as Carrie and Louise are able to bond through Louis Vuitton, so these women in Abu Dhabi are able to articulate their sameness with the American girlfriends through fashion. The Western designer labels function to signify the Arab women's freedom and civilization, as well as reinforce their likeness with the *Sex and the City* girlfriends. Fashion is a signifier of the postfeminist and essentialized norm: women love to shop and to covet designer labels. Indeed, fashion is constructed as existing in a girlish fantasy land outside the matrix of power. Just as the postfeminist woman is defined through her ability to consume, so (correct and lavish) consumption binds different women together.

Neither *Sex and the City* films received critical acclaim and the second, in particular, was panned by the critics. Tellingly, much of the criticism is directed at the women's bodies. Philip French in *The Observer* describes Carrie as 'equine' (French, 2010). In the *Telegraph*, Sukhdev Sandhu dismisses the women for 'all getting older', especially Carrie who looks, 'if you happen to go for human pipe-cleaners, absolutely fabulous'. He also describes her as being 'a cross between Worzel Gummidge and Bride of Chucky'. Miranda, on the other hand, 'looks badly embalmed' (Sandhu, 2010). In the *London Evening Standard* Andrew O'Hagan writes,

> Carrie Bradshaw is 45 and Samantha, her blonde slut friend, is 53, and it's more than difficult to love them. Why? Because they are greedy, faithless, spoiled, patronising, women-degrading morons who confuse their common vulgarity for camaraderie, that's why.

In addition, 'These girls are so hung up on looking great they've forgotten there are several ways to be ugly.' The women behave like 'materialistic whores' (O'Hagan, 2010). This is precisely the misogynistic discourse that generated the image of the bridezilla and which girlfriends like Ellie and Jules in *Cougar Town* internalize and relate through. Part of the reason why these journalists (and their editors) allow their misogyny and slut-shaming full rein is because the film invites it. In particular, the character of Samantha is humiliated. Her obsession with sex and aging are played for laughs and she is ridiculed by the camera. In a public office, in front of her assistant, she pulls her underwear round her ankles to rub ointment on her vagina. She drops condoms on the ground and scrabbles in the dirt to pick them up. It could be compared to *Bridesmaids*, another girlfriend movie that privileges slapstick humour and laughs at female bodies. However, because *Bridesmaids* does not market a relentless commercialized perfection, it manages to keep the characters' dignity intact. Or rather, it displaces the closed boundaries of the dignified female middle class body in favour of a more fluid performativity. Contextualized within a cultural tradition of fearing the female body, as well as within the contemporary privileging of girly femininity, the portrayal of Samantha is one of prurient abjection. Moreover, if the East is a foil to Western realities, then this landscape is apt for Samantha's punishment as an older successful woman.

However, the utilization of Arab women to comment upon Western femininities seems to refract differently according to the characters. The female mirroring across difference covertly slut-shames Samantha through negatively contrasting her with the contained sexualities of the Arab women. In the case of Carrie, however, the Arab women seem to reflect back her authenticity. Indeed, Carrie's only 'sluttish' gesture is when she almost makes out with an ex-boyfriend. She is wracked with guilt and confesses her misdemeanour to Mr Big, who eventually forgives her. At the beginning of the film, when Carrie comments on the veiled woman's eating of fries, there is a moment when the two women's eyes meet, and Carrie smiles in a nervous reaching out of friendliness. Like Louise from St Louis, the Arab women hold up an authentic mirror to Carrie. The film harbours a deep anxiety over glamorous postfeminist older women and so positioning their femininities (with the exception of Samantha) through an axis of friendliness with the Othered women is an attempt to validate them. Indeed, the Arab women are harnessed through the film's sexual economy to slut-shame the white women. White women seeking recognition and wholeness from Orientalised women has a long history dating back to the travel writing of Lady Mary Wortley Montagu, through to Lady Elizabeth Craven and Lady

Hester Stanhope. In *Sex and the City 2* the misogyny at the heart of the film, which becomes overt in reviews, is harnessed through juxtaposing the integrity of the veiled women with the girlfriends' relentless appetites.

If the strategic networks of girlfriend culture cultivate and maintain power among women, and this power is defined as being white and middle class, then what happens to low-income women and women of different ethnicities, races and cultures? In the womance, as well as the corporate sisterhoods of the Manhattan dramedies, the function of women of colour is primarily to make white lives better. This is either through their subservient servant status or because they provide a mirror of authenticity to render the self-branded and consumer-obsessed girlfriends less fake. In most girlfriend texts racial and cultural difference are organized as insurmountable. With the exception of Mia and Victory (and to a lesser extent Alicia) in *Cashmere Mafia* and *Lipstick Jungle*, women of colour are excluded from the aspirational luminosities of postfeminist neoliberal success. On the whole, African American women are disqualified from representability, and this disqualification is written at the level of the body; skinniness is white and lucrative, while blackness is located as fat and low income. Women of colour are, in general, excluded from the paradigm of normative distinctiveness and, as a result, they are discounted from the policing and competitive networks of girlfriends. Although *The Devil Wears Prada* and *The Women* feature African American girlfriends, they are marginal to the plot. In addition, although there are many films that solely feature African American girlfriends such as *Waiting to Exhale* (1995) or *Down in the Delta* (1998), girlfriends do not relate equally across racial difference. They are segregated.

White feminism: *2 Broke Girls*

Rather than representing girlfriends relating with and through intersectionality, the market segments into niches that target specific racial, ethnic and cultural demographics. This is particularly evident in the structuring of American and British television. Banet-Weiser critiques the trend of niche market cable channels, arguing that marketers' processes of segmentation have rendered demographic groups such as African Americans 'distinct and closed'. Intersectional identities become commodified and separated. This reinforces the understanding that identified niche markets have no relation to the mainstream or to other demographics:

The result is not a harmonious multichannel, multicultural media universe but one in which a host of niche channels stand in their discrete corners, while the mainstream audience channels continue to dominate the stage and define norms of representation.

(Banet-Weiser, 2012, 35–36)

Beretta Smith-Shomade identifies how the cable channel Black Entertainment Television (BET) makes 'black folks synonymous with consumer products' (Smith-Shomade, 2007, 179). Indeed, commodifying identity reifies it and this is problematic if racial prejudice is enacted through the same objectifying strategies. In Banet-Weiser's words, racial identity becomes a hegemonically constructed thing, 'rather than relational, intersectional qualities that are constantly subject to reinvention' (Banet-Weiser, 2012, 36).

Black and white women are rarely represented as relating through the complexities of girlfriendship. Their relationships are either superficially or marginally represented as in *The Devil Wears Prada*, unproductively antagonistic (as in the *Sex and the City* episode 'No Ifs Ands or Butts'), or problematically sentimentalized such as in *The Help*. Girlfriends tend to be represented as relating with and through girlfriends who are 'like them', and this division is heightened through niche marketing and, as I discuss below, the postfeminist privileging of whiteness. The sitcom *Girlfriends* (UPN 2000–2008) focuses on the friendships of four African American girlfriends. Despite being a comedy, the show tackles difficult issues such as jealousy, betrayal and loss. Season 7 begins with Joan (Tracee Ellis Ross) mourning the loss of her best friend Toni (Jill Marie Jones) while struggling with the devastation of Hurricane Katrina in New Orleans. The comedy is one of the longest-running series featuring a predominantly black cast since *The Cosby Show* (NBC, 1984–1992). A spokesperson from the network called it 'the most-watched program on television by African Americans since it premiered in 2000' (LA Times, 2006). I am not suggesting that *Girlfriends* would have been a more valid show had it represented long-running relationships between white and black women. Indeed, shows that demarcate themselves from the white postfeminist landscape of girlfriendship and privilege all black spaces are to be welcomed. However, I am identifying how there are very few representations of women relating through the full range of friendship affect – including its ugly feelings – in a productive and ethical way. This is especially the case with women relating across intersectional identities. There is an absence of racially diverse friendships on television. This critique is not about *Girlfriends*, but rather

I am using it (alongside *Girls* and *2 Broke Girls*) to demonstrate how the complexities of relating across race are frequently excluded, and this is both a consequence and a cause of the problematic segregation of markets.

Girlfriends never aired in the UK and the fact that it did not have distribution here may be linked to Bim Adewunmi's criticism of the whiteness of *Girls*, the HBO series which screened on Sky Living in 2012. Adewunmi argues, 'that none of the unrelatable stuff' about the programme 'was down to my race':

> And that made me feel sad because, in a world where I can easily see myself in these women's lives and experiences, the message fed back loud and clear to me is that they cannot see themselves in my skin, my life.
>
> (Adewunmi, *The Guardian*, 2012)

Girlfriends' black female identities perhaps meant that British television networks believed their audiences could not 'see themselves' in their lives. (Or rather, they did not fit the consumer profile which the networks wish to target, as identified by Greenblatt in relation to *The L Word*, discussed in Chapter 3.) Adewunmi critiques a culture that has 'no interest in putting non-stereotypical portrayals of people of colour onscreen'. Moreover, she protests that if 'you can research medieval feasts or make up magical worlds with different breeds of dragon, then surely you can look into the lives of contemporary brown people and write them into a 30-minute sitcom?' (Adewunmi, 2012). Indeed, many of the American imports to British networks have predominantly white casts, which is reflective of the normative girlfriend femininities which I have been identifying.

The economic downturn offers a space for less-reified performances of femininity on American television. However, relationships between women across the borders of their intersectional identities are still problematically segregated. The television programmes *Girls* and *2 Broke Girls* focus less on having it all and more on having very little. In response to the financial crisis, New York City is no longer the glamorous commercial feminine space of the Manhattan dramedies. Instead, the action is primarily located in the less ostentatious and more culturally diverse borough of Brooklyn. These two programmes challenge the luminosity of postfeminist girlfriends who mobilize affluent happy subjectivities that reap the pleasures of entitled shopping in a global power. Both *Girls* and *2 Broke Girls* depict women in their 20s struggling with their economic situation; financial uncertainty is central to their reflexive girlfriendship. The girlfriends are depicted as insecure and ambivalent about their position in life, and they continuously make mistakes, especially in relation to sex and money. They are sexually harassed by men, a situation which is both humorous and imprisoning. Their bodies are not flawless, and they are confused in a cynical society that refuses to financially embrace them.

These shows maintain elements of the girlfriend genre through centring the conduct of friendship and representing strong emotional bonds with women that surpass those with men. The girlfriends attempt to make sense of their position in the world through an interpersonal girlfriend reflexivity. Whereas the power girlfriends of the Manhattan dramedies support each other in maintaining a hyper-feminine masquerade and corporate power, these shows portray girlfriend sociality as necessary to economic survival. The friends in *2 Broke Girls* and *Girls* give each other food and shelter rather than being dependent on each other to create a self-brand or a coherent narrative. They are mutually reliant in order to learn the basic mechanics of femininity, as well as to protect from male abuse – whether this is emotional, physical or sexual. The fact that they are young makes their precarious lives more palatable (I doubt we'll ever see a compassionate *2 Broke Cougars*) as they do not have to strive for girlhood. The girlfriends' youth also means that their cynicism and lack of designer clothes are not abject because the programmes pivot on the hope that they will eventually make it. Nevertheless, they deconstruct the high-end and commercialized glamour of much girlfriend media.

2 Broke Girls was created by *Sex and the City*'s Michael Patrick King and the comedian Whitney Cummings. It centres on the growing friendship between working class Max Black (Kat Dennings) and the fallen heiress Caroline Channing (Beth Behrs), who both work in a diner. Caroline's father is in prison for fraud and when Caroline initially starts working at the diner Max takes a disliking to her, pointedly asserting: 'Whatever that is, it doesn't belong here' ('Pilot' 1:1). However, when she discovers that Caroline is sleeping on the subway, she invites her home. Subsequently, she helps Caroline at work and proffers her hand of friendship: 'Here, let me take some of those... everyone needs help sometimes' ('Pilot' 1:1). The programme self-consciously mimics the working class and uniformed femininities of Flo and Alice in *Alice* (CBS 1976–1985) as well as the close dyadic intimacies in *Kate and Allie* (CBS 1984–1989). Max is cynical, acerbic, and angry. She throws out such unaspirational one-liners as, 'It's life. Lower your expectations' ('And the Spring Break' 1:19), and (to Caroline): 'We're not family until we testify against one another in a manslaughter trial' ('And the Secret Ingredient' 1:13). She refuses the performance of serenity essential to a postfeminist femininity – 'I'm so many kinds of bitches I've lost count' ('And the Very Christmas Thanksgiving' 1:10) – and is aggressive in her treatment of the diners. She insists that she does not do 'girlfriend stuff', telling Caroline that she is a dude not a girl's girl ('And the Pretty Problem' 1:7).

Women in popular culture are visual indices of the economy, as such they are represented as embodying contemporary anxieties around commercialism. Consequently, whereas Carrie Bradshaw was the signifier for financial optimism, so Max reflects the economy in its downturn (indeed, she *works* in a diner which Carrie would not have even frequented). In *2 Broke Girls*, BFF stands for 'Broke Friends Forever' and 'Bang Bus Friends Forever' referring to Max's birthday present to Caroline: a bus ride to visit Caroline's father in prison. In the penultimate episode of season 1 we see Max act out anger by punching cheesecakes. In the final episode, she pushes a woman who has insulted Caroline. Max's repartee is bawdy and, occasionally, very funny. She is white, young and beautiful, but she challenges the skinniness of the postfeminist girl through continually pointing out her big breasts and enjoying her curvy body. Through these gestures and behaviours, the character of Max is deliberately polarized from the perfect self-brands of the Manhattan dramedies. In addition, the actor Dennings is Jewish (whereas the character Max is unsure of her origins) and this is ironically referred to when Max makes cupcakes for a Hasidic Jewish family and the mother repeats to her, 'It's like looking in the mirror' ('And the Kosher Cupcakes' 1:17).

Sex talk is not a means to accumulate erotic or social capital as in *Sex and the City*. Nor is it a way to create more serene and happy femininities for men, or a perfect branded commodity for self-promotion. Max's sexual carnivalesque is not the self-hating misogyny of Ellie and Jules in *Cougar Town*. Instead, Max's visceral experience is at the centre of her classed self-expression. She plays with the ungirly aspects of her sexuality in a refreshing manner, joking about the yeastiness of her vagina ('vagina' being her favourite word) or the pleasures of masturbating. In addition, she does not pretend to be in control of her life, frequently referring to her pot-smoking, lack of money, and dubious sexual liaisons. Her persona is more reminiscent of the pervasive slacker masculinities; except that she works really hard. The fact that she does not aspire to, and is not represented through, a perfect girly skills set, means that she can exploit abjection without resorting to misogyny. Unlike the flawless girlfriends of *Sex and the City* who have to project sexuality on to their freakish men, Max embodies the pleasures and pains of sex. She uses her libido in a vital and humorous way, rather than to demonstrate commercial and cultural control.

Partly because of their 'imperfect' relationship to the body and sexuality, Caroline and Max share a loving relationship which, to some extent, subverts the girlfriend gaze. Instead of replicating the misogynist conversations of Ellie and Jules in *Cougar Town*, Max and Caroline take pleasure in abjection. Max is having an on-off fling with a street artist named Johnny (Nick Zado). She and Caroline take on a catering job at a party in an art gallery which, it transpires, is hosted by Johnny's girlfriend, Cashandra (Marsha Thomason). Both Johnny and Cashandra are present and this tension drives Caroline and Max to drink copious amounts of the free wine. They will not be paid until all the cupcakes have gone so, drunk, they stuff the cupcakes down each other's bras and escape. The next morning, when they wake up in the same bed, cake is plastered on their faces and falling out of their clothes ('And the Really Petty Cash' 1:9). Here we see female intimacy celebrated through imperfection, slapstick and lack of self-control. Indeed, because they do not regulate each other – especially around body image – their relationship is libidinous and more like a bromance. Max and Caroline do not control each other and when Caroline does attempt to govern Max, this becomes a point of humour.

Boyle and Berridge (2012) argue that most female friendship films focus on already established friendships and consequently they lack the passion and depth of the bromances. They maintain that shared histories between friends dilute the intensity of the homosocial bond. *2 Broke Girls*, however, evidences a developing and intriguing relationship between women. Max and Caroline are both fascinated and repelled by each other's disparities. Indeed, the complexity of their intersectional identities creates an energetic polarity between the girls which runs deeper than the typical incongruence in hair colour that usually typifies female difference in popular culture. Caroline and Max's contrasting pasts heighten the bonds of their friendship as they love each other despite, or because of, their varying outlooks. The celebration of slapstick combined with the relaxed and pleasurable relation that Max has to her body endows their friendship with passion. For example, in 'And the Messy Purse Smackdown' (1:21), they are forced to scrabble around in a dumpster in order to find a tax return. Angry at each other, they fight and throw garbage. Max rubs noodles in Caroline's hair. The amalgamation of the atypical girlfriend mise-en-scène and their mutual rage provides their relationship with a depth, tenderness and libidinal energy that supersedes the controlling networks of much girlfriend media.

Like many girlfriends, Max and Caroline are estranged from their mothers. Consequently, their feminine subjectivities are cultivated through their girlfriend reflexivity. However, this reflexivity refracts differently from the Manhattan dramedies because of the different socioeconomic climate. The 'artfulness' of their friendship is partly learnt and developed through their lack of assets: Max teaches Caroline how to survive on a low income and Caroline shows Max how to have entrepreneurial aspirations. They buy clothes in secondhand stores and shop for groceries using coupons. Max tells Caroline, 'It's not a big deal. Lots of people use coupons. Yes, people like us. Poor people.' Caroline replies, 'The same food for less money? [...] Max, coupons are genius!' ('And the Secret Ingredient' 1:13). Economic realities dominate their lives as many of the jokes pivot on their lack of money, such as Caroline waxing with duct tape. Over time, they profess their loyalty and commitment to each other. Caroline sells her jewellery so that she can buy a purple oven for Max, telling her, 'our future means more to me [...] I'm in for the long haul' ('And the Pop-up Sale' 1:12). In response, Max gives Caroline payment from a drug trial so that Caroline can hire a lawyer and visit her father. Care trumps making money. In the episode, 'And the Really Petty Cash', discussed above, Johnny hangs a painting of him and Max kissing in the art gallery. Perceiving that Max needs to get over him, Caroline buys the artwork and demands that Max destroy it. In this way, she hopes that Max will go some way towards moving on. Max's emotional welfare is more important to Caroline than saving up for the cupcake business.

As with all girlfriend media, *2 Broke Girls* has an aspirational narrative. This is evidenced in the entrepreneurial venture of their cupcake shop. Caroline realizes that Max has expertise in making cupcakes and consequently uses her own financial acumen developed at Wharton business school to set up their business. After each episode we are given a tally of their savings. It is significant that their hope machine is not romance or marriage. Again, we see how economic security and success is ensured through female networks rather than heterosexual marriage.[2] In the second season, Max and Caroline succeed in buying a space to sell their cupcakes (which they eventually lose). Caroline's knowledge of branding strategies and her calculating mind (she manages to manipulate a homeless man into donating two dollars towards the business) is partly parodied and undercut. The two characters balance each other out: Max is cynical but down to earth – 'I'm too poor to have a fear of success', and Caroline has entrepreneurial dreams: 'I have nothing. I really need the cupcake business [...]. Please let's do this [...] I believe in your dreams' ('And the Break-Up Scene' 1:2). In the final episode of the first season, Max and Caroline enact a Cinderella makeover sequence as they try on designer dresses for a ball where they hope to meet Martha Stewart and promote their cupcake business. The sequence both parodies itself as a stock trope in intimate publics, and plays up to the aspirational hope machine of the fairytale. The girlfriends eat junk food and are distinctively unladylike in their carnivalesque dressing room romp. Simultaneously, however, the final dress is portrayed through the signifiers (tears and gasps) that conventionally accompany finding the perfect wedding dress or 'the one'.

Significantly, the programme has been criticized for its racism. Max and Caroline are the only white American characters. The chef Oleg (Jonathan Kite) is Ukrainian, the owner Han Lee (Matthew Moy) is Korean, and the money-taker Earl (Garrett Morris) is African American. There is also the Polish Sophie (Jennifer Coolidge), who owns a cleaning business. Most episodes include an ethnic group that is parodied, such as Hasidic Jews, wealthy Arab women, or Italian Americans. The characters all represent niche market demographics, but this is not necessarily defined through race as the most ridiculed group, for example, are hipsters. Nevertheless, a hipster identity is a changeable one, which can be outgrown. In contrast, race is defined as unchanging and in this way racial identities are reified within the show's format. Indeed, each character – apart from Max – performs a stereotype in their one-dimensionality. This includes, of course, Caroline, who could be straight from *The Hills* (although Caroline changes and grows throughout the series). The prejudiced jokes, which mainly come from Max and the characters' generic behaviours, are startlingly racist. This is exacerbated by the (presumably edited) live audience laughter track. Indeed, the laughter track prompts the viewers to laugh when a particular character is playing up to their stereotype. The reified identities are part of the show's retro-ethic and intersect neatly with the short diner dresses and low-cost format. Oleg is a sexual harasser, Earl is (or was) a womanizer and ex-criminal Han is infantile; the gay characters are extravagantly camp. Problematically, the interactions and the humour based on race reveal the assumption of a post-racial time, where stereotypes can be re-introduced and ironized for entertainment. That is, the programme's racial and cultural identities merely evidence niche marketing in branded cultures, and this glosses over the history and legacy of racism.

In the episode 'And the Really Petty Cash', where Max first meets Johnny's girlfriend Cashandra, Max complains that she is, 'black and British. The two cool things I can never be.' Max calls Cashandra 'black and British' twice in the course of the episode and then for the rest of the season Cashandra is just 'British' – perhaps because the writers realize it betrays a too-overt commodification of race.[3] Cashandra's race is objectified within the comedy format of the sitcom because everybody's ethnic, sexual or racial identity is up for parody, including Max's. However, Max directs the show's laughter and so Cashandra is distanced from the viewers both because she is not a recurring character and because she is Max's rival for Johnny's affections. Cashandra plays true to racial stereotype as she performs, 'The Evil Black Woman' (Springer, 2008). For example, as discussed above, she insists on Max and Caroline finishing the cupcakes before they can get paid for catering at the art gallery. Moreover, she tells Max: 'Johnny loves chocolate. Sometimes he tries vanilla but he always comes back to chocolate.' It is a crass joke which both superficially reproduces Cashandra's racial stereotype and reifies racial identities. Indeed, the audience laughs but there is also a note of protest and anxiety in the laughter. This note of anxiety in the live audience/laughter track recurs in the episode where Caroline and Max go to cupcake decorating classes run by two Italian American cousins. The Mafia jokes multiply and the relationship between the cousins and the girlfriends are antagonistic. This culminates in Caroline calling them 'the Robert DeNi-hos' ('And the Pretty Problem' 1:7). Aside from the joke being poor, the audience's laughter also includes cries of protest. This is presumably a means for the show's producers to obfuscate responsibility for the girlfriends' quips.

The overt racism functions to accentuate Max's postfeminist normativity. That is, contrasting her with the characters of colour renders her more white and more conventionally American. Her low-income status, aggression and bawdiness are so unusual in girlfriend culture – outside the reality television format – that polarizing her from bodies which are marked through difference reduces or masks her subversiveness. Racism functions here to detract from Max's radicalism. It obfuscates the transgression of her gender performances through demarcating her from Otherness. The white waitresses are clearly separated from people of colour, and this glosses over their liberal Anglo-American feminism which, consequently, offsets the gendered politics of the show.

This is particularly evident in the episode where Max is at her most liberal feminist and Han is most retrogressively stereotypical. When he increases the price of tampons from 25 cents to 75 cents, Max retaliates in outrage, demanding that he return to the original price. Caroline remarks, 'You're taking advantage of women. If men were the ones who got periods, tampons would be thrown free from floats like Mardi Gras beads.' Max puts tampons in the straw dispenser, distributes them with the bill, and informs the diners that Han is the man, 'who thinks your menses should be more expensees' ('And the Secret Ingredient' 1:13). At the end of the episode she pretends to smoke a tampon. Han plays up to Asian-American stereotypes by bowing, waving and through his prudery around sex (he won't even look at the tampon machine). He is also small – a physical trait that draws much mockery from Max. His man-child asexual and money-grabbing demeanour is relentlessly exploited for laughs. Max's power is generated from her deft one-liners and Han's weakness is produced through his infantilized speech patterns. When Max waves tampons around the diner, he cries, 'Didn't your mother ever teach you that is secret no-no private lady thing?' To represent an angry fight over the price of tampons on primetime television is unusual. To have such an overt consideration of the realities of the female sexual body and to intersect it so precisely with economic factors, not to speak of Max's vocal and active 'rage against the [tampon] machine' is a radical departure in girlfriend culture, and it seems that this subversiveness must be undercut or legitimated through the commodification of racial identities.

However, there are some productive aspects of having a multicultural cast in a working class setting. Because we see the characters every week at the diner, their one-dimensional and commodified identities become, to some extent, multi-dimensional. Evolving friendships replicate those of sitcoms like *The Mary Tyler Moore Show* (CBS, 1970–1977), *Laverne & Shirley* (ABC, 1976–1983) or *Cheers* (NBC, 1982–1993). Because their identities are relational, they are subject to change and this renders them less commodified and less reified. For example, Oleg metamorphoses from being a peasant-like sexual harasser to a loyal and devoted lover of Sophie. Sophie subverts the girlfriends' assumption that she is a pimp by revealing that she runs a very successful cleaning business. She eventually exposes her generous and loving nature as she gives the girlfriends money to buy ballgowns and later donates $20,000 so that they can buy their cupcake shop. In addition, the fact that the girlfriends do interact regularly with culturally, racially and ethnically different people (who are not their PAs, doormen or homeless) is, in the context of girlfriend culture, highly unusual. Earl is Max's close friend and they maintain a tender intimacy which runs throughout each episode. Max is devastated when he has a heart attack and finds him his own hospital room. He is affectionately proud of her when he tells her how far she has developed in relation to her cupcake business and in her life. He also threatens a customer who is sexually harassing her.

In the episode which centres on filing tax returns, Max, Caroline and Earl share one of the diner's booths in a scene of friendship and mutual support. Earl asks Caroline to fetch his racing fixtures. The fact that two white women and an African American man – who are not all middle class – sit together in a position of equality is rare in girl-friend culture, as is a working class African American man asking a white woman to run an errand for him. By stating this I am not advocating *2 Broke Girls'* racial politics. Rather, the fact that there is a multiracial cast which does not portray clearly demarcated hierarchies reveals and throws into sharp relief the segregation of the girlfriend culture of which it is a part. In addition, the representation of girlfriends within a culturally plural context is useful. At the very least it opens up a space of debate. This contrasts with the closed whitewashed spaces of the Manhattan dramedies, where symbolic violence and racial prejudice are only evidenced through the absence of people of colour. The representation of girlfriends interacting outside their intimate sphere of white girlfriendship succeeds in revealing and pointing up the commodification of race, sexuality and class that lies at the heart of a postfeminist girlfriend identity.

Deconstructing girlfriendship: *Girls*

One of the main criticisms levelled at *Girls* (HBO, Sky Atlantic, 2012) is the whiteness of the characters.[4] Across the blogosphere and in the press, most of the debate is centred on the racial politics of the programme: if this is about all girls (as the universality of the title seems to imply) then where are the girls of colour? What is significant here is why *Girls* is perceived as more guilty of whitewashing than other girlfriend texts. Most of the media that I look at in this book reify white youth-ful skin and yet these texts not discussed with the same rigour. I suggest that the passionate debates about race in *Girls* are due to the fact that it is heralded as a liberal feminist text and, in this celebration, the exclusionary processes of Anglo-American feminism itself are thrown into sharp relief. In other words, if *Girls* is representative of feminism in the new millennium then this feminism is predominantly white.

Girls' narrative centres on the friendship between Hannah (Lena Dunham), Jessa (Jemima Kirke) and Marnie (Allison Williams) who were classmates at college, as well as Shoshanna (Zosia Mamet), who is Jessa's cousin. The first episode opens with claustrophobic grey shots of the New York landscape. Bleak economic realities are on display, signifying that this is not the entitled safe place to shop that was represented pre-crash. Like Max and Caroline, Hannah and Marnie sometimes sleep in the same bed. The first episode shows Hannah spooning Marnie before they shower together. Hannah sits naked in the bath eating the ubiquitous cupcake, while Marnie is wrapped in a towel and shaving her legs. Their intimacy is physically close. In a later episode, Marnie and Jessa make out in front of Jessa's future husband. Although the girlfriends do not have sex with each other and do not come out as lesbian or bisexual, sex is not rigidly foreclosed in the same way as it is for the corporate power babes discussed in Chapter 3. The girlfriends have not yet developed strategic means of relating in order to maintain their representability and cultivate their erotic capital.

The programme was created by Dunham, who is head writer, executive producer, and who directed five of the first season's episodes. She also wrote and directed *Tiny Furniture* (2010), another film that explores the complexities of female relationships, but in the familial triangle of a mother and her two daughters; indeed, the film is useful for its portrayal of the difficulties of female relating. Dunham states that *Sex and the City* was about 'women who figured out work and friends and now want to nail family life'. However, in *Girls* Dunham wanted to address the lives of young women before this life stage when friends have not yet been 'worked out'. She admits that she reveres *Sex and the City* 'just as much as any girl of my generation' (Goldberg, *Hollywood Reporter*, January 2012). The first episode of *Girls* explicitly and ironically references *Sex and the City*. Shoshanna points to the show's poster on the wall of her apartment and tells Jessa: 'You're definitely like a Carrie but with some Samantha aspects and Charlotte hair. That's like a really good combination' ('Pilot' 1:1). Marnie, like Charlotte, works in an art gallery, Jessa enjoys sex with strangers, and Hannah is an aspiring writer.

However, Dunham is clearly demarcating her show from *Sex and the City* and this is partly achieved through critiquing girlfriend self-help culture. *Girls* overtly subverts the magazine format of *Sex and the City*, particularly its rules about feminine conduct. When Shoshanna reads aloud advice from a dating book which is a combination of *The Rules* (1995) and *He's Just Not that Into You* (2004) (itself a spin-off from a *Sex and the City* episode), Jessa angrily questions the author's address to 'The Ladies', demanding, 'who are The Ladies?'. She storms off, telling

Hannah, 'This woman doesn't care what I want [...] I am not The Ladies [...] I don't like women telling other women what to do or how to do it or when to do it' ('Vagina Panic' 1:2). She overtly distinguishes herself from the expertise of mediated intimacy. Girlfriend culture is further critiqued when Hannah is groped by her boss and her female co-workers advise that 'you'll get used to it', and 'I know it's gross but he's really nice'. They assure her that it is worth it as he doesn't complain if they are late and buys them gifts for their birthdays ('Hannah's Diary' 1:4). Hannah does not protest and indeed encourages him because it means that she can be 20 minutes late for work. Here, sexuality is overtly linked to commercialization. That is, rather than employing the techniques of hypervisibility in order to capitalize on one's erotic capital, the exchange is mundane and disempowering, although mutually beneficial. A woman's body is not only an asset that she controls but something that can also be manipulated and abused. In a scene which takes place in the work bathroom – a typical girlfriend mise-en-scène – Hannah's co-workers comment on her oily skin, patchy eyebrows and give her guidance in applying makeup: they are ladies advising other ladies what to do, but their expertise is represented as highly dubious. The postfeminist values of empowerment and freedom are here exposed as hollow and unrealistic.

Girls also deconstructs the technologies of self-branding. Season 1 opens as Hannah's parents refuse to give her any more financial support. Consequently, Hannah is no longer able to be 'busy trying to become who I am' ('Pilot' 1:1). Hannah is an intern, then a cleric in a law office where she is sexually harassed, before she takes a job in a coffee shop. In addition, the programme pokes fun at the girlfriends' privilege. For example, one of the male characters observes that watching the girlfriends 'is like watching *Clueless*' ('Pilot' 1:1). Although Hannah does not have money, we are encouraged to see her as talented. Indeed, this provides the aspirational narrative. Just as the cupcake business provides the entrepreneurial reflexivity of *2 Broke Girls*, so Hannah's writing career prevents her from appearing too hopeless and confused. Her humiliating sexual experiences become fodder for her book.

Unlike the reflexive girl talk of *Sex and the City*, the girlfriends' negotiation of sexuality and the body is experienced by the characters as baffling. None of the characters seem to take pleasure in sex; it is something that they are compelled to perform. *Sex and the City* might depict an uncomfortable heterosexual coital moment where the girlfriend is unable to express her dismay or discomfort to her male partner, but then it will cut straight to the Manhattan power babes processing the moment together through a mutual reflexivity. In contrast, the girl-friends in *Girls* are portrayed as lost and unable to garner humour together from the encounter. The camera lingers on the sex, drawing out its atomized and alienated affect. In addition, profiting from one's sexuality intersects with self-diminishment. In another parody of *Sex and the City*, Hannah is depicted in her room typing on her laptop and we are privy to the words as they appear on the screen. However, instead of cultivating her erotic capital in pithy statements about contemporary sexual lifestyles, Hannah is investigating sexual diseases. Afraid that she might have an STD she searches for 'diseases that come from no con-dom for one second' and 'stuff that gets up around the side of condoms'. Bemused and wrapped in a towel, she explores her vagina.

This is not the assertive and autonomous girlfriend of the Manhattan dramedies. The show portrays her relationship with Adam (Adam Driver) as made up of misunderstandings, miscommunication and power struggle. The first time that we see Adam and Hannah having sex, he commands her to hold her legs and take her clothes off while he fetches lubricant. She struggles with her clothes and worries that he will have anal sex with her: 'please don't do that. That feels awful.' Later, she asks, 'do you want me to move more [...] I'm sorry about the wrong hole thing' ('Pilot' 1:1). The second episode opens with Adam acting out a Lolita-style fantasy while Hannah pretends to participate. He mastur-bates on her and aggressively presses her face down. 'That was so good', she lies to please him, 'I almost came' ('Vagina Panic' 1:2). After Adam sends her a picture of his penis wrapped in squirrel skin (followed by a text saying that the picture wasn't meant for her, which suggests that he is dating someone else) she texts him a picture of her holding her breasts ('Hannah's Diary' 1:4). Hannah is not one of the empowered girlfriends entitled to good sex and an opportunity to work her erotic capital. She responds eagerly to Adam's rejections. Although the sex, like in *Sex and the City*, might be freakish, Hannah is in thrall to it in the first season and implicates herself further in her relationship with Adam.

The programme is subversive because of its portrayal of the female body. Dunham depicts Hannah's body in such a way as to puncture the normative bodies of postfeminist girlfriend culture. She chooses shots that accentuate Hannah's non-normative figure (non-normative in the context of the postfeminist popular culture I am exploring), especially in moments when she is having uncomfortable sex or is naked. This trans-gression is accentuated through the way in which the show plays on autobiography. That is, just as *Tiny Furniture* depicted Dunham's real-life sister and mother, so we are expected – to some extent – to see Hannah as conflated with Dunham. When we see Adam pinching Hannah's belly and asking her why she has never thought about losing a few pounds, we are also seeing Dunham's belly ('All Adventurous Women Do' 1:3). Consequently, when Hannah tells him that she has better things to think about, her character expands to include the woman who plays her.

Indeed, the programme gains its complexity from the potential identification between character, actor, writer and creator. Hannah and Dunham conflate – sometimes ironically – such as when Hannah articulates in the first episode: 'I am the voice of the generation [...] or a voice of a generation.' As well as seeing Dunham's body shape, we are also voyeurs of Dunham's tattoos. Hannah explains to Adam that she had them done when she was at school in order to 'take control of my own shape' ('Hannah's Diary' 1:4). Adam is sceptical but this scene is pertinent as it addresses the tyrannies of slenderness, and represents a girlfriend who refuses to conform to its dictates; a girlfriend who could also be a highly successful writer and director. What is interesting here is that although Hannah is depicted as bewildered by her predicaments, she does not embrace her victimhood in the same way as Andy in *The Devil Wears Prada*. She does not lose weight in a punishing culture in order to appear empowered and to assert her sexual control. Moreover, Dunham – whose body we are watching – is hypervisible, despite not conforming to the dominant discourses of body image.

These are the Manhattan girlfriends before they become 'Plastic'. They have not yet developed a means of strategically relating. Their friendships are highly ambivalent and emotionally messy; they are libinized. Marnie and Jessa make out together. The girlfriends are nasty about each other, and Hannah is overtly selfish and narcissistic in the pursuit of her career. When Marnie's boyfriend reads Hannah's diary and discovers that Marnie no longer wants to be with him, Hannah's main concern is whether the diary was well written and not how Marnie is feeling. Part of the liberal-feminist pleasure of the television programme is the girlfriends' imperfection, which creates and reveals the messy reality of female relating. Their friendships are not calculating. However, like *2 Broke Girls*, imperfect femininities on television are counteracted by racist codes, whether these are through overt stereotypes or through exclusion. In order to render the transgressive girlfriends less abject, they are positioned in the normative paradigm of a postfeminist popular culture which reifies whiteness.

6
Catfight

You have been weighed, measured and found lacking.

(Sorority Girls)

The Hills (MTV, 2006–2010) is a hybrid reality series (Hearn 2010) that traces the social lives of a group of affluent Californian young women. It follows the friendship between Heidi Montag and Lauren Conrad as they move in together in the first episode, through to the pain endured as they subsequently grow further apart. The womance between Heidi and Lauren is the emotional and narrative focus of the first and second seasons and is dragged out as a subplot until Lauren eventually leaves. Heidi laments to her ex-BFF Lauren: 'I never thought in my wildest dreams that this would be how things ended up [...] the only thing really missing in my life is you' ('I Heidi Take Thee Spencer' 4:20). Although these two girlfriends broke up in season 1, the show milks the affect of their broken womance until Lauren finally leaves in season 5, but not before she confesses to Heidi, 'I still love you', and Heidi replies 'my favourite stories are my stories with you, my favourite memories are my memories with you' ('Don't Cry on Your Birthday' 5:1). Heidi and Lauren's girlfriend break-up veers from sentimentality to crisis. Moreover, the suffering induced by their conflict is heightened because it is created by an unreliable and untrustworthy male – Spencer. Because of him, the segregated spaces of entitled girlfriend love are gate-crashed by one of girlfriend culture's omega men.

This is the era of 'emotional capitalism' (Illouz, 2007). Our relationships are increasingly played out through systems of exchange, but our mediated lives and our relationships with commodities and brands are more affective. The reality shows *The Hills*, *Paris Hilton's My New BFF* (MTV, ITV 2, 2008–2009) and *Sorority Girls* (E4, 2012) exploit emotions through the tropes of intimacy. This chapter examines the ways in which these programmes summon the affect of friendship in order to yoke viewers into co-participatory practices. The shows are produced through product synergy and so the signifiers of friendship are an effective means to generate an emotional engagement between the viewers and the branded cultures. Appropriating Kavka's theoretical framework for understanding 'reality love TV', I argue that these shows evoke a 'deep script' that 'undergirds the affective operation' of female sociality. Indeed, this deep script of friendship 'precedes and exceeds the framework of television' and it is through this that the programmes gain their meaning (Kavka, 2008, 106).

Branded sociality: *The Hills*

A semi-scripted show with high production values *The Hills* combines a soap opera format with 'real life'. It brings together the womance of the girlfriend flick with the female-only spaces of the corporate sisterhoods, and adds the value of 'authenticity'. The programme opens up and represents the friendships of a set of highly affluent women: Lauren, Heidi, Whitney Port, Audrina Partridge and, in later seasons, Lo Bosworth and Kristin Cavallari. The girlfriends are in their 20s but their bodies are further girlified through veneer teeth, groomed hair, careful makeup, designer clothes, tiny waists and plastic surgery. The girlfriends' lifestyles are intricately bound up with the products that they consume and the commercial spaces through which they socialize. Their lives are embedded in an aspirational branded lifestyle and product synergy. Lauren and Whitney work for *Teen Vogue* and Heidi is employed by an event-planning firm, Bolthouse Productions. We follow and understand the characters through their promotional togetherness: shopping for 'cute' clothes, drinking in Les Deux, or eating in Café Sushi. Because the show follows a reality TV format and the protagonists are not professional actors, we are dependent upon the girlfriends' conversations in order to follow the plot. It is through their girlfriend reflexivity that the plot is evident: who is friends with whom, who is dating whom, what is going on in other girlfriends' lives. They are rarely shown on their own unless it is to express Lauren's melancholia at the loss of Heidi. Together they talk through their personal lives, confess their emotions and relate their intimate experiences and aspirations.

Jack Bratich maintains that reality television does not *represent* the current conjuncture, rather 'it interjects itself into the conjuncture and enhances particular components required by it' (Bratich, 2007, 7).

Consequently, the programme does not merely represent the girlfriends relating with one another, it also intervenes and augments those relationships. Because the show is semi-scripted, the emotions of their sociality are, to some extent, divorced from context and 'performed' between the characters. The womance between Heidi and Lauren, for example, illustrates what Illouz terms 'cold intimacy'. That is, their emotions are partly performed outside the context of their production. Indeed, *The Hills* is a pertinent example of how emotion has shifted into the performative. Rather than being a spontaneous and pre-rational expression of the inner self, emotions are commodified and acted out as a form of display. Consequently, they are harnessed as social, cultural and erotic capital. The girlfriends' emotional lives – as they confess them with and to each other – are their assets. Their interpersonal activities are their labour; their sociality is their work.

Significantly, the girlfriends' position within the show's format only makes commercial sense through the ways in which they talk to each other and consume together. The leveraging of these commodified emotions determines the girlfriends' worth as visible postfeminist subjects. How they talk to each other builds their public profile as it provides the content of the show. The conduct of correct girlfriend conversation is essential in revealing the girlfriends' affluent postfeminist subjectivities. Indeed, because emotion talk is also historically and sociologically bound up with success in the world of business, so 'emotional competence' or self-awareness is a means to advance one's cultural capital. As Illouz argues, one's emotional attitude defines one's social identity. Therefore, it is crucial to the building of advantageous networks and accruing social capital (Illouz, 2007, 66). As I discussed in Chapter 3, talking about sex and emotions are components of girlfriend reflexivity. It is the way that the girlfriends maintain, monitor and police each other's visible identities. Talking about emotions is a skill that is learned, flexed and constructed between girlfriends as part of their feminine skills set. This girlfriend talk is produced through a combination of womantic lexicon, therapy talk, and feminine consumption.

Lisa Taylor argues that *The Hills* has a 'subtle moral pedagogic agenda' (Taylor, 2011, 128). She develops the work of Annette Hill (2005), who employs qualitative research to demonstrate how audiences 'become intrigued by adjudicating, decoding and *learning from* the "people-watching" element of reality television' (Taylor, 2011, 120). This pedagogic element is manifested by representing how the girlfriends manage their emotions through talking together, and also by portraying how they manage each other's visible identities. Indeed, a significant component of *The Hills'* pedagogic agenda is to demonstrate how to relate with and through an aspirational and branded girlfriend sociality. The pedagogic elements are heightened through the affect of friendship that spreads to the viewers, drawing them into the show's intimate sphere. The tropes of womance summon an emotional engagement between the audience and the characters, and so the sociality of the women on the screen is extended to the viewers. Spaces of intimacy are produced through inducing audience identification and emotional involvement with the characters' interpersonal connections.

Sam Binkley argues that friendships are reflexive projects and that they are cemented or consolidated 'from the artfulness with which they are produced and maintained by participating parties'. Disembedded from institutions and from faithfulness to duty or collective purpose, contemporary interpersonal bonds evidence a plasticity; they are 'objects of informed technique and skilled craft' (Binkley, 2007, 166–167). *The Hills* (as well as *Paris Hilton* and *Sorority Girls*) offers guidance in the performance of this 'artfulness'. The rules of friendship are delineated by Lauren. She guides her girlfriends in the art of correct girlfriend sociality. Lauren provides the voiceover at the beginning of each episode, recapping the plotlines from her perspective. Because she positions her relationships with women as central to her identity, so she directs the viewers' emotional standpoints. The viewers are privy to the events that she sees but that other characters are denied. For example, we observe, along with Lauren, Spencer flirting with a woman other than Heidi.

Lauren is the friendship rule-maker. Friendships are constantly under evaluation in order for Lauren to determine which are the 'real' ones and which will last 'forever'. There is a hierarchy of friendship with best friends having constantly to prove their worth. Lauren (and the show's narrative) relegates men to a marginalized place in a girlfriend's life. Lauren's primary rule of friendship is never to choose a guy over a girlfriend. Consequently, she accuses Heidi of 'having chosen' Spencer over her and because of this they cannot be best friends. Heidi insists that she wants her in her life: 'You're my best friend and I love you more than anything [...] I'm reaching out. I'm trying to have a conversation with you' (2:6). The episode ends with Heidi lingering at Lauren's bedroom door before she eventually leaves with a suitcase to the soundtrack of Dido's 'Don't Leave Home', a song which heightens the volatility of the womantic break-up. Another friendship rule prohibits girlfriends from dating each other's exes. *The Hills'* girlfriends set up boundaries so that they do not involve themselves in sexual competition or sleep with each other. They develop limits in order to preserve trust, loyalty and individual representability.

The Hills markets a girlfriend lifestyle through the flow of media convergence. Consumers can buy into the girlfriends' lives through the clothes, spaces and performances that the televised friends enact. The promotional strategies in girlfriend culture function through inciting the desire not 'to be like her' but 'to be friends with them'. That is, to be conjoined in a mediated sociality is to be tightly bound up with strategies of promotion. To be emotionally invested in the programme is to be emotionally invested in the brands through which *The Hills* girlfriends interact. Indeed, a significant way in which *The Hills* teaches friendship is through the branded locations that stage the girlfriends' sociality. Because of this commercialization of intimacy, these reality programmes evidence how social skills fall victim to a consumer logic. They are guided primarily by conforming to a regulatory neoliberal consumer culture. As Binkley argues, the skills of intimacy and friendship are exploited and mined for commercial transaction.

Because reality television as a genre operates at the level of intervention rather than straightforward representation, viewers are encouraged to interact with the show and therefore invest emotion in their consumption. This could be through voting, through having the possibility of being in the text, or through overt identification with the participants. Through these systems of involvement, reality television creates 'a new participatory relationship between the viewer and the screen', where we are simultaneously both audience and participant (Skeggs and Wood, 2012, 39). This has significant implications in the context of *The Hills*, which is tightly bound up with branding cultures. Indeed, the show's pedagogy extends to the processes of self-branding that the characters perform. As Hearn argues, *The Hills* demonstrates 'the means for individuals to produce their own image personae, or "branded selves"' (Hearn, 2010, 61). Because the girlfriends are scripted through branding strategies – this is a version of their lives after all – the show represents and teaches how, in Gareth Palmer's words, 'submitting oneself to selling oneself is actually good and proper' (Palmer, 2011, 136). This is evident through the ways that the girlfriends maintain and promote their hypervisibility. But these processes of self-branding reach beyond the show into other mediated formats. The characters – especially Lauren and 'Speidi' (a neologism of Heidi and Spencer) – have successfully used the show as a launch pad to market themselves as celebrity brands, whether this is through chat show appearances, writing a book, or further reality-mediated formats.

However, once Lauren leaves the show, the rules governing the correct – and strategic – sociality implode, and the processes of self-branding are depicted as monstrous. Without Lauren's moral guidance, girlfriends are depicted as out of control and the affect of bestfriendship is suffused with the signifiers of meanness. Lauren and Heidi's womantic conflict is replaced by a catfight through the persona of Kristin. The sentimentalization of girlfriendship is replaced by overt rivalry, as the characters increasingly 'act out'. Kristin is cast as the competitive Mean Girl to Lauren's BFF. With the appearance of Kristin there is more swearing, more fighting between girls, more plastic surgery, more drugs and more violence. She is frequently filmed in her bikini (in juxtaposition to the more conservative Lauren) and she socializes with boys rather than girls. She is associated with an addiction to cocaine. Kristin quickly breaks Lauren's rules of friendship by dating other girlfriends' boyfriends. She openly fights – sometimes physically – and she complains to Spencer's sister, 'Why do we all have to be best friends?' Spencer's sister calls her a 'mean person' with a 'bitchy attitude' ('Rumor Has It' 6:2). Exclusion and competitiveness provide the emotional drama of the show. Kristin might be a Mean Girl but she also controls the perspective through the voiceover, and consequently disrupts the moral centre as the show changes its narrative drive to foreground women's rivalry, envy and recklessness.

As the show progresses, the ambivalences of a branded culture (Banet-Weiser, 2012) are brought to the fore. This ambivalence is located in the bodies of the women, especially Heidi. In the final season, Heidi has extensive plastic surgery on her face and body. The programme is edited to generate suspense through the narrative of Heidi's procedures. Consequently, we are shown her altered body almost at the same time as her mother does. There is a build-up to the final reveal as we follow the back of Heidi's head as she travels to her childhood home to visit her family. Because we are not shown her changed face the tension is heightened until we see her mother's pained expression on first sighting Heidi. Later we are shown Heidi's new face as she and her mother talk on the sofa. Corporeal, familial and public spaces of consumption merge. Heidi's surgery evidences the show's authenticity: this is not a performance but the real. And Heidi's body is the signifier of this authenticity.[1]

Heidi is the sacrificial lamb who legitimates the show's real-life credentials. By acting herself out to excess she leverages her celebrity brand, especially as it has been publicized on a global scale. Furthermore, her surgery increased the number of viewers who were then dispensed to the advertisers. The strategies of self-branding which were represented, evoked, disseminated, forged and fetishized throughout the preceding seasons become located on her body. This body is depicted, talked about and analysed within the show and elsewhere in order to court prurience and controversy. Indeed, Heidi becomes the locus for contemporary anxieties over the commercialization of intimacy and the dehumanization of a branded culture. Nevertheless, because the show fetishizes the girlfriends' wealth and because they profit from their collusion, criticism of exploitation is circumscribed. Contextualized within the show's neoliberal pedagogic agenda, the female body is sold as an entrepreneurial project, suggesting that the more it is penetrated the more the individual can be validated as self-brand. But although the show profited from and relished in Heidi's surgery, the narrative was framed in such a way that the surgery was not easily condoned. The market's incursion into her body – through the processes of celebrification and cosmetic procedures – was problematized. This was primarily executed through the demonization of Spencer and the portrayal of Heidi as a victim of the privatization of their marriage, as she strays from Lauren's correct girlfriend conduct. Spencer is violent and volatile. He spreads rumours that Lauren has a sex tape, he throws Heidi out of his car when she refuses to move in with him, and he develops a bizarre habit with new age crystals, among other pathologized performances.

On *Access Hollywood* on 19th October 2012, Heidi claims that 'I would never do it again and I never recommend it for anyone [...] I wasn't told really the repercussions and what would happen, emotionally and psychically, and the pain I would be in'. She sells a narrative of losing her sense of self when being in *The Hills*. Through this interview Heidi extends the performance of revelation – especially of inner feelings – that was an integral part of the girlfriends' sociality and therefore of the programme's content. Because the show is only partly scripted and we only know the plot through the girlfriends' conversations there is a powerful sense of confession underpinning the conviviality we are privy to. This confessional rhetoric often feels exploitative. That is, we are consuming the girlfriends' exposition of their intimate emotions – however much this is acted out. Heidi's story about her surgery is part of this confessional way of speaking. It is also part of her 'emotion work' as a dysfunctional celebrity self-brand. Nevertheless, her story highlights the ways in which the configuration of consumer agency and choice is highly problematic, revealing the exploitation that can be obfuscated in the promotion of the self as brand. In other words, the problems of a branded culture become individualized as a personal choice located in the body of Heidi. The show's multiple perspectives and its ambivalence towards condoning Heidi's surgery mean that she holds sole responsibility. It becomes a private decision and therefore an issue that is disconnected from the seductive visuals which promote and fetishize blonde, thin girls socializing in high-end consumer spaces. On *The Hills*, and through the figures of Kristin and Heidi, women are scapegoated for the excesses of free market deregulation, while the programme and the branded cultures that are intricately bound up with their sociality remain untarnished by human abjection.

Rivalry: Paris Hilton

Paris Hilton is a self-confessed brand 'like no one else' (Lawson, 2009, 29). She is, of course, not the only self-brand in contemporary popular culture. However, her assertion that through branding herself she has become more distinct, more visible, and more successful at leveraging her femininity than anyone else reveals the competitive nature of the self-brand. What is of interest here is that the feminine masquerade is commodified as part of a woman's brand. In her cross-over feminist-populist text, *Catfight: Rivalries Among Women, From Diets to Dating, From the Boardroom to the Delivery Room* (2003), Leora Tanenbaum argues that femininity is a competitive game. Giving a self-reflexive account she states that:

> The success of another woman translates into my failure. And my success translates into her failure – which makes my success all the more sweet. Although I am a feminist, committed to the idea that every woman should be given the opportunity to succeed in whatever endeavor she chooses, there is also a part of me that feels reassured if a woman on the same playing field stumbles.
>
> (Tanenbaum, 2003, 15)

According to Tanenbaum, to be feminine is to have an edge over other women in the marketplace, whether this is in marriage or the boardroom. Because femininity entails trapping a better mate or being more attractive – 'Who is the thinnest of them all?' – it is a gendered performance that a woman 'wins' at (Tanenbaum, 2003, 119, 20). Paradoxically, according to Tanenbaum, femininity is also defined through the *foreclosure* of competition. She argues that the only way out 'is for a woman to be competitive but to *pretend* that she is not' (Tanenbaum, 2003, 21). That is, to be normatively feminine, one must be serene and self-contained as the insecure manifestations of comparison and envy are deemed pathological. Whereas the practices of competition are an integral component of what it means to be conventionally masculine, it is unseemly for women. Although, as Tanenbaum maintains, femininity and competition 'go hand in hand', this partnership must be obscured (Tanenbaum, 2003, 20). She states that there are few sites where women can openly compete and as a consequence of this a woman must pretend that she is not competitive. This masquerade – which disguises an illegible rage as discussed in Chapter 3 – means that women are stereotyped as catty and cunning. This is a problem in reality television formats where the women want to appear feminine but at the same time they want to win.

In the reality TV programmes, *Paris Hilton's My New BFF* and *Paris Hilton's My British Best Friend* (ITV2, 2009) – as well as *Sorority Girls* – femininity is explicitly linked to competition. Female contestants are drawn into an aggressive format so that those who are the most normatively feminine will win. These shows offer the possibility of participating in celebrity culture and consequently they overtly market the dream of being hypervisible. That is, the winner will be the most visible and distinct in a normative postfeminist paradigm of femininity. In a neoliberal culture where subjectivities are increasingly recognized as brands, it is essential for the entrepreneurial self to be better than the others. Indeed, Tanenbaum's understanding of femininity as competition becomes conflated or linked with the competitive status of brands. That is, the most lucrative self-brands are those with the most competitive edge. This is most clearly evident in the case of Paris. But it is also played out by the contestants in her show as they compete to be Paris's BFF.

Paris's brand is built on her absolute pink-packaged individuality, but her 'emotion work' is partly produced through her sociality and her best-friendships. She draws on the affect of girlfriendship in order to promote her self-brand. For example, she starred with her then best friend, the socialite and television personality Nicole Richie in *The Simple Life* (Fox, E!, 2003–2007). This was a 'celebreality' programme where the girlfriends were placed within a working class family or in a working class town (or, in the final season, in a van crossing America) and expected to work. The show gains its entertainment from the fact that these girlfriends have never worked and do not need to. Instead, they perform pranks and humiliate their colleagues. The labour that they actually perform on the show is that of girlfriendship and the two are depicted as clowning around and laughing together while simultaneously evidencing 'the insouciance of [class] exploitation' (Hendershot, 2009, 255). The status of Paris's bestfriendships is one of the ways in which she gains publicity and coverage in celebrity and gossip culture. Consequently, the ups and downs of her and Nicole's girlfriendship are speculated upon in the media as part of the promotion of her brand. Paris's friendship with Lindsay Lohan is also a component of her celebrity narrative. For example, a video was posted on YouTube where she laughs uncontrollably as a male friend abuses Lindsay, calling her a 'firecrotch' (Hilton, YouTube). Elsewhere, she gives her earrings to a woman who mistakes her for Lindsay, and Paris informs the viewers that 'if I was Lindsay I'd be stealing those earrings not giving them away' (OMGthatcom, YouTube).

My New BFF ran to two seasons and there was also a version shot in Dubai and aired on MTV in 2010 (but which was never shown in Dubai). In the first season, 18 girls (and two men) vie to become Paris's best friend. The show is structured like *The Bachelor* (ABC, 2002) or *The Bachelorette* (ABC, 2003) where contestants compete to be the chosen beloved of the single bachelor or bachelorette. After each episode, a contestant is eliminated until there are only two remaining. In the case of Paris, the contestants live together in a luxurious mansion and undergo a series of trials in order for Paris to choose the most authentic and appropriate BFF. The show plays on the affect of normative cruelties. The contestants, like Cady and Gretchen in the film *Mean Girls*, subject themselves to a tyrannical friendship in order to experience belonging through visibility and fame. Paris dictates the paradigms of the ultimate girlfriend: her ideal BFF should be 'real' rather than fake and always look hot on a rollercoaster ('Sayonara' 1:3). She should be able to handle gossip, dance, secure a hot guy (but not be sluttish), surrender to makeovers, and perform successfully in an advert. The ideal friend is frequently alluded to and analysed as Paris cries and professes her love for the contestants. Paris purposefully mines the affect of loving meanness and her self-brand veers between BFF and Mean Girl. She both cries when the participants are eliminated, complaining that she hates the exclusion process, while simultaneously waving her wand and stating: TTYN (Talk To You Never).

Bratich identifies the effectiveness of social bonds on reality television in cultivating affect in consumers. He examines the creation and exploitation of pair-bonds, or couples maintaining that the complexities of their relating are exploited in order to create a narrative drive. The representation of, and intervention into, their bonds produces 'an affective intensification (even volatility)' that generates entertainment value (Bratich, 2011, 63). In *My New BFF* the couple bond is the imagined one between Paris and the potential BFF. The aspirational womance of this goal is the emotional drive of the programme. Before Paris makes her final decision about her BFF, she takes the remaining two contestants out on dates. She impresses them with the heterosexual accoutrements of hedonistic romance: an expensive meal, a ride in a helicopter, jewellery. The girlfriends are depicted as in love with Paris through their confessions of adoration – both to her and the camera – and they are situated in an equal bubble of straight intimacy with Paris in order to heighten the suspense of the final disclosure. Their gaze is a striking mix of envy (they want what she has), competition (they want to win), acting out, and desire for Paris which is 'straightened' through the cynical and competitive format. A queer spectatorial position is enabled but also pathologized through, for example, Vanessa, whose love for Paris is framed as creepy and similar to a stalker ('Best Friends Forever' 1:10).

Volatility is also produced through the bonds between contestants. Conflict is organized among the girlfriends from the outset as they are competing for Paris's affections and the attendant femininities that this will bring. Like the final seasons of *The Hills*, the show draws on the performance of the catfight. At the end of each episode, one, and sometimes two, of the participants are eliminated and the other girlfriends are often asked by Paris for their opinions on their rivals, or forced to decide the exclusion themselves. The friendships among each other are ignored or attacked in favour of jealousy and bitchiness, which make better television. The girlfriends physically fight in the show. One girlfriend is suspected of being racist and the others gang up on her through ostracism, outright abuse, and the gay male participant cleans the toilet with her toothbrush. Lingering shots are used to incite judgment, whether this is to focus on the contestants' fear over being eliminated, their disgust at a fellow participant, or their jealousy. In one episode the contestants' ex-friends are invited onto the show in order to cast their damning verdicts on their former friends.

The fact that the contestants want to be Paris's BFF forecloses intimate relationships with the other participants. Antagonism is produced, scripted and edited to highlight the women's differences, jealousies or possessiveness. Female interactions are sold as relationships of power and regulation. This produces anxieties similar to those represented in the girlfriend flick: Who is to be trusted? Who is real? Who will sabotage Paris's representability? As an heiress, Paris can be particularly strategic when compiling her friendship portfolio. She can choose – or be seen to choose – those who will develop the promotional myths of her brand. Consequently, the show plays on, and critiques, the liquidity of neoliberal relationships where friends can be picked out by the affluent. However, as with all of Paris's pink brand, it is often difficult to discern what is being ironized and what is being validated within the programme's visual framework. Indeed, it draws upon and exploits the assemblage of affects evoked by friendship, including normative cruelties, catfights, belonging and authenticity.

On reality television there is 'a pull towards validating those that (appear to) have been "true" to themselves' (Holmes, 2005, 17). Season 1, episode 4 is entitled 'Real or Fake?' and the contestants are grilled by celebrities, including the American gossip blogger Perez Hilton. The fact that Paris (and Perez) is judging them on the level of authenticity is laughable and, indeed, Paris's favourite contestant is voted by the other contestants as the most fake. The participants are caught in a bind, however, as Paris wants a friend rather than a person who is ambitious. Consequently, they are continually trying to prove their authenticity, while at the same time being hot, sexy, fun and able to handle media pressure. Contextualized within the programme's friendship epistemology, being a BFF is both a commodity and a performance. The girls (and boys) vying to be Paris's BFF must disguise the desire for commercial success that appearing on Paris's show might confer. Simultaneously, they must market their suitability for Paris's mediated lifestyle. In the context of *Paris*, it is Paris herself who wields the girlfriend gaze. Consequently, she polices and monitors the contestants' bodies and personalities, and assesses their ability to strategically enhance her brand. In addition, the contestants do not want to look good for a man; they want to look good for Paris. This is a business venture as they want the celebrity status and visibility that being Paris's friend will bring. However, they need to negotiate the contradictions between appearing normatively feminine and competing with the other contestants. This is frequently represented as cattiness, and is exploited in order to court prurience.

The show draws on the deep script of friendship to generate the affect of normative cruelties through the figure of Paris who plays the Mean Girl. It is a commercial enterprise for the television network and for the promotion of Paris. It is an opportunity for girlfriends to aspire to fame through being on reality television and consequently 'sticking' to Paris. Indeed, *My New BFF*, like *The Hills*, reroutes the impulses of the market as a personal interaction between women. Competition is exploited as a means to promote oneself as self-brand by vying for proximity to the Paris brand. The show is edited to represent women being competitive. Significantly, the winners of the second season as well as of the UK version, were men. This reveals how little Paris trusts the girlfriends vying to be her BFF. It seems that she is influenced by the programme's representation of the envious nature of women. In addition, she is represented as a character (albeit blessed with more expertise around the strategies of self-branding). Therefore, the volatility of the affective relationship is not only the potential womance between her and the winner, but also the catfight covertly acted out between her and the contestants. She competes with the contestants as they fight out the superiority of their hypervisible feminine performances. And through choosing a man, Paris wins.

The contestants are examples of women who are in the process of succeeding in celebrity culture. Consequently they signify aspiration and fame in a meritocratic society. In addition, through the contestants, viewers of the programme are transmogrified from being passive consumers in thrall to celebrity stardom to having the possibility of hypervisibility. This means that the practices of celebrity aspiration and its attendant femininities are potentially universally applicable. As I discussed in Chapter 1, because celebrity media proliferate across multiple platforms that encourage users to interact, engage and participate, so the bar of feminine perfection becomes raised for all. The contestants fit neatly into a normative postfeminist paradigm, but they are still represented as 'ordinary' people, so the viewers are marketed the possibility of being like them. *My New BFF* demonstrates how – with hard work and the right brands – celebrity lifestyles can be our lifestyles. Like *The Hills*, *My New BFF* celebrates and normalizes postfeminist branded identities and it does so through its product placement, sponsorship and branded spaces. These feelings of belonging become associated with the branded cultures promoted by the show.

This has important implications if the self-brand is achieved through a ruthless system of female sociality. The assemblage of affect acted out on screen with and through the contestants is violent. The highly charged sphere of the staged catfight de-individualizes the participants' feelings as they operate within a public space. This public space is extended to include the viewers who become conjoined in the emotions of competition, comparison and envy generated between the participants. Viewers become affectively embroiled in the ugly feelings acted out on screen which pass between bodies. Moreover, these feelings gain traction if the viewers are also relating to the pedagogical aspects of the show. That is, rivalry is also marketed as necessary to the postfeminist self; one should be inculcated in the systems of judgment, feedback and evaluation if one is to succeed. Consequently, viewers are coerced into participating in the processes of comparison between the contestants, and encouraged to ask, in Tanenbaum's words, 'who is the thinnest of them all?' while simultaneously denying this.

Slut-shaming: *Sorority Girls*

In *Sorority Girls* (E4, 2012), five American 'Sorority Sisters' choose five British students (out of 14) to become part of the first British sorority. Through this format, it is as if Regina and the Plastics from *Mean Girls* take on, and compete with, British femininity. The voiceover at the beginning of each episode salaciously informs us: 'now for the first time the secret world of the sorority has come to the UK' but warns that 'the road to sisterhood is tough'. The show's emotional emphasis highlights the qualities of intimacy, secrecy and competition. Like *My New BFF*, the British contestants fight it out to be the chosen girlfriends. The contestants are moved into a house in Leeds where, under the care of the house mother, they sleep together in a dormitory for the duration of the programme. The American Sorority Sisters live upstairs in their own pink-furnished rooms. Through this division, the Sorority Sisters are given the position of 'affective domination' as they judge, scrutinize and police the British students (Weber, 2009). The contestants must undergo a series of trials in order to prove their worthiness to the Sorority Sisters. If they fail they will be 'cut' in the weekly elimination ceremony. Viewers are called into an engagement with the show as the discursive frame or grammar of friendship 'creates the setting for the generation of emotion' (Kavka, 2008, 107). In addition, the audience experiences responses to the house mother, the rules and the chants of the Sorority Sisters almost simultaneously to the contestants, which draws them into an intimate connectivity (Kavka, 2008, 107).

In *Sorority Girls*, normative femininity is produced through a girlfriend reflexivity. To be a Sorority Sister the contestants have to be able to function as a team. As one of the Sorority Sisters maintains, 'we want girls who are supportive of each other' (1:4). The ideal Sorority Sister needs to be able to self-promote, perform and market herself. However, she must be able to do so in a way that takes into account the visibility and representability of her girlfriends. The Sorority Sisters condemn 'unsisterly behaviour' as they seek a cohort of British sisters who will promote and pass on their values. The contestants are split into two teams who compete with each other. This means that the girlfriends within the same team need to cultivate a reflexive togetherness in order to be successful. The tasks they are meant to perform reveal their feminine competitive edge as well as their ability to work strategically with other women.

They must also prove their commitment to the sorority by participating in a number of rituals, including expressing a vow to leave old friends and family behind, and publicly devoting themselves to their sisters. When one of the participants, Cristiana, is involved in some 'unsisterly gossiping', she is cut. The Sorority Sisters maintain that 'if you do not invest in your sisters then we do not invest in you'. According to them, a sorority produces friendships of 'a higher standard', so it is encouraged that girlfriends 'rat each other out' in order to root out 'inappropriate sisters' (1:4).

We are privy to the American Sorority Sisters laughing at or criticizing the participants' clothes and bodies. Bitched about and held up for scrutiny, the participants are judged through their gestures of a specifically classed taste. They are also dumped in public. In the opening credits of each episode, one of the Sorority Sisters tells an eliminated contestant: 'you have been weighed, measured and found lacking'. The Sorority Sisters worry whether certain participants are there for the right reasons or whether they are pretending to be someone else in front of them; as in *My New BFF*, contestants are judged for being real or fake. In the first episode, the pink pristineness of the American girls is contrasted with drunk, smoking British students on a night out, shaking their breasts at the camera. The American Sorority Sisters are associated with taste and respectability, as well as authenticity through their condemnation of fake tan, fake eyelashes and fake nails. When the Sorority Sisters choose their 14 contestants in the first episode they reveal that they 'dislike when girls are sloppy' (1:1). They demand poise and an academic attitude. Indeed, cultural difference between the Americans and the British contestants is exaggerated and exploited. In particular, both feminine cohorts act out nationally inflected performances of gender. In the first episode, the Sorority Sisters are introduced in the context of their home settings alongside the camped up signifiers of Americana. Dressed identically, surrounded by pink walls draped with American flags, they are represented in heightened contrast to the contestants (and the viewers). When they allow the British students to give them a makeover, they profess reservations about drinking snakebite and their new 'slutty looks'.

In fact, the femininities that the Sorority Sisters advocate are delineated through the signifiers of the British class system but, within the show's framework, this is also reconceived along the lines of national difference. Slut-shaming intersects with class as the Sorority Sisters prohibit the accoutrements of British working class glamour: fake tan, fake nails, hot pants and high heels. The American Sorority Sisters slut-shame the contestants. In a departure from other girlfriend media, this slut-shaming is explicit and develops the dynamic of school friendship groups, as identified by Ringrose where 'jealousy gets sublimated into a socially acceptable form of social critique of girls' sexual expression' (Ringrose, 2013, 93). A 'Rush Slut' is a potential Sorority Sister who is considered undesirable. Girlfriends must know how to leverage their erotic capital, both as individuals and as part of a group. In particular, their behaviour and appearance cannot be 'sluttish', as this might incite sexual jealousy, as well as revealing class pathologies. The Sorority Sisters comment, 'that girl's looking a little slutty' or, as they more politely put it, that she is 'Slooter Cahooter' (1:1). When Dominique – one of the Sorority Sisters – hears about the concept of an Ann Summers party she appears to be genuinely shocked: 'That's disgusting! A sex toy party!' (1:7). In episode four, a team of Fraternity Boys enact a 'raid' on the girlfriends' house in order to test how the contestants act out their sexuality. The Frat Boys must choose their favourite girlfriend and crown her 'queen'. They claim that the queen 'has to be a bro but not a ho' and that 'she has to carry herself with self respect'. The Sorority Sisters can be seen as the handmaidens to the Frat Boy's misogyny as they regulate the contestants' sexuality (1:4).

Class exploitation is masked through the personalization of systems of governance achieved by highlighting national difference. However, although the American Sorority Sisters dictate the norms of sisterhood, viewers are offered positions from which to critique these norms. The Sorority Sisters take particular exception to Claudia, who gains pleasure through dressing up in these banned components of femininity. Indeed, towards the end of the series, as the competition becomes fiercer, the Sorority Sisters claim that 'we're going to be watching them more than ever' (1:6). This surveillance extends to the contestants' Facebook pages, including their profiles and photographs. Wardrobes and suitcases are rifled through and analysed. The Sorority Sisters police Claudia and eventually find a reason to eliminate her. She is cut in week five, when the Sorority Sisters discover images of her breasts posted on Facebook. They publicly shame her in the elimination ceremony, until Claudia is humiliated and outraged. As she is cut, she tells the participants – her supportive girlfriends – that 'Dominique is a stuck up bitch – and the other American girls...' (1:5). None of the women of colour reach the final chosen five so that the elected British sorority exclusively represents white middle class taste: they are perfect normative postfeminist girlfriends.[2] Nevertheless, Claudia's reaction to Dominique, as well as some of the contestants' dismissal of the Sorority Sisters as 'cheesy', mean that the Sorority Sisters can be held to account by the viewers just as much as the contestants (1:1). This reinforces the intimate rerouting of symbolic violence, however, as the American Sorority Sisters and the British contestants are pitted against each other in a fight for the most normative feminine skills set.

In the episode with the Frat Boys, Dominique warns one of the contestants, Maxine, that 'you came across vulgar and slightly flirtatious with the Fraternity boys. They described you as Maxine Obscene' (1:4). Significantly, the other participants rally round Maxine. They are indignant that she is being regulated in this way. Consequently, they offer a spectatorial position from which to critique the programme's affective domination. Through this display of sisterliness the contestants protest their sexual regulation by the Sorority Sisters but they also evidence their own girlfriendship. Indeed, there is a powerful focus on the love that is being formed between the contestants. Maxine confesses: 'these girls are like a massive inspiration because I've never had so close friends as these girls before' (1:4). This has important ramifications for the viewers as the girlfriends' friendship offers the possibility of being drawn into their visceral and emotional performances. The viewers become implicated in the deep script of friendship and the externalization of its emotion, as well as the affective systems of control.

Surveillance, comparison and the self-brand

Femininity in a neoliberal postfeminist society is promoted as a performance that one wins at. The narrative format of programmes like *Paris Hilton* and *Sorority Girls* forces women to catfight as they compete with each other in order to become normatively distinctive, but also to prove themselves as the most innovative potential celebrity. They compete for the approval and approbation of other women, and are regulated and judged in a spectacular display of normative cruelties. These reality television formats tease out and make overt any feminine rivalry as a short cut to generating entertainment value and in order to court prurience from viewers. This is problematic as it plays on a misogynist understanding of the catfight, where women can only position themselves as rivals. This gendered configuration of competition differs from 'healthy male competition' because it is represented as pathological and out of control. Kristin, or the contestants who fight in *My New BFF*, are represented as abject. Indeed, on the one hand the shows market feminine intimacy as structured, strategic, goal-oriented and future-focused; as formed through the logic of business. Simultaneously, however, they portray and provoke the volatility of these processes. Like the bridezillas discussed in Chapter 4, women are depicted as having the ability to be excessive and monstrous. Contextualized within the ambivalent spaces of branded cultures, women embody the anxieties induced by reckless market forces. Through the gestures of envy and rivalry, contemporary ambivalence over the ethics of relating through the marketization of the body and the self are rerouted as personal issues between catfighting women. This is not to say that women do not experience competition, envy, and comparison among themselves. Indeed, girlfriend culture is powerful precisely because of its harnessing of a complex assemblage of affect generated through social relations – I discuss this further in the conclusion. However, the strategic networks of comparison and policing that are enacted in girlfriend culture mean that postfeminist identities – like the logics of branding – are aggressive. In order to be a successful brand, one must evaluate oneself in relation to others, as well as being open to feedback from them. As Banet-Weiser argues, in relation to digital networks:

> Self-branding, much like the branding of other products, only works if you enable other people to rank your product, which in this case is yourself [...] Self-branding does not merely involve self-presentation but is a layered process of judging, assessment, and valuation taking place in a media economy of visibility.
>
> (Banet-Weiser, 2012, 87)

In the context of these reality shows, these processes of feedback are set up through a competitive format where the contestants are evaluated during the elimination ceremony. This feedback is intricately bound up with the programmes' circuits of surveillance. That is, the contestants are judged by their competitors as well as those who are in the position of affective domination. The participants survey and are surveyed by each other in the shows' gynaeoptic format. Moreover, in the context of these shows, this regulation is linked to class. Through the girlfriend gaze, women like Claudia who evidence class pathologies (signified through not knowing how to leverage one's sexuality according to postfeminist precepts of taste and respectability) are publicly shamed.

In *The Hills*, the girlfriend cast perform the illusion of a closed intimacy. They are not dependent upon anyone apart from themselves, they demand little from the flaky men who they date, or from a wider political or global arena. Nevertheless, the viewer is always aware that these so-called private lives are being filmed. This knowledge is exploited in the final episode when the camera pans out to reveal that the programme – or at least the final scene – was shot on a set. These processes of surveillance are more explicit in *My New BFF* and *Sorority Girls*, where the contestants are often shot on CCTV-style footage. The girlfriends' labour is their ongoing performance in a social relation. They have agreed to have their bodies held up for scrutiny. Consequently, *The Hills* and *My New BFF* produce, perpetuate and feed into the affective experience of constantly being watched. And, furthermore, of being watched by women. These processes of surveillance are marketed as essential to the creation of the perfect postfeminist self-brand.

Because the reality television format intervenes in and evokes real people's intimacies, it summons and strengthens affective bonds between the viewers and the participants. Intimate connections merge powerfully between the mediated and the real. Misha Kavka maintains that reality television 'involves a performance of reality which generates intimacy as its affect'. Acknowledging that the settings of the shows are usually artificial, she also identifies how they are 'chosen or constructed to simulate the scene of intimacy'. Because the participants are removed from their normal surroundings and stripped 'to nothing but the performative space and affect of social interaction', then this artificial or simulated setting '*stimulates* feeling' (Kavka, 2008, 25). Even though this situation is amplified, both for the participants and for the viewers, intimacy is still generated as we gain knowledge of the participants over roughly the same timescale as they do each other. We become affectively conjoined in their experience. The emotional volatility of the discrimination and selection processes also serves to heighten the affective engagement.

This affect is channelled through the signifiers of female friendship that have a powerful regulatory force because they summon feelings of belonging while simultaneously manipulating the terrors of exclusion and shame. Whereas in childhood or adolescence the reasons for not fitting in are often elusive or inexplicable, these shows dissect what is wrong and offer a solution. The tools for normativity are played out and explained. Importantly, the shows offer answers to the feelings of non-belonging that they themselves have produced in their evocation of girlfriendship affect. Indeed, part of the pleasure and catharsis of watching these programmes is experiencing the activation of old wounds in a safe space, as well as achieving resolution. This resolution is produced through observing and learning the techniques that go into creating the healed self. That is, a coherent and successful self-brand.

Part of the labour of being a brand, as evidenced through the figures of Paris and the Sorority Sisters, is to have one's body held up for analysis and to voluntarily put oneself under media surveillance. Moreover, if having a celebrity subjectivity is marketed as available to all, then this also means setting oneself up for scrutiny and analysis by the gynaeopticon. Skeggs and Wood argue that the 'desire to watch and be watched can be seen as part of the endless pursuit of the confirmation of selfhood among the loss of other more certain life trajectories: I see/I am seen, therefore I am' (Skeggs and Wood, 2008, 180). But being subject to the girlfriend gaze also means being complicit in its perpetuation, and this mutual surveillance is marketed as desirable. It is not just that the few see the many, or the many watch the few, but that the many girlfriends watch the many self-branded girlfriends. This means that the many mediated girlfriends affectively participate in the viewers' reflexivity of togetherness, and the viewers are implicated in the networks of control.

7
Class and British Reality Television

There's a bit of jealousy there [...] a bit of envy.

(*What Not to Wear*)

In the spoof documentary *Trinny and Susannah: What They Did Next* (2004), Susannah claims, 'This is a relationship that's been going longer than 14 years.' 'It's lasted longer than my marriage', chimes in Trinny and the camera lingers on their sullen faces. In this 'mock-umentary' Trinny and Susannah camp up their class, celebrity and friendship through portraying themselves in country houses, riding horses, being massaged and reaping the benefits of an upper middle class lifestyle. They simultaneously laugh at themselves through their self-representation in career meltdown and friendship bust-up. Coined 'the princesses of makeover', they perform themselves as alcoholic, hysterical and heading for failure. Here, Trinny and Susannah take the class signifiers that were so evident in their UK television show (BBC, 2001–2007) and bring them to excess. This chapter examines how this excessive manipulation of classed subjectivities is employed as a means to generate conflict between women. I explore the affect of friend-ship and female sociality in the UK 'social work' television programmes (Skeggs and Wood, 2011, 42), *What Not to Wear*, *Cook Yourself Thin* (Channel 4, 2010–2012) and *Wife Swap* (Channel 4, 2003–2009). Not all these programmes are overt examples of girlfriend culture as they do not all represent friends. However, they do enact and enable the girlfriend gaze through their policing networks.

In the absence of a traditional script, inequalities and prejudices are convenient short cuts to narrative opposition (Skeggs, 2010). This is obvious in programmes such as *Wife Swap*, where wives are taken from different socioeconomic and cultural sites and relocated to another's wife's home. *Wife Swap* exploits class or cultural difference between women to produce antagonism from the outset, in the quest for entertaining television. The women in these shows are clearly identified through classed subjectivities that are then edited to produce personal tension. Differences are exaggerated to generate overt disagreement; as Imogen Tyler argues, the affects of hate are lucrative (Tyler, 2008). However, this conflict is also evident in shows structured through a presenter-contestant format. The upper middle class presenters in *What Not to Wear* and *Cook Yourself Thin* are also depicted as characters. I argue that this complicates the power relation of top-down governance because the presenters are also held to account. Because they are cast as characters, this means that the authority structure and its subsequent power struggle between the presenters and (predominantly) working class participants is partly reconfigured as personal, emotional, intimate and female. In this way they function as effective components of the intimate networks of neoliberal control.

The contact zone: *What Not to Wear*

In one episode from *What Not to Wear*, 56 'glamorous sisters' send in 'video nasties' of their 'dowdy siblings'. Trinny and Susannah meet the sisters and deliver cruel comments such as, 'But isn't this your mum?!' Four women are initially chosen and must stand in a mock-up identity parade for inspection. Trinny and Susannah survey the criminal suspects through one-way glass while they decide which two will go through to the next stage and learn 'what not to wear' (the suspects are watched by their more glamorous sisters, as well as the viewers). Addressing the line-up through a microphone, Trinny asks each woman to step forward so that her performance of femininity can be dissected. Once the presenters have made their choice they hug the women who they are going to transform. Through the friendly gestures of touch, female familiarity is harnessed from the outset. This intimacy is foregrounded and heightened through the affect of bestfriendship that is performed by Trinny and Susannah, as discussed in Chapter 2.

Female affection and competition conflate in this episode as the siblings are overtly compared and one is found lacking. Indeed, what is particularly significant here and throughout the episode is the way that Trinny and Susannah play on the affect of the catfight. Pitting the sisters against each other they repeatedly evoke the emotions of comparison and envy between women, referring to potential rivalries between the glamorous and dowdy siblings. They psychologize the contestants' need for a makeover by insisting that one of the main reasons identified for these women's apparent self-neglect is the fact that 'there's a bit of jealousy there [...] a bit of envy'. Trinny and Susannah locate the ways in which the dowdy sisters have competed with their prettier siblings and failed. They diagnose that, due to these earlier experiences of failure, the dowdy sisters have let themselves go. Through this analysis Trinny and Susannah link body image with emotional trauma produced through intimate relationships, and invest the makeover with a deep significance for health and wellbeing.

The relationship that Trinny and Susannah have with the makeover participants is also portrayed as an intimate one. Indeed, the intimacy cultivated through centring the show on the relationship between siblings interconnects with Trinny and Susannah's friendship, the participants, and the viewers. The contestants are invited into the apparently private or closed sphere of Trinny and Susannah's BFF friendship group. Once ensconced within this close relationship, they are represented as freely choosing to put their bodies and dignity into the hands of the best friends. The dynamic between presenters and contestants is suffused with trust in the conventionally private sphere of female knowledges. Through the course of the episode, Trinny and Susannah adopt the clothes and lifestyles of the women who they are going to regulate. For example, Trinny masquerades mockingly in one of the contestants', Saira's, clothes. Sitting at Saira's desk in her home, Trinny feigns boredom, simulating Saira's apparently drab lifestyle; Saira's sartorial choice has seeped into the rest of her life, rendering it dull. Trinny's sculpted and postfeminist body invades Saira's home and chats intimately with Saira's family. Trinny interviews the criminalized woman's work colleagues about Saira's lack of self-esteem. She also mimics the intimate girlfriendship of *Sex and City* as she chats with another contestant's female friends about sex over lunch.

The most overt representation of intimacy – or violation of privacy – is when they place each dowdy sister in a 360-degree mirrored closet and humiliate her. For example, Saira is a British Asian tax consultant who they dismiss as putting 'brains before beauty'. We have already been introduced to Saira's sister who states, '[Saira's] look is not a good look', as well as Saira's friends who confess that she is 'drab'. Trinny and Susannah mock Saira's life and guess at her lack of sex as a consequence of her working too hard and therefore letting herself go. When Saira is in the mirrored closet they bully her through asking her age and then telling her that she 'could be ten years older'. They provoke primal feelings of shame and envy through asserting that 'it must be very difficult for you to stand up in a row with your sisters' and 'you're so nervous of being feminine'. When they ask, 'what has led you to this point?' Saira breaks down and cries, at last confessing that she is ashamed of herself. This scene neatly fits into Foucauldian paradigms of surveillance.

Indeed, Martin Roberts argues that *What Not to Wear* overtly employs the fashion police metaphor through the policing rhetoric, the cameras and the criminal structuring of the relationship between the presenters and the participants. Each episode mimics the successive stages of law enforcement from observation and arrest through interrogation, conviction and release, to ultimate rehabilitation (Roberts, 2007, 234). The offender is a person – usually a woman – who has not fulfilled, or has not been a full participant in, the citizen's duty of consistent self-renewal and consumption for an aspirational body image. In addition, a significant component in this fashion policing process involves shaming and stigmatizing the offender. Roberts states that the subject's transformation is 'presented as a *self*-transformation, freely accepted and undertaken, rather than a form of social discipline'. In this way, governmentality is able to 'erase its own operations in the freedom of its subjects' (Roberts, 2007, 241). The show is constructed to give the appearance of freedom and choice. That is, the contestants are choosing their place on the show and selecting to take or reject the presenters' advice.

The cruel encounter between the two friends and the shamed Saira is played out in the intimate site of a mirrored closet. Saira is regulated through the affect of loving meanness, but also through the exploitation of the complex relations between sisters. Trinny and Susannah enact what Weber calls 'affective domination'. That is, they dominate Saira through their power as presenters but also through the insistence that they are doing this for Saira's own good. Because they are represented as caring, it is all done through the power of love. Indeed, because Trinny and Susannah are best friends, so they powerfully harness the affect of school girl normative cruelties. Once Saira has broken down into tears and confessed her shame, Trinny and Susannah enter the closet to prevent her from leaving. They grab her body and tear at her top until the camera zooms in on Saira's cleavage. Trinny and Susannah then take off Saira's glasses. Here we see two upper middle class white women using the narrative of their loving care to vindicate their sexual harassment. They physically cultivate Saira's erotic capital to heighten her (as well as their) visibility. It is a shocking scene of sexual invasion but it is legitimized through the containment of female intimacy and the affect of friendship.

McRobbie maintains that Trinny and Susannah are complicit in the remapping of social class in gender terms. She notes how they, as upper middle class women, play a key role in the reproduction of a class society by humiliating the working class participants (McRobbie, 2004, 105). Their bullying produces 'new social divisions through the denigration of low class or poor and disadvantaged women by means of symbolic violence' (McRobbie, 2004, 101). Indeed, the reality television shows that I look at here, like many others, are structured through class relations where the working class is over-represented and depicted as inadequate. Training and guidance in respectable and tasteful conduct is sold by the programmes' format as aspirational. Middle class femininity is visualized as caring, respectable and tasteful, and thin middle class bodies become the habitus of a governing normativity. Moreover, as Sara Ahmed argues, the shame and humiliation levelled at the participants generates from an established ideology of social abjection that has expelled the female working class body, and through that expulsion finds it to be disgusting (Ahmed, 2004). Ahmed argues that signs become 'sticky' with repetitive use, and this shapes perceptions of others. In the case of reality television, where bodies are configured as sticky with disgust and criminality, the participants are judged as unfeminine or unwomanly. There is a pervasive power structure at work: the presenters perform their expertise, evidenced through their cultural capital, whereas the participants are represented as ignorant and lacking. Class exploitation is manifest through Trinny and Susannah's camped up performance, but also through the career profile that they accumulate through their labour, as well as their remuneration.

This class exploitation is complicated in the case of Saira, who is a middle class tax consultant. Her performance of femininity is overtly criticized by Trinny and Susannah because she has put brains before beauty through privileging her career. (She also has a child and husband and the presenters maintain that through letting her body image go, Saira has let her family down.) Nevertheless, Saira's class is partly undercut by her race and the 'sticky' signifiers associated with being an Asian woman in contemporary Britain. When Trinny and Susannah maul her body and rip at her clothes they are participating within a colonialist paradigm where it is acceptable for white women to violently coerce women of colour into postfeminist femininities (Weber, 2009). Indeed, the scene can be interpreted as a 'contact zone'. A contact zone is a social space where 'cultures meet, clash, and grapple with each other, often in contexts of highly asymmetrical relations of power, such as colonialism, slavery, or their aftermaths as they are lived out in many parts of the world today' (Pratt, 1991, 34). White knowledge over femininity is pitted against Asian knowledge. The women compete in the intimate space of the closet and the Asian female body is found wanting. However, the top-down governance as identified by Roberts and the symbolic violence noted by McRobbie are complicated through affect. The affect of friendship and intimacy glosses over the processes of neoimperialism, governance and symbolic violence being acted out. Trinny and Susannah are also cast as characters within the show's power struggle. Their class signifiers are edited and heightened as though their own expertise is up for scrutiny by the contestants as well as the viewers; they are portrayed as personalities who are also judged and mocked. Trinny and Susannah's upper middle class English accents are their main signifiers of their class, but their stock phrases are also primary indicators. For example, they gush 'hello there', they call each other 'dahling' and Trinny calls Susannah 'Sooz'. The contestants are 'girls' and 'ladies' who look 'pretty dreadful' and 'ghastly'.

Affect complicates the straightforward viewing regimes of television. In *Reacting to Reality Television*, Skeggs and Wood argue that because the genre functions through affect, and affect cannot be controlled, so viewers' responses to reality television are often unpredictable. They maintain – along with Annette Hill – that reality television has a powerful draw because it gives the viewer the possibility of an empathetic positioning. Through their ethnographic research with British focus groups Skeggs and Wood found that their working class respondents put themselves in the position of 'as if' when watching and discussing reality television. That is, they think themselves into the position of the reality participants as if they were them; they 'constitutively actualize' themselves into the same situation (Sobchack, 1999). The viewers place themselves in the same position of value as the participants and 'the workings of emotion and melodrama elevate the affective currency of immediacy over the signifying practices of representation' (Skeggs and Wood, 2012, 40–41).

Skeggs and Wood identify how viewers situate themselves as both the judged and the judge. This self-positioning and its attendant feelings of empathy, sympathy or identification – however short-lived or contested – are pertinent. Significantly, the respondents take great pleasure in de-authorizing the presenter's governance 'as a viewing practice' (Skeggs and Wood, 2012, 221). Skeggs and Wood found that their middle class respondents often dismissed the advice as not directed to them, whereas the working class respondents would become outraged at the guidance being disseminated. In response, the working class respondents resisted the imposition of authority from those whom they refused to authorize. For example, they would de-legitimate 'those whose knowledge was clearly based on very different economies of time', such as those who could afford nannies (Skeggs and Wood, 2012, 221). Viewers challenge the symbolic violence and the guidance that presenters dictate on behalf of the women who they are seen to be regulating.

This indicates that many viewers of reality television shows like *What Not Wear* also critique the middle and upper class presenters. Indeed, they are presented in such a way as to invite this viewing location. Trinny and Susannah are held to account by the viewers (and the camera's gaze). In *Formations of Class and Gender: Becoming Respectable* (1997) Skeggs identifies the social pleasures of constructing femininity as her working class respondents dress for a night out. She observes the space of dressing up as a site of intimacy that is distanced from men as well as middle class women. In the context of *What Not to Wear*, this private space, constructed through and by groups of working class women, is infiltrated by Trinny and Susannah who redirect the rules of femininity according to the signifiers of their class register. All the women (within the show's narrative) are affectively conjoined through a clearly delineated class structure. However, because not all the participants accept the presenters' advice and not all the viewers confer authority on to the presenters, it becomes a dispute over femininity. The middle class presenters armed with their expertise present their femininity as better than the working class women; or in the case of this episode, a British Asian woman. The show represents a contact zone configured through the practice of dressing up where women feud over correct feminine behaviours.

Because this contact zone is situated in the conventionally private and feminine spaces of the changing room, the fight is depicted as intimate. The contact zone becomes a site of personal conflict between women and through this women are hooked into networks of regulation where the female body is the site of analysis and harm. Moreover, by presenting the experts as characters, symbolic violence is reconfigured as personal, and neoliberal control is re-routed as a catfight. We can see how surveillance culture and its attendant symbolic violence is increasingly enacted, enforced and perpetuated through personal relationships. This masking of governance through self-mockery around class (as evidenced by Trinny and Susannah), combined with tropes of friendship, strengthens postfeminist networks of control. It is harder to be alienated from these networks as they are located in the participatory and interactive practices of a girlfriend convergence culture; they are pervasive and insidious because they are intimate.

Loving meanness: *Cook Yourself Thin*

Cook Yourself Thin is not as intrusive as a show like *You Are What You Eat* (Channel 4, 2004–2007), which overtly links working class bodies with dirt and pathology through extending its surveillance to looking at the participants' faeces. Nor does it replicate the bullying irony of Trinny and Susannah as they mock and denigrate women's taste and bodies. In addition, because it focuses on one woman, it does not draw on affective friendliness in the same way as *Skinny Bitch* or the Fearne and Holly co-brand. Nevertheless, the show is pertinent because it structures a relationship between two women where, from the outset, one woman ostensibly holds epistemological and representable power. Normative cruelty is acted out by the female presenter's shaming of other women's bodies through long close-up judgment shots that are edited to court scrutiny and prurience from the viewers. The show is spliced with misinformed eaters scoffing the wrong food in the wrong places. Their failure as entrepreneurs of the self is coded through the disgust generated by watching them eat meat pasties in front of the television.

Cook Yourself Thin pivots around the presenter, Gizzi, who enters the homes of the female participants (and in season 3, two men), scrutinizes their cupboards and fridges, and makes judgments on their food choices. She then designs three meals in order to train the shamed eaters into 'cooking themselves thin'. The participants are primarily working or lower middle class women who have families. Gizzi, however, is depicted as a girl. She is brisk, cheerful, happy, healthy and mimics the style and taste of Holly Golightly through her 1960s clothes, eyeliner and beehive. The relationship between Gizzi and the participant is one of symbolic violence. Gizzi's power is signified through her girly visual and rhetorical markers, as well as her remuneration as a media personality. The soundtrack mimics 1960s domestic comedies like *Bewitched* (ABC, 1964–1972) and the opening credits mimic the domestic retro femininities of an era when women apparently knew how to look after their homes. It exploits the same period signifiers as *Mad Men* and *The Help* – as discussed in Chapter 5 – with all the attendant classed and raced power relations that this evocation summons.

In season 3, episode 14, Gizzi disciplines a 31-year-old single mum called Yvonne who is a psychology student and has a three-year-old son. Yvonne wants to lose a stone and a half. The episode is spliced with repeated footage of Yvonne walking in the street while eating a doner kebab. The long held close-up shot in a grainy CCTV quality highlights the criminality of Yvonne's body as evidenced through her fat. Her body apparently reveals a lack of discernment around her food choices as well as exposing her failure to participate in an entrepreneurial self-reflexivity. Her self-confessed crimes are that 'I don't plan my food' and that she cannot control her appetite: 'I can't help it'. This has impacted on her body and she has 'let it go'. Yvonne confesses to liking 'fast' and 'instant' food, including takeaways. This goes against the strategic planning of a successful neoliberal subject, but it also reveals her lack of female knowledge in the space of the home. Yvonne's life is represented as out of control.

In contrast, Gizzi opens the episode striding purposefully towards Yvonne's front door. She calculates the extreme proportions of Yvonne's body and holds food up for analysis through giving statistics: grams of fat, calories and 'fat allowance'. According to Gizzi, Yvonne is 'making so many mistakes' and Gizzi advises her that 'we need to teach you how to cook properly'. Furthermore, Yvonne's inability to make the right choices around food also extends to her mothering skills, as she confesses that she does not have the energy to play with her son and is teaching him the wrong eating habits. Gizzi suggests that if Yvonne played with her son by lifting him up to sort out her 'bingo wings', she could lose weight. Gizzi's symbolic violence is played out on the level of body hatred through the term 'bingo wings'. However, because this term of abuse is located in the intimate sphere of female knowledges, it is configured through a loving meanness rather than being an outright articulation of misogyny. In addition, correct mothering skills are intricately bound up with a normative body image, implying that how Yvonne looks is the measure of how much she cares for her family.

Gizzi distinguishes between wrong and right food through the indices of calories. This is disingenuous as she is actually teaching the participants how to cook middle class food. The meals that she demonstrates take much more time and planning to produce, as well as being more expensive. This is never indicated. Gizzi demands cherry tomatoes on the vine, field mushrooms and venison sausages. She advises on using an oil spray and a griddle to dry fry bread. Through demanding dearer food and kitchen utensils, as well as more time – but not defining them as such – Gizzi reduces class exploitation to choices around food and weight gain. These choices are indexed through personal responsibility rather than money. There is an assumption that time and money are plentiful, while fat is a personal failure that reveals lack of control, planning and knowledge. Through these factors, the show attempts to erase the power operations that generate and produce class inequalities, and it glosses over the strategies through which the middle classes exploit and other the working class in the maintenance of hierarchy. Gizzi, in the role of postfeminist missionary, listens to the participants' confession and offers the solution. The comparison of her success (she used to be a model and is a professional cook) is juxtaposed with women who do not have her body. Instead, they have a body riddled with let go, where food has been solely about functionality rather than health, and ease rather than planning.

Dawn Nelson is a black woman who is 38 and a receptionist, living in Hackney, London, with her partner and two children (3:12). Dawn likes her food 'quick, easy and piled high'. She is filmed eating in front of the television and the camera produces CCTV-style shots of her criminalized body. She is diagnosed as lazy when it comes to cooking. In addition, she apparently lacks control, as evidenced when she confesses, 'I don't know when to stop'. In the context of a show that pits Gizzi's visual and classed signifiers against the participants, Dawn is pathologized. Dawn's body is analysed – like the bodies in *Heat* as discussed in Chapter 1 – on the *Cook Yourself Thin* website:

> Age 38
> Height 5' 1"
> BMI 41.5
> Current weight 16 st.
> Lightest weight 10 st.
> Heaviest weight 16 st.

Dawn's appetite and apparent compulsive laziness hamper her role as a mother. Dawn confesses: 'I want to be there for my children and getting bigger is not good for my heart'. Gizzi promises to teach her 'a new way to cook', warning Dawn that 'people who cook and eat fresh food are thinner'. During the course of the episode, Dawn is, in Gizzi's words, 'introduced to a whole new world of food and aroma'. This includes suitably ethnic dishes like 'Gizzi's Caribbean Chicken Jerk with Coconut Salad and Griddled Plantain'. Note that Gizzi marks the meal as hers through her name, but problematically tailors the food for Dawn through its Caribbean flavours. It is one of many instances in this episode – and the programme as a whole – when race and class are reified through the indices of food. Food choice is depicted as embodying the subjectivity of the participant. Different food stuffs become signifiers of identity and it is through the markers associated with eating that classed and raced subjectivities are controlled and fought over. According to Gizzi, Dawn cannot control herself. Gizzi observes to the camera: 'The thing that terrifies me is her portion control [...] if you want to lose weight you have to control what you put in your body.' Later in the episode, the presumably still terrified Gizzi advises Dawn: 'This is a normal portion size. This is what an average person would eat.' She tells the viewers, 'She doesn't need to eat as much as she does. She just has to accept that unfortunately.' Contextualized within the show as a whole, this derogatory diagnosis of Dawn's habits is a typical example of symbolic violence wielded by the middle class expert over the ignorant 'ordinary' (Bromley, 2000) or working class participant. It is yet another example of women competing (in an unequal power relation) over a correct and normative skills set. Gizzi represents what is normative for a woman: self-control and restraint.

However, contextualized within Pratt's understanding of the contact zone, there are also more pervasive power structures being enacted. This episode plays on a long legislative and socioeconomic tradition of subjugating black women. This was justified through the apparently scientifically proven discourse of black women's bestial bodies. Consequently, Gizzi's discourse operates within and gains traction from the racist paradigm of black women's bodies as excessive, uncontrolled and insatiable (McClintock, 1995; Hill Collins, 2004). Gizzi's body – signified through middle class whiteness – is contrasted favourably against Dawn's. In a neoliberal culture intersectional identities are commodified into niche market demographics and through this process history becomes erased. Through the strategies of marketing in a branded culture, the power struggles underpinning identity politics are obfuscated (Banet-Weiser, 2012). In this apparently post-racial culture, where the logics of the market dominate, a white middle class woman telling a black working class woman that she cannot control her appetite is deemed acceptable and proper.

We do not hear how Dawn or Yvonne fare after the episode is over. We do not know whether Gizzi has succeeded in passing on her knowledge or whether Dawn has submitted to her gaze. *Cook Yourself Thin* does not follow up the participants. Instead it arms them with normative expertise (but not the time and money to realize it), and leaves them to self-regulate. Significantly, *Cook Yourself Thin's* moral framework does not so much advocate thinness as a *striving* for thinness. The ideal citizen is perpetually in training, continually aspiring to be thin, and this means that they are continually engaging with weight loss media.

Indeed, Dawn or Yvonne's actual weight is not the issue. Rather, it is their apparent reluctance to perceive the self as a reflexive project. Moreover, they are punished within the show's pedagogic agenda because they resist the feminine network of constant body weight surveillance and its attendant girlfriend gaze that are necessary components of the feminine entrepreneurial self.

The *Cook Yourself Thin* website states that: 'If Dawn swaps her dishes with Gizzi's healthier options, and does ten minutes of hula hooping everyday, she could lose two and a half stone in a year. Now that's how you cook yourself thin!' (www.cookyourselfthin.co.uk). This cliffhanger functions as a classed judgment, but it also provokes consumers into co-participating in the *Cook Yourself Thin* brand. *Cook Yourself Thin* is part of a media convergence culture. Viewers can be members of the dieting programme that is promoted on their website. This will give access to the sociality of other participating dieters, as well as delivering a plan for losing weight. As I discussed in Chapter 1, women's interactivity can be mobilized as 'a gendered requirement of neoliberal citizenship, an ongoing, mundane regimen of self-empowerment' (Oullette and Wilson, 2011, 549). Maintaining and controlling body image can be understood as part of the 'second shift' of housework as being a good mother and wife also means preserving one's visibility (Hochschild, [1989] 2003). We can see how Saira, Dawn and Yvonne are all represented as letting down their families because they have let their bodies go. Through relinquishing the networks of neoliberal and postfeminist control that are played out on their bodies they have failed in their intimate life. The surveillance systems of a convergence culture make the domestic sphere visible through the bodies of women.

Gizzi's performance is a means to incite shame or self-doubt in the participants, as well as the viewers, in order to make them change. This has further poignancy and power if we see her as performing a character rather than just being a mouthpiece for neoliberal governance. As such, from the start of the programme the viewer is enjoined to speculate on who will win: the upper middle class expert or the 'ordinary' person? Like the presenters of *What Not to Wear*, Gizzi is a component in the artificial set up of the reality television format. Although she is represented as successfully participating in the circuits of control through her thinness and her dissemination of 'thin expertise' she is also a figure of entertainment. She might be salaried and have a desirable career profile, but she (like Trinny and Susannah) acts out her upper middle class girly status. Her beehive, eyeliner and retro style also distance her from the viewers. The way in which the viewers are alienated from Gizzi's moral authority is exacerbated through the voiceover, which is different both from Gizzi and the participants.

Through the figure of Gizzi, class inequality is both foregrounded and simultaneously represented at the level of personality. This understanding gains traction within the context of the show which is about makeover and transformation. The contestants are participating within the aspirational narrative of the transforming subject, where becoming is more important than being. They are represented as being 'made over' rather than being made middle class. Consequently, class signifiers are reconfigured as character traits that have the potential to be freely chosen. Class is rerouted as a decision about making a beetroot and trout pitta over buying a doner kebab. It is conflated with discerning shopping. The participants and viewers are marketed the possibility of consuming their way into a different lifestyle. Because class (within the context of the show) is ostensibly codified through making the right kind of choices then having what Gizzi has is sold as achievable. Viewers are marketed the possibilities of being like her, and socioeconomic realities are obfuscated as personal failings.

If class can be achieved through choosing the right kind of food then paying to be part of the *Cook Yourself Thin* brand means adopting aspects of Gizzi's femininity. Gizzi is the signifier used to coerce consumers into the neoliberal networks of control, and as such she is represented to inspire envy and competition. Admiring her lifestyle choice as it is marked on her body also means engaging in competition with her; it means contrasting and comparing one's body or lifestyle to the one that she promotes. If to be successfully feminine is to perform it better than another woman, as Tanenbaum suggests, then to think that Gizzi's advice is useful is to find oneself lacking. However, part of the pleasure of watching reality television is also becoming immersed in the complex and intimate affective social relations that it generates, and viewers are offered a position of resistance. The battle between Gizzi and her participants over a correct and normative feminine skills set is also being played out between and through the programme's affective relationship with its viewers. Indeed, part of the pleasure provided by reality social television – as evidenced in Skeggs and Wood's research – is the articulation of rejection. Because the viewers can adopt the empathetic position of 'as if', so part of the gratification of watching the show is refusing its representation of authority. Nevertheless, whether the audience is enjoined in a relationship of comparison, competition, resistance or rejection, they are situated in an antagonistic relation with another woman, and this conflict is played out on the female body configured as lack. Moreover, it is a fragile resistance, which is solely located in the cathartic space of the reality television format rather than enabling wider political ramifications. Again we see hegemonic power structures being reconfigured as intimate and female.

The other woman: *Wife Swap*

Wife Swap overtly pits two women against each other. The gendered focus of the title is powerfully affective as it appropriates what is central to these women's femininity – their partner and family – and relocates them under the care of 'the other woman'. The title has a sexual frisson and so competitiveness between women is implied from the outset; each episode is set up as a personal conflict. Skeggs argues that 'everyday female television participants (usually working class women) perform their value to millions of viewers' (Skeggs, 2010, 30). In *Wife Swap* we observe the ways in which the wives repeatedly perform (or fail to perform) their conjugal, domestic and familial selves for the camera. The programme is then edited to exploit potential antagonism as part of its narrative push. Tension drives the narrative leading up to the final scene or 'judgment shot' (Grindstaff, 2002), where the wives eventually encounter each other. Although the men participate during this confrontation, it is the women who have entered each other's households and consequently it is their value as wife, mother and carer that is primarily thrashed out at the table. Normative femininity is being fought over.

The voiceover for the episode 'The Ahmeds and the Escotts' tantalizingly promises to reveal 'what happens when religion clashes with sexuality'. Nuzhat is a 'strict Muslim' who works for the council, studies accountancy, and runs her house single-handedly. She has a 'tight rein' on her children. She is filmed performing her faith to excess. Consequently, the show is edited to highlight provocative statements such as, 'in Islam cleanliness is half of the faith' and 'how can people live without a religion?' The family that she enters – the Escotts from Liverpool – have a lesbian teenage daughter (Bex) and a husband who does most of the housework. Nuzhat 'wife swaps' with Debs who works for a theatre company and is described by the voiceover as 'liberal'. Nuzhat disagrees with Bex's sexuality – 'this lesbian and gay is not acceptable in Islam at all' – and reduces her to tears. She also asks Bex to cover up her body, but Bex fights back: 'There are certain things about covering oneself or one's head that I don't agree with.' Nuzhat is also pitted against Debs through her nightly confessions:

> This family is so damaged. I hope that when Debs come back she will be a loving caring mother like me. Maybe that's too much to ask.

When the wives eventually encounter each other, Nuzhat tells Debs:

> I think your house is really messy and really dirty [...] Andy does too much in the house. He's not being appreciated [...] You need to have a relationship with Bex. She is screaming for help and she is screaming for love. As a mother I would never say giving up on my child.

Debs retorts:

> I think maybe you've just come in and maybe been quite judgmental. I felt like a slave in your home...

Through the show's editing, both women are caricatured in order to make their differences more stark and the potential catfight more explosive. Debs vocalizes, and is a vehicle for, dominant discourses about Muslim women – that they are slaves. Traditional morals are articulated through the voice of Nuzhat. She expects that a woman's place is in the home and that a wife should nurture her husband, as well as producing a clean environment. However, Nuzhat, as she is presented in the programme, is not the kind of woman who would choose to appear on a reality television show, especially not *Wife Swap*. The woman who works at the council, studies for accountancy, and wants to be on reality television is a more multi-dimensional character than the one who is being portrayed.

Samantha A. Lyle maintains that *Wife Swap* is structured through a middle class gaze that 'encourages a preferred reading by the audience in terms of class identities' (Lyle, 2008, 328–329). Even though the middle class gaze is not monolithic (it functions on and from the participants, the producers of the programme and the audience in different configurations) it favours those with access to modes of self-narrativization as they are able to present themselves as persons of equal value. The participants, viewers and producers are all surveying and surveyed but those invested with cultural capital are more able to distinguish themselves from the regulatory gaze (Lyle, 2008, 328–329). The producers (for whom the show will be part of their career profile and remuneration) create a site for class antagonism and symbolic violence which is acted out by the participants who receive considerably less in terms of economic and cultural return.

We see this middle class gaze being harnessed in the episode 'The Berrisfords and the Pearson-Faiths', which exploits sexuality as well as class to highlight and enhance insurmountable differences between women. The Pearson-Faiths are a married lesbian couple from Essex. Jess, 'the wife', receives benefits and lives in a council house. Her partner remains at home to receive the Berrisford wife, Mandy, and to take care of the children. The show is structured to pathologize and shame Jess through comparing her negatively with Mandy who is from 'a traditional farming family'. Although there is no governing middle class presenter, Mandy becomes the voice for hegemonic discourses. The programme affectively mines the women's class and sexual identities in order to threaten a catfight. It is class rather than sexuality that is the overt source of competition between the women as evidenced when Mandy despairs:

> That's money that my family are working really hard for and we give it to people like this.

In the final confrontation scene Mandy wins as Jess breaks down as if in a confessional. Jess admits her classed inferiority: she has failed as a mother and her family is not as perfect as the Berrisfords.

In these reality television programmes, women are pitted against each other along the lines of class for commercial gain, and it is white middle class women who are represented as regulating and maintaining this symbolic violence. The programme's producers harness the middle class gaze in their judgment of the working class participants and it is also through this symbolic violence that they make their profit margins. Working class women perform their value for other women and through the regimes of looking incited by the middle class gaze, they fail. That is, they are portrayed as lacking the qualities of caring, mothering and domesticity. The commercial impulses of the programmes mean that normatively distinctive (middle class and girly) female bodies are privileged and their regulation is enacted by and between women. Working class women are portrayed as being excluded from knowledge about the correct procedures of consumption, and they are symbolically misrecognized as responsible for their own exclusion. The participants are depicted as complicit in their own denigration.

Patriarchy is obfuscated by representing class exploitation as a personal antagonism between women. Whereas neoliberal elites enjoy the power garnered through mutually enriching networks (Harvey, 2005), female consumers are encouraged to compete with each other in order to achieve normativity. Through foregrounding conflict, these television programmes cement hierarchies between women and foreclose solidarities or alliances across the intersections of class and race. This is especially the case if these are sites where political anger is rerouted as a personal catharsis enacted between women.

Nevertheless, by configuring power relations as clashes of personality, the programmes also *reveal* the ways in which women perpetuate symbolic and racial violence through the talk, posturing and interaction of intimacy. The register and rhetoric through which the women speak to each other, as well as their body language and gestures, demonstrate the ways in which symbolic violence is channelled on and against women. Significantly, the way that we see power structures being woven into interpersonal spaces is pertinent for feminism. It evidences how ideological exploitation intersects with the affect of normative cruelties and loving meanness in a staged interaction between two women. To perceive *Wife Swap* in this way – as a relationship between women – is not so much to personalize what is a class or race issue, rather it is to observe the multiplicity of ways in which exploitation is repeated and consolidated between women. Symbolic violence is performed through replicating the normative cruelties of female relationships – including the affects of belonging promised by striving for normative distinctiveness – while simultaneously regulating through gestures of shame, humiliation and exclusion. The problem with reality television is that it does not offer a productive or creative exploration of these affects. It can, however, provoke one. It can be a valuable trigger for engaging with shame, humiliation and exclusion, and perhaps for formulating strategies for understanding more deeply how they manifest and function. I discuss this further in the conclusion.

8
The Friendship Market

Whether you have a little or a lot to loose [sic], join the rest of the 2013 brides to be with a weekly weigh in every Sunday!

(youandyourwedding.co.uk)

In *The Program: Fifteen Steps to Finding a Husband After Thirty* Rachel Greenwald appropriates techniques from the Harvard business model to advise women on how to transform themselves into successful brands.[1] Making oneself into a brand, she enthuses, will ensure the ensnaring of a husband – even after 30. Greenwald advises that the potential bride brand will be more authentically herself and, simultaneously, meticulously crafted and cultivated through marketing strategies. These strategies combine branding techniques that have been honed at Harvard along with the purloining of traditional attributes and performances of femininity. According to Greenwald, most men prefer feminine women; this means that they 'prefer longer hair [...] that is soft to touch' (Greenwald, 2004, 45–46). She tells her readers:

> Part of evaluating your look and how you are perceived by men requires a frank assessment of whether or not you **look** and **act** feminine [...] I have seen time and again that men are usually more attracted to women in skirts than in trousers [...] *most* men seek women who exude feminine qualities.
>
> (Greenwald, 2004, 52)

She advises on how to position oneself as an object to the managerial self and, consequently, how to be both brand and producer. Greenwald counsels on how to manage one's femininity strategically, including how to give the appearance of being 'pursued' when one is actually 'capturing' a man's interest (Greenwald, 2004, 52). In a culture of self-branding, this is not a paradox. On the contrary, perceiving oneself as a project is key to one's success in neoliberal society. This chapter explores how discourses of self-branding intersect with postfeminist digital sociality through forums and social media. It examines how branding interconnects with the neoliberal citizen who is expected to be self-responsible and to perceive themselves as a project to be worked upon. In the first section I look at British wedding media, and argue that they address themselves to networks of women, whether this is established familial and personal friends, or ones that have been cultivated through digital sites. The postfeminist girlfriend landscape in popular culture is dotted with weddings, or what Renee Sgroi calls the 'wedding imaginary' – the heterosexual cultural logic which centres on weddings (Sgroi, 2006, 114). It is populated by wanna-be brides, brides-to-be, bridezillas and sometimes jilted brides. However, it is also occupied by girlfriends who assume the identities of hens and bridesmaids in the run-up to the big day. Indeed, the wedding imaginary enables female sociality. Examining how brides are encouraged to emulate celebrity wedding ceremonies, I maintain that the idealized figure of the bride is a pertinent example of contemporary self-branding. Wedding media replicate Greenwald's business model approach through addressing the bride as a traditional feminine figure, as well as a strategic brand manager. In the second part of this chapter I develop my analysis of digital networks to look at sites that harness the affect of friendship such as Facebook.

Here comes the brand

Although wedding discourse is usually one of individualism, it addresses itself to networks of women, particularly female family members and friends. Wedding media configures the planning, preparations and the big day as a site for postfeminist sociality. Indeed, much of wedding media is troped through the feminine and intimate signifiers of the womance. Wedding media's primary target market is the bride and, in particular, the bride as part of a closed female group.[2] The bride as flawless spectacle is not merely locating her self-commodification. She will be an object of admiration, but she will also be addressed as events coordinator, wedding planner, accountant, and marketing consultant. Part of the success of her brand will not just be that she looks 'perfect', it will be that she has successfully and strategically planned a distinctive and innovative spectacle for others to participate in. She will have been a successful and visibly entrepreneurial self.

The ubiquitous wedding mobilizes the spectacle of the girl through reconfiguring traditional femininities such as the perfect bride and the white wedding. This is not necessarily linked to an essentialization of femininity (although it borrows heavily from these discourses and their affect). It is more that traditionalism is a particular branded feminine identity that can be bought and which a potential bride can choose to perform. The whiteness of the bride – in all its raced and gendered connotations – draws on girly femininities, however ironic or self-conscious. By branding I mean not only the narratives generated by commodities, such as the Vera Wang dress, but also the branding and brand management of the entire wedding event, including the bride. Wedding media increasingly borrow from brand management discourse and persuade their consumers to theme, and to strategically manage their weddings. *Hello!* magazine's website, for example, directly addresses the practice of branding through promoting five wedding 'brands' which include 'Vintage Vixen', 'Modern Mini' and 'Fairy-tale Princess'. Choosing and planning are offered as means to create a distinctively unique and authentically personal spectacle. The dizzy proliferation of blogs and websites, never mind the choices that each mediated platform offers, reinforces the sense of autonomy and the power to create a distinctive wedding. On youandyourwedding.co.uk, for example, the planning section includes the following links: events, venues, gift list ideas, readings and speeches, entertainment, hen party, favours and thank yous, photographers, cakes, flowers and stationery. Under each theme there are up to 50 articles offering advice, from a DIY best man's speech template to cupcake-making hen dos.

Wedding media can be seen as part of the makeover and reinvention genre which saturates popular culture. However, instead of just drawing on the 'affective currency' (Weber, 2009) of shame to induce an image overhaul, wedding media promotes perfection and the ideal one-off spectacular experience. McRobbie defines the makeover as 'the transformation of self with the help of experts in the hope or expectation of improvement of status and life chances through the acquisition of forms of cultural and social capital' (McRobbie, 2004, 99). Rather than being an enforced victim of patriarchy, the makeover participant is coerced through a rhetoric of entitlement – she *is worth it*. In this way, she is both object and empowered business woman, who has agency and control over her life. Commenting upon this culture of transformation, Orbach argues that women are encouraged to aspire to physical perfection through a rhetoric of authority: 'It's about transforming that sense of feeling powerless into feeling powerful. It transforms the image of you as the victim into thinking, "Oh, this is a real opportunity! I could do it this time"' (Orbach, 2009b). In addition, 'the makeover endeavors to offer subjects either the reclamation or the first-time-ever experience of me-ness' (Weber, 2009, 9).

Just as brand management literature stresses the need to reinvent constantly in order to keep consumers hooked, so makeover privileges continual change and the process of '*becoming*', which is represented as 'more desirable than *being*' (Jones, 2008, 12). The postfeminist girl must continually change her look, keeping it up to date and edgy in order to be normatively distinctive. Greenwald locates the importance of 'packaging' when creating the self as brand. The 'packaging' chapter typically advises the reader to lose weight. However, the emphasis is not so much on maintaining a slender ideal, but on being transformed through the process of recurrent change: 'the most important success criterion is your level of commitment to the search' (Greenwald, 2004, 6). In wedding media the focus is not on frequent image conversion, but on a time-bound specific event. Nevertheless, the language of authenticity and the revelation of the real self holds true for wedding media. The wedding is about being perfect, but it is also about being the best person that you can be, and illuminating your authentic inner beauty. The wedding spectacle is also marketed as something that is distinctively about you and your relationship. The day will be set for posterity through photographs and memories, both of which increase the pressure of producing the perfect experience.

Self-branding explicitly addresses the self as a product and fragments the product in order to create a more authentic and yet sellable self. This self is structured through a coherent narrative. Greenwald advises the potential bride: 'You, the reader, are the "product", and *The Program* is a "strategic plan" to help you "market" yourself to find your future partner' (Greenwald, 2004, 2). She assures us that 'A well-defined, memorable brand is absolutely essential for any successful product'. According to Greenwald, brands serve four main functions: '(1) to help customers remember the product, (2) to convey a complex message quickly, (3) to help customers distinguish the product from similar products, and (4) to create positive appeal to entice someone to buy the product' (Greenwald, 2004, 69).

People have brands, 'just like products', but communicating this is complex (Greenwald, 2004, 70). She outlines four rules:

1. The brand rings true to who you are, both as you see yourself and as others see you.
2. The brand will appeal to a wide range of men.
3. The brand should be memorable and unique.
4. The brand should position you as 'lifelong partner or marriage material'.

(Greenwald, 2004, 74)

Once the personal brand has been developed, the self-brander must learn to advertise 'the brand' and make it 'consistent in all details of your packaging'. The self-brander must also 'reinforce' the brand with online dating and other dating activities: 'you will extend your brand across your entire "product line"' (Greenwald, 2004, 80). We can see how this branding of the self is a means to create normative distinctiveness as one must be both 'memorable and unique' while simultaneously 'marriage material', with all the conventional feminine attributes that that connotes.

This calculated attitude towards heterosexual coupledom is typical of girlfriend culture. Promoting oneself on the marriage market has traditionally been key to women's economic and cultural success. However, Greenwald's explicit dissection of the process, which is written through the language of empowerment and business, is specifically linked to contemporary branding practices whereby the body and femininity are approached as erotic capital that is accumulated by women. What is interesting about Greenwald's approach to the self is that emotion is siphoned off. Romance is high risk and messy, whereas business models are pragmatic and reliable. Marriage, which has always partly been a business arrangement – however glossed over – becomes overtly so in Greenwald's conduct book, where she advises on how cultural capitals can merge to create future economic success and stability.

Celebrity brands

The wedding is a way of extending the celebrity profile, as well as adding value to the individual's brand through wedding stories that can be spread across media platforms. Analysing David and Victoria Beckham's wedding feature in *OK!*, Andy Milligan argues, the 'Beckhams chose to turn their wedding into a brand event, a decision that brought them cash, positioned them as true celebrities and broadened interest in them still further' (Milligan, 2010, 108). Referring to their media coverage, Milligan notes that the representation of the wedding boosted their couple-brand: Posh and Becks's 'co-branding relationship is one of the most high-profile joint-venture brands ever' (Milligan, 2010, 157). Celebrities also add to their value by extending it to wedding products. The *Hello!* magazine website links to brands such as Littlewoods that feature a range of celebrity branded dresses for weddings, such as 'The Holly Willoughby Bow Front Dress'.

The telling and selling of celebrity weddings in *Hello!* and *OK!* reinforce the decreasing value placed on the groom, as evidenced throughout girlfriend culture. Their narratives focus on the spectacle, the commodities and the dress, and in both magazines there are frequent references to the cost of the weddings. A piece in *OK!* features the summaries of a range of celebrity nuptials, celebrating them under the headline 'extravagant weddings'. These descriptions commonly include details of abundant ceremonies lasting a number of days, usually at luxury venues. Footballer Wayne Rooney and Colleen's wedding is described as a 'four-day Italian wedding extravaganza with Colleen's five stunning white Marchesa gowns'. Details include a masked ball on a luxury yacht with pink champagne and lobster buffet: 'The 16th century Abbey of La Cervara had been festooned with white blossoms and fairy lights and the couple released doves, were serenaded by opera-singing waiters and were surprised by an incredible fireworks display' (Guiltenane, *OK!* 18 August 2009). Here, the exceptionality of celebrity weddings is conferred by the degree to which the bride builds her distinction through extravagant consumption. In addition, the emotional significance of brands is evident in being represented as the ideal medium through which brides express their marital vows: 'Can't think of a better way to say I do, than to say it with Tiffany's.' The perfection of branded products is also bestowed through their role as a substitute for the ideal husband: 'the one'. For example, TV presenter Andrea Mclean 'looked stunning in a Caroline Castigliano dress and tiara', and she enthuses that 'the first dress I tried on, I knew it was the one' (Dowdeswell, *Hello!* 28 September 2009). Significantly, 'the one' is usually found and shared with and through women at the ubiquitous bridal fitting. Here, we see women socializing through the tropes of womance summoned by brands.

It is not just their ability to consume conspicuously that makes celebrities and their weddings so fascinating. Celebrities are also icons of the transformational process of brand management, and are explicitly recognized as human brands. Celebrities such as J. Lo, Beyoncé and

Paris Hilton perform the role of brands with their own logos, packaging and product lines, but they have also 'become products themselves [...] you can buy their representations' (Cashmore, 2006, 3). Because the focus in branding management is 'less on giving a brand meaning, and more on giving it *life*', celebrity brands have added emotive power (Braun, 2007, 158). Wedding media persuade women to emulate celebrities' high visibility and encourage them to engage in a brand management process of transformation. Wedding blogs and websites profile both 'real weddings' and 'celebrity weddings' in order to provide inspiration for the planning bride. Like the magazine, the *Hello!* website affiliates celebrity with weddings, and 'Brides' and 'Your Weddings' are two of its main sections. It represents this wedding perfection as unique in being financially unavailable for its consumers, but at the same time suggests ways in which it can be emulated. The inspiration of celebrities is emphasized in a section called 'Jet Set Wedding Inspirations – Tying the Knot Celebrity Style'. Its introduction states: 'The rich and famous can afford to indulge their every whim when it comes to celebrating the happiest day of their lives.' It gives a number of examples of 'the different approaches chosen by stars', intended to be guides to achieving distinction.

The degree to which readers of wedding media are encouraged to emulate the self-branding promotional spectacle of celebrity brides is apparent in the back pages of *Hello!* The 'Hello You' section offers readers the validation of being seen through publishing readers' wedding photographs alongside celebrity weddings. The *Hello!* website also offers gallery space for consumers to post their wedding photographs and, again, enjoy a quasi-celebrity moment alongside real celebrity brides. They are asked to give a brief description of their wedding and, as with the narratives of celebrity weddings, these invariably relate to the designer dresses worn, the lavish consumption, as well as what made their wedding special. For example, Anna Hanson married Ian Black in the church where Anna's parents were married and which was also the home to her maternal grandparents' ashes. What conferred their wedding with distinction was their 'Classic Glamour' brand:

> the bridesmaids wore floor length one shoulder dresses in a stunning shade of African violet. The gorgeous purple colour continued throughout the theme of the entire wedding, with the floral arrangements, venue decorations, and even the lighting including shades of deep purple.

Emulating celebrity culture, 'Anna herself wore a crystal encrusted Sophia Tolli gown in pure white, along with crystal shoes that the groom had custom made for her' (hellomagazine.com). The copy is illustrated with photographs and because they are posted alongside celebrity weddings we can see a convergence between the ordinary and the extraordinary. This is also signified through the places where the weddings are held. Nick and Nikki Edwards married in 'a stunning beach ceremony in Palma de Mallorca':

> The ceremony itself was held at Mood Beach as the sun shone down on the couple, followed by drinks on the champagne terrace and a reception in the beach club at Mood. The beach club is a truly glamorous venue with celebs such as Cristiano Ronaldo hiring it for private parties.
>
> (hellomagazine.com)

The conspicuous consumption that merges with the space and name of a celebrity within the copy, gives added value – and validation – to the wedding spectacle. The consumers' interaction with, and investment in, celebrity branding through these sites is part of the co-production process of wedding media brands.

The planning and promotion of the wedding is not enough as the body of the bride is also up for scrutiny on the best day of her life. There is a huge market for brides who want to improve their appearance for the big day. In the UK there are hundreds of personal trainers who market themselves specifically to brides. There is even a bridal boot camp in Wokingham that offers intensive ten-week weight loss programmes with prices starting at £1300. It is sold as a no-nonsense approach that uses the language of force, control and punishment. It ostensibly counteracts the excess of choice and emotions that play havoc with the bodies of women. However, this disciplining approach is actually yet another choice, another commodity to be consumed. There are also conduct books such as *Perfect Bride* by Janet Wright. Published for a UK market in conjunction with *You and Your Wedding* magazine, the rhetoric of Wright's is covertly that of strategic management interwoven with the persuasive and regulating language of normative cruelty. It is pragmatic, time-bound, future-focused, and addresses the bride through a language of scrutiny and surveillance. For example, Wright informs the reader that six months before the wedding she should be choosing the dress, being aware that 'a full-skirted ball gown hides a multitude of sins' (Wright, 2005, 31). Brides are told to, 'Take a critical look at yourself, not to denigrate your shape but to check if you've slipped into bad habits of standing or moving that don't do you any favours' (Wright, 2005, 64).

However, guidance over the bride's event, as well as her 'packaging', is not limited to this conventional top-down expert and consumer relationship. Consumers also participate in the dissemination of advice and the co-production of brands. Sky Living TV's *Four Weddings* is a pertinent example of the wedding being marketed to, with and through networks of women (although the grooms also sometimes participate). The website describes the programme as 'four brides-to-be put their special day under scrutiny, inviting three rival brides to critique their nuptials, all in a bid to win every newly wed's dream prize – a luxury honeymoon'. (http://skyliving.sky.com/fourweddingsuk). It was first screened in summer 2009 and so far has run to four seasons. There is also a US version (TLC, 2010–). Each bride creates and projects her packaged personality, reflected in the wedding theme and spectacle. The wedding is divided into four categories – dress, venue, food, experience – and the contestants mark each other out of 25. After all, if the wedding is individual and unique it must be so in relation to something or someone else.

The competitive format of this programme provokes, courts and exploits feelings of envy and rivalry between women. The women must compare their wedding with the other contestants and this process of evaluation and feedback is essential for choosing the winner. Judgment and scrutiny are important components in the development of the self-brand, but in the context of this show it is also a means to play on and manipulate stereotypes of women as competitive and catty. We can see how the surveillance and normative cruelties of *Sorority Girls* are combined with the peer evaluations of *Wife Swap*. *Four Weddings* also plays on the trope of the bridezilla evident in the girlfriend flick (as well as the much more volatile American reality television series *Bridezillas* [WE, 2004–]), where the brides are depicted as acting out the competitive consumption of the narcissistic and avaricious bride. It is usually the brides who have spent the most money – and consequently have most closely achieved celebrity exclusivity – who win.

Episode 1, season 1, portrays Ada, 'who naturally compares weddings anyway'. Her ceremony is branded as the '£15,000 big African wedding'. We see the church ceremony, the vows, the reception and the edited comments of the other brides. Her racial identity is reified through the labelling of the wedding and also through the show's particular focus on the food, which is heavily criticized by the other white contestants: 'My lips are, like, numb', and 'I was struggling to eat the food.' The venue is also dismissed: 'It's not really weddingy' and, 'The venue's not fantastic; it's a kind of sports hall'. They make normatively cruel remarks about the other weddings, too: 'definitely not my kind of dress'; 'Barbie bridesmaids!' and 'there wasn't anything about the dress I liked'. The pursuit of the special day is more important than friendliness and support, and female relating is portrayed through the enactment of judgment and jealousy. As the competing brides are interviewed, they act out the cruel scrutiny of the girlfriend gaze, while simultaneously dispensing feminine expertise against the backdrop of the wedding imaginary.

Weight loss convergence

The self as brand is most clearly exemplified in the figure of the celebrity and, as celebrity culture becomes apparently more accessible to all, so emulating their promotional strategies becomes achievable. Moreover, with the possibilities of self-marketing and self-publicity offered on social networking sites so the ability to create a distinctive brand becomes more relevant. Brides also look for support in the planning of their wedding and their self as brand on internet forums hosted by consumer sites such as confetti.co.uk, youandyourwedding.co.uk, hitched.co.uk. Brides-to-be network and meet virtually in order to support each other. We can see the market's lines of flight producing and intervening in women's virtual sociality. These forums create a space for women to share in the pleasures of intimate publics and homosocial spaces. They are sites where women can reveal doubts and fears that are generated in a neoliberal and punishing postfeminist culture, as well as co-participating in the pleasures of 'trying on' femininities.

In digital wedding media, users can congregate in order to support each other in losing weight. Their sociality provides the content of the digital site. The forums evidence the perceived need for a change in body image, with many brides aiming to lose up to three stone for their weddings. Weight loss packages sold by diet brands Slimming World, Weight Watchers, and Rosemary Conley, plus those advertised by the websites themselves, are frequently discussed and compared. Prospective brides ask for support in the anticipation of being 'weighed in' on a weekly basis, and one chatroom user on hitched.co.uk has coordinated a forum weight loss group where women can indicate their target weight and use each other for support in achieving this. The language shared is primarily one of self-deprecation and failure, charged with taking control. A typical example reads:

> I would like to lose 7lbs this month. Had a disaster over the summer holidays and really need to get back into this. Children back at school on Monday so my routine should be back to normal. I really have to knuckle down. Won't put my total weight loss on here as it's not good as I have put quite a bit on. Once I'm back to where I was I will put it back on here. This is it!!
>
> (hitched.co.uk)

Interestingly, women often return after their wedding (and after they have put the weight back on) to take part in this community working towards image change. This indicates the value of a virtual community, but it also evidences the pleasures of socializing through the narrative of weight loss. This could be linked to the desire to take control of one's life as this is recognized as being achievable through regulating the body. It also evidences the contemporary obsession with body image and the pain accrued through this. Moreover, just as celebrities do their emotion work and also garner publicity through fluctuating weight, so ordinary people can forge networks through sharing a narrative of controlling the body.

On confetti.co.uk, the threads are posted under the section 'live talk' that is accompanied with a photograph of two women affectionately engaged in conversation in order to flag up the intimacy of the forum. Indeed, the comments are personal, confessional and expose the users' vulnerability. It seems that the virtual privacy of an online community means that it is possible to reveal insecurities and shame. Interestingly, just as digital networks can be harnessed in the cultivation of the self-brand as evidenced in the work of Banet-Weiser, it can also provide an antidote or solace to this relentless hypervisibility. Although the women congregate digitally through weight loss as part of the 'second shift' of housework that puts huge emphasis on body image, they are also utilizing this intimate sociality to reveal the pressures of postfeminist subjectivities. These virtual networks can be a means to reveal the self in a culture increasingly focused on marketing the self as competent and coherent. Moreover, in an era when familial and community structures are liquid, these forums can be invaluable sites of support where an ethics of care structures the technologies of interaction.

On youandyourwedding.co.uk there is a weekly weigh-in. Here, the body is subject to analysis in a similar way to *Heat* magazine and *Cook Yourself Thin*:

> Whether you have a little or a lot to loose [sic], join the rest of the 2013 brides to be with a weekly weigh in every Sunday!
>
> My starting weight is 78.3kg. (I am going with kg as I am using the wii fit).
> My BMI is 29.84 (Overweight)
> Aim – to lose at least 13.3kg
> Let's cheer each other on!
> I used this website to calculate my BMI
> http://www.dropadresssize.myforever.biz/nutrilean/ calculators/bmi. html

As members join they give their measurements: present weight, ideal weight, as well as the lightest weight they have ever achieved. Armed with statistics, information and each other's support, the women unite against their recalcitrant flesh. They socialize via the networks of control that analyse the female body and in these surveillance systems they interact through the regimes of sight configured in the girlfriend gaze.

Weight loss is not only a concern in wedding media, however. On 31 July 2012, Candy Crate posted on the enormously popular mumsnet.com:

> I have a stupid belly that I need to get rid of. I am 5'10 [sic], have no idea how much I weigh but I'm a size 12. I would be perfectly happy with my body except since I had DS [darling son] two years ago my belly just seems to always be big and sticks out over my jeans!
> (mumsnet.com)

In response, users advise on work-out videos, diets, control pants, tummy tucks or the MuTu System, which is 'great because you get connected with other mums also trying to get/stay in shape. Brilliant.' Another mum – 'tittytittyhanghang' – suggests that Candy Crate has split stomach muscles and developed a 'mum tum'. puds11 posts:

> hate to say this, but you may never get rid of the saggyness of your belly (if that is what it is?) but you most certainly can get rid of the excess weight although it will be hard work. I am embarking on a

belly blitz myself starting today. So far i have had my SF shake for breaky and have done 100 sit-ups and a 30 min cycle ride. Now i have no intention of doing a 30 min cycle ride everyday but i am aiming to do 200 sit ups per day. If you like i shall report back after a week to see if the intense sit up madness has made any difference?

Other users are eager to hear about how puds11 develops, and through this online community she is inspired and supported in her attempt to rid herself of something that brings her pain. It is significant that the women use misogynist language to describe their bodies, whether this is 'tittytittyhanghang', 'bingo wings' or 'stupid belly'. This mimics other political re-appropriations of words that were previously abusive, and indeed there is a strong sense of solidarity among the users. The shared knowledge of the tyranny of slenderness and the catharsis that this engenders is valuable. However, in a context where women are striving to change their bodies and so perceive them as flawed and in need of transformation, it evidences body hatred. It mimics the gestures of *Cougar Town* where women unite through bawdiness but are simultaneously complicit with the industries that perpetuate misogyny.

In mumsnet and youandyourwedding.co.uk we can see how networks of women are mined in the corporate spaces of social media in order to spread brand loyalty. In particular, women who congregate through body anxiety are a prime demographic. Brands need the right balance between body hatred and the desire for transformation. These social spaces – configured through the empowering rhetoric of postfeminist sociality mixed with misogyny – are a key market for brand ambassadors and brand spreaders; that is, users who are employed to covertly market a product. These sites are suffused with the affect of female friendship and its complex assemblage of pleasures and pains. youandyourwedding.co.uk, for example, provides a virtual interactive sociality around its own products and those of the other retailers it promotes. Users on the websites cited above spread information about weight-loss brands such as the MuTu System, Slimming World, BMI websites, Slim Fast or the 30 Day Shred. The forums are crucial places for these products to develop deep loyalties among consumers, especially if the interaction is through group participation in weight loss; the brand enables and consolidates women's sociality. Significantly, the emotional investment that women put into their friendships can work to personify a brand and give it human qualities. Female knowledges and expertise, which play an integral part within women's intimacies, can render a brand's narrative more reliable and trustworthy.

Whereas texts like *Heat* magazine offer the celebrity body to be consumed, online women offer their own bodies for surveillance. Significantly, women socialize and connect not through the pains of a heterosexual coupling narrative, but by speaking through and against the body as disappointment and/or aspiration. Girlfriend media provide sites for women to participate in the sharing of the flawed or fabulous felt self. Women congregate intimately to complain and care about their bodies, but also to share, consume, test and take pleasure in solutions for their fluctuating faces and flesh. Although it is silently (and sometimes vocally) accepted that the perfect body is an illusion created by the beauty complexes, there is no attempt to politicize this fact. On the contrary, there is a pervasive ambiance of resignation and a mutual acceptance of the status quo at the same time that an immense social pleasure is shared in the construction of a feminine performance.

These virtual networks and friendships function to provide support, advice and empathy, but they are also necessary for the promotion of the self. Losing weight is a bid for individual recognition and self-profiling. Consequently, these relationships are built around systems of exchange: women support each other in becoming more visible and therefore apparently more empowered. As the male gaze is mystified as retro, discipline is meted out between girlfriends. In this way, virtual networks have value in promoting erotic capital. The social value of various forms of capital responds to historical change, and in an era of social networking we can see that having, and being seen to have, social capital is increasingly necessary. Digital networks are essential in the cultivation of the hypervisible self.

Facebook friends

Sociality is Facebook's value. Facebook claims ownership to everything that is posted, which means that users' friendships are its content, its market and its worth. Facebook is privately owned and is the most used global social networking site. There are 1.06 billion monthly active users worldwide and these users are mainly located in the US. It is used for individuals to connect but it is also mined by employers, businesses and brands 'as a way to distribute information about people, groups, and products' (Banet-Weiser, 2012, 82). The 'like' function means that a brand can colonize new consumer territories that have already been opened up through friendship networks. This is particularly effective as it can mine the intimacies of private relationships in order to extend the reach of its demographic, as well as 'spreading' through the affects of peer pressure, including the pleasures of belonging and its potential normative cruelties. As a space for sociality, Facebook is a goldmine for the spreading of brands and the vacuuming of data for consumer profiling. As Banet-Weiser notes, its genealogy helpfully illustrates its present context as a platform for postfeminist self-branding. It was originally created by Mark Zuckerberg as a site for college students to rate the 'attractiveness' of women's photographs that were voluntarily submitted by other users. This clearly ties in to the current emphasis on visibility. Indeed, the lower-ranked faces were deleted.

Friendship networks are essential in providing the necessary loop of feedback, comparison and control needed in the creation of the selfbrand. Users can upload photographs and pictures, and these have differing degrees of visibility. The 'profile picture' illustrates or marks one's Facebook identity and it accompanies all comments and posts as well as having a prime position on a user's home page. The 'cover photo' epitomizes one's public self or brand. There are also albums that illustrate parts of the user's life that they want to share. This emphasis on visuals means that the self-brand can incorporate the cultivated body as part of its 'packaging' and this body can be subject to further analysis by networks of acquaintances, family and 'close friends'. This self-marketing is both enabled and glossed over through the affect of friendship.

Friend is both a noun and a verb. Users are called 'friends' and they are able to invite and befriend other friends; there is also an 'unfriend' function. Indeed, profiling the right kind of friends is an excellent form of self-promotion. The affect of friendship coheres its consumers and also creates a prime market for the creation of emotional ties to brands. Different categories of friends can be created depending on the content that users want various social cohorts to be able to access. There is a 'mutual friends' box that displays the people that users have in common. Users are also able to view each other's friends and in this way friends become primary indicators of one's visible social profile; the amount and quality of these friends is up for analysis, feedback and comparison. Friendship networks also function as social capital because they can generate further possibilities of self-branding. Not only is there the option to friend and unfriend chosen people, but the invitation function means that networks can be personal, exclusive and also distinctive. That is, you can choose friends who will enhance your social profile.

In order to garner better and bigger networks necessary to the self as brand one must be continuously marketed. If I am linked in to Spotify or guardian.co.uk, for example, my friends can see the tracks I am listening to, the articles I am reading and, when I accept invites, the places where I am going. The self-brand needs constant maintenance in order not to slip up (both from myself and through the systems of feedback garnered through my friendship networks). I am a free advertisement for the brands I use. It is in the interests of Facebook, and other corporations, that consumers enjoin in the discourses of self-branding. After all, the larger the networks of friends, the more chances that branding myths can extend their lines of flight into untapped demographics, and deliver users to diverse companies and corporations. In addition, the brands used and 'liked' could also advertise a user as a potential friend who could consolidate someone else's social capital. The more that individuals buy into self-branding, the more they will consume, use and develop social networking sites in order to extend and personalize their social profile. We can see new systems of social value being created.

Insecurities over self-profiling are exploited by the advertising banners that appear alongside the web pages. Because data are collected by marketing companies, we are specifically targeted, particularly along the lines of gender. My Facebook page tells me that Adele has dropped over two stone, and that 5351 people like this. Underneath is an advert by Fitness Advice Guru, which promises to teach me how to lose two stone in one week: 'Learn how to shed pounds and pounds of weight from your belly by following this 1 tip!' There is that hideous female belly again – hopefully not making a spectral appearance in any of my photographs or profile pictures and thus devaluing my self-brand. If I 'like' these brands then this will signify to my friends and acquaintances how repulsive I find a big belly. It will show how I trust a particular product to cure me – and them – of this excessive marker of libidinal womanhood. I will make it appear more vital and necessary by giving it a story and, depending on how my mediated friends view me, rendering it more reliable.[3]

Banet-Weiser critiques the postfeminist insistence that empowerment can be reached through constructing oneself as a self-brand. She argues that empowerment in these branding contexts 'potentially distracts individuals from what empowerment might mean in a broader sense' (Banet-Weiser, 2012, 82). Indeed, these processes are in fact exclusionary and contribute to the racism and symbolic violence endemic in neoliberal cultures:

> This individual entrepreneur, validated within postfeminism and interactive digital media, unfolds within preexisting gendered and racial scripts and their attendant grammars of exclusion. Certainly, as I have argued, producing a self-brand *is* cultural participation, but

this kind of participation – what it does, and for whom – needs to be critiqued as a commercial practice.

(Banet-Weiser, 2012, 89)

This critique must be understood within a feminist paradigm and it is to feminism and its role in women's sociality that I now turn.

Conclusion: Feminism, Friendship and Conflict

Women friends constitute my most precious relationships as well as the most complex. Eichenbaum and Orbach identify the exquisite intimacy of female friendships while also noting how they have the potential to generate powerful negative feelings: 'Behind the curtain of sisterhood lies a myriad of emotional tangles that can wreak havoc in women's relationships with each other' (Eichenbaum and Orbach, 1988, 10–11). Indeed, my most cherished friendships are precisely those knotty ones in which we have found ourselves exposed, vulnerable, hurt, but also loving; where we have created an alchemy of relating unique to us and which has illuminated much about ourselves and each other. These 'emotional tangles', however, have also caused the dissipation of some friendships and their loss continues to be a source of grief. Eichenbaum and Orbach identify how feelings like anger and betrayal are not easily expressed and, as a consequence, collaborations, networks and intimacies can be destroyed. If conflicts between women do not have a collective space to be unpacked then solidarities can implode, leading to the dissolution of projects and manifestos.

It is these 'emotional tangles' that initially generated my fascination into girlfriend culture; into exploring mediated female sociality and how women are provoked, perceived and portrayed as acting out the 'threshing floor of friendship' (Apter and Josselson, 1999, 7) in an era of neoliberalism. In this book I have focused on a misogynist harnessing of ugly feelings by looking at how converging branded cultures exploit antagonisms produced through intersectional identities, as well as manipulating stereotypes of women as envious and avaricious. I have examined how they evoke feelings of competition in order to strengthen bonds between consumers and producers. Indeed, neoliberal postfeminist culture prizes a competitive edge. It encourages loops of comparison, feedback and aggression among women in order to normalize the drive for hypervisibility in the quest for the distinctive self-brand. Women and girls are encouraged to both admire and envy celebrities in order to buy into the brands they are selling. The complex affective relations between women are harnessed in a neoliberal culture as a means to negate the self, as well as to destroy potential political solidarities.

A productive understanding of difficult emotions is useful, therefore, in loosening the grip of branded cultures. If brands exploit and manipulate feelings of rivalry then to understand these feelings more creatively would go some way to recognizing the ways in which the market functions so insidiously and so pervasively, particularly around the libidinal female body. Envy can be harnessed as a political tool to negotiate the power of brands in a postfeminist context. As Sianne Ngai argues, envy can be a means 'to critically negotiate' certain models of femininity that we have been accultured into admiring. In her words, a fruitful reflection on envy could 'facilitate a transition from desire to antagonism that might enable me to articulate what I have been trained to admire as something threatening or harmful to me' (Ngai, 2005, 163). Experiencing envy can be a signpost to inequality and injustice, and consequently offers 'an ability to recognize and antagonistically respond to, potentially real and institutionalized forms of inequality' (Ngai, 2005, 129). Maud Perrier suggests that envy's 'critical potential resides in its ability to protect the subject from fully idealizing the coveted object' (Perrier, 2012, 10). Furthermore, using envy can be a means to unpack or queer the straightness of the gynaeopticon; to think creatively about jealousy could enable the recognition of discounted desires underpinning sociality among women.

Knotty emotions exist in social relations. Indeed, they are an inevitable part of 'the ambivalence that beats at the heart of being human' (Skeggs, 2004, 29). Feelings of competition and comparison gain traction in a neoliberal popular culture, but they have deep roots. To maintain the illusion of a utopic sisterhood unencumbered by conflict is damaging, both because it is false and because it prevents a truer understanding between women. It is useful to imagine a space where antagonisms can be recognized and approached productively. They can make possible a deeper understanding of oneself and our interpersonal relations. In her discussion of sibling relationships, Apter discusses the 'inevitable ambivalence we have to negotiate to keep the relationship alive'. She advocates the importance of 'recognizing the mixed elements in ourselves and in our attachments' in order to reach a more integrated and truthful vision of female bonds in general (Apter, 2007, 277). Conflicts between women could be approached dialectically as forms of energy and creativity. But in order for this to manifest we also need to devise a site of collectivity where these deeply exposing inner realms can be carefully brought to light.

Rather than being merely individualized feelings or internal failings, competition, shame, anger and envy are historically produced within specific socioeconomic and gendered contexts. Similarly, racism, sexism and class exploitation are partly perpetrated through personal relationships, or through the mediated and staged intervention into these relationships; the personal and emotional interface with discursive violence. This is not to flatten out or erase political conflict by reading it as personal antagonism. Rather, it is to explore the ways in which technologies of oppression structure the gestures, conversations and interpersonal reflexivity enacted by and between women. Mariana Ortega argues that white women can be unknowing 'participants and perpetuators of a racist system' (Lugones, 2003, 72–75; Ortega, 2006, 68). Moreover, the intimate mechanics through which women relate are pertinent for revealing the ways in which exploitative systems are propagated on a micro and interpersonal level. Personal female relationships do not lie outside a feminist politics. As politically situated subjects we participate in the regulation of dominant femininities, whether this is through overt resistance or covert complicity (Mohanty, 2003, 203). This includes the ways in which we absorb, appropriate, spread, resist and share in dominant ideologies.

Divisions and inequalities across lines of class, race and sexuality are still prevalent in feminism, as well as popular culture (hooks, 2000, 114; see also Carby, 1997). Mohanty argues that an uninterrogated universal sisterhood ends up 'being a middle-class, psychologized notion that effectively erases material and ideological power differences within and among groups of women, especially between First and Third World women' (Mohanty, 2003, 116). In their investigations into feminist movements in Spain, Norway and the UK, Line Nyhagen Predelli and Beatrice Halsaa identify how 'relations between ethnic majority and ethnic minority women have been complex and ambivalent'. They argue that the actors in majority women's movements have paid little attention 'to their own racial and ethnic positions' and that minoritized women's political voices 'have yet to be included as equal partners in women's movement dialogue, claims-making and lobbying'. However, they also note that 'responsibility for dialogue, inclusion and solidarity cuts across racial and ethnic lines' (Predelli and Halsaa, 2012, 192). They maintain that feminists perceive racism as an issue that lies outside feminism and, moreover, that there is 'a fear of perpetuating racist and discriminatory attitudes towards minoritized communities' (Predelli and Halsaa, 2012, 263). Predelli and Halsaa argue for the importance of forging coalitions or collaborations that are alert to interpersonal micropolitics. There needs to be a paradigm through which women are able to unpack the antagonisms that are created and reproduced through difference along the axes of race, ethnicity, religion, sexuality and disability. In particular, feminists of the majority ethnicities need to reflect on their own whiteness (Lorde, [1984] 2009, 93–94; Predelli and Halsaa, 2012, 264).

It is feminism, moreover, that can provide the space for a productive exploration of conflict. As real and destructive affects, ugly feelings need an ethical framework through which they can be unpacked in order to expose the power dynamics that structure them. Indeed, this would bolster feminism against the frequent media representations of feminist harpies at each other's throats, as disagreements between women are often exploited in a misogynist popular culture to reveal the inevitability of feminism's disintegration. In response to this, Perrier argues for the critical potential of antagonism. She perceives it not as a phase to overcome in order to enable kinder feelings, but rather as a permanent condition. She persuasively suggests that this is not in order to reveal the authentic love or compassion that lies underneath antagonism. Being a political movement, feminism is not seeking friendship between women as a goal; rather it is fighting for justice and liberation. Indeed, antagonism can play an important role in sustaining political movements. As Ngai maintains, 'If aggressive acts of not identifying can play as active a role as identification in facilitating the transition from single to group femaleness, this usefully highlights the primary and [...] even constitutive importance of antagonism to collective political formations' (Ngai, 2005, 161). As Perrier argues, 'feminism is actually strengthened by this kind of dis-identification':

> This suggests a different way of valuing the conflicts and differences between feminists. Rather than seeking reconciliation, we can unpack uncomfortable affects for their regenerative power. This would mean that difficult conversations between young feminists and old feminists, post-structuralists and modernist feminists,

western and developing world feminists are something to hold onto rather than overcome.

(Perrier, 2012, 10–11)

I would like to imagine a space where a shared commitment to feminist practice can productively hold and explore conflict as an exciting and renewing force.

Notes

Introduction: Girlfriend Culture

1. Although I have not had time here to focus on the differences between the two cultures, some distinctions are striking. These are especially foregrounded in programmes which cross over between American presenters and British contestants, such as in *Sorority Girls* and *Paris Hilton's My New BFF*. In general, US media are more consistent in their fetishization of the figure of the girl, and there is more girlfriend regulation around slut-shaming. In addition, girlfriends in the UK tend to eschew the high-end commercialized glamour of their American sisters. I have not had the space to include the British *Lipservice* (BBC, 2010–2012), *Mistresses* (BBC, 2008–2010) or *Scott & Bailey* (ITV, 2011–). This is partly because the femininities that they depict do not adhere fully to the postfeminist girlfriend that I am identifying, although I would include them within girlfriend culture. Indeed, as a definition in flux, emergent texts continually redefine the parameters of 'girlfriend culture'. For example, *Scott & Bailey* draws more on a tradition of British crime drama as it portrays two tough and relatively ungirly characters with a fascinating interaction.

1 The Girlfriend Gaze

1. Within the polysemy of *Heat's* article, Josie's body has the possibility of being a site of dissent. Her transgression of celebrity norms provides an instance of gossip, and debate. Nevertheless, it is still a woman's body being held up for analysis among networks of women.
2. Indeed, third wave feminists have already advocated the empowerment accrued through harnessing one's sexuality for capital gain. As third-wave feminists Jennifer Baumgardner and Amy Richards argue, being in control of your sexuality – like Madonna – makes you smart (Baumgardner and Richards, 2010, 141). Just as Madonna appropriates her sexuality as an asset in a promotional culture, so a savvy girlfriend must know how to yoke her libido to a business model in order to channel and control the flow of money; she must know how to market herself.

2 BFF Co-Brands

1. 'BFF' is a commonly used acronym that stands for 'Best Friends Forever'.

3 Strategic Sisterhoods

1. The *Sex and the City* movies were panned by the critics, but enthusiastically attended by groups of women. Indeed, the show became a point of contact through which friends could relate. Anna Pickard notes in her *Guardian* review of *Sex and the City 2*'s opening night that women were responding and reacting to the events and spectacles on the screen as part of their mutual interaction. They consumed it as friends and the film became part of their communication. The *Sex and the City* franchise is marketed across media platforms as a site for women to play out their own friendships; to frame, explain, stimulate and perform their girlfriend selves 'with their own Carries, Mirandas and Charlottes' (Pickard, *The Guardian*, June 2010). Indeed, there are moments in *Sex and the City 2* when the viewers are implicitly addressed, such as when Miranda and Charlotte bond over the difficulties of motherhood and drink a toast to the mothers without nannies. The characters extend their hand of friendship to the viewers and thus give added emotional value to the brands through which they are produced.

4 Womance

1. This is partly due to the structure of the genre as the filmic texts derive their narrative drive from climax and resolution, whereas the television format generates pleasure through the steady reassurance of weekly girlfriend intimacy.
2. In a pivotal scene in *In Her Shoes* (2005), Ella (Shirley Maclaine) buys cable television so that she can bond with her granddaughter, Maggie. Maggie initially ignores Ella and her friends until she hears *Sex and the City*'s Carrie recounting how one of her girlfriends laments a time 'when dinner was followed by dessert, not lubricant'. Hearing Carrie talk about sex with her girlfriends signals a turning point in Maggie's relationship with her grandmother and with her estranged sister. The show melts Maggie's defences against Ella and she tells her, 'I've seen this one. It's funny'. Later, she admits, 'half the fun of sex is talking about it'. This scene is pertinent because it references *Sex and the City* to point up and develop bonds between female viewers. It echoes Wolf's assertion that women are connected through the mediation of friendship being privileged in *Sex and the City*. This scene also reveals how homosocial girl talk trumps having sex with men. In a popular culture where men are usually cast as emotionally illiterate or closed, the ability to negotiate one's (difficult) emotions is crucial. As the primary subject of the girlfriends' conversations, men are depicted as a lifestyle; they are constituted as a choice – bad and good – to entertain the girlfriends. Moreover, sex with men is a commodity to be enjoyed, selected and exchanged as intimate conversation. As Maggie says about her sister in *In Her Shoes*, 'without her I don't make sense'. For these girlfriends to 'make sense' they need their girlfriends to co-create and work through their self-narratives; they need to narrativize with them through the conviviality of sex and emotion talk.
3. In *13 Going on 30* (2004) Marcia DeBonis is typecast as the bullied secretary due to her 'unhappy' body size: 'Please don't sack me!' she pleads. DeBonis

is a PA in *Lipstick Jungle* and is sacked as the wedding planner's secretary in *Bride Wars*; her female boss states scornfully that she 'will be dead her whole life', implying that she is too fat to be a postfeminist bride. Weight indicates victimhood; it is the proof that women do not have the capacity to rationally negotiate the proliferation of choice. It seems that women cannot have their cake without stuffing themselves. Moreover, because supportive girlfriends are controlling it is an easy step for this to be employed as abuse and for girlfriends' bodies to be used as their battleground. We see the natural progression from normative cruelty to pure cruelty. After all, supporting or sabotaging body image amounts to the same thing: maintaining the illusion of an ideal and holding the body up as a site of analysis.

4. David Hansen-Miller and Rosalind Gill argue that 'lad flicks' signal a movement away from the subjective pleasures of masculine identification and towards an 'examination of objectified masculinity as a troubled cultural category' (Hansen-Miller and Gill, 2011, 36).

5. Melissa McCarthy's character is not quite the symbol of the unmarriageable woman as played by DeBonis. She is too gutsy, and draws too many laughs for that. Nevertheless, she is (like the other bridesmaids, apart from Annie) one-dimensional in her feminine stereotype: the grotesque and embarrassing fat girl who is played for laughs.

5   Making White Lives Better?

1. *Mad Men* is a period drama set in a prestigious Manhattan-based advertising agency in the 1960s. Portraying the 'creative revolution' taking place in the advertising industry at the time, it centres on the beguiling but mysterious white ad man, Don Draper and his team of colourful secretaries and whisky-drinking, besuited white male colleagues. Up until season 5, which attempts to explore the experience of the African American secretary, Dawn (Teyonah Parris), black characters are primarily cleaners. They legitimately lurk behind the scene as a spectral reminder of the bad old days. Their speechlessness enacts a poignant and self-congratulatory bid for period realism. Their histories or stories are marginal to the stylized fetishization of the white characters. In season 2, one of the copywriters has a black girlfriend, Sheila (Donielle Artese), towards whom the head secretary Joan (Christina Hendricks) expresses a deep and racist hostility (2:2). In this episode, there is an attempt to explore women relating across the power structures of racial difference. Nevertheless, the fact that the show refuses to explore the inner lives of the black cleaners is significant – their stories are still perceived to be insignificant or abject.

2. Although, as in *Bridesmaids*, running one's own cupcake business is not necessarily a secure career trajectory. In addition, cupcakes are potent and sugary signifiers of the tantalizing danger of eating in a postfeminist popular culture. They can make you fat but they are small, girlish and hypervisible.

3. Comedy has always been a vehicle for racism. Moreover, racism has usually been associated with the working class. Because it is Max who delivers most of the offensive jokes against the other characters (and is chided by Caroline for

doing so) she plays up to her class stereotype and lets the middle class viewers off the hook.

4. Although this is addressed in the second season, which had not aired in the UK at the time of this book going into production. Hannah's mishandling of her relationship with a Republican black man is an astutely observed imaging of white middle class ignorance.

6 Catfight

1. Fascinatingly, Heidi's surgical procedures meant that she sculpted a 'year-zero face'. That is, she mimicked the fashion to look 'done', which inevitably means looking like an older woman wanting to look like a girl. That is, a woman performing the postfeminist masquerade. As New York plastic surgeon Douglas Steinbrech tells *W* magazine:

> There's this new mentality that if you do not look a little bit fake, then the surgeon hasn't done his job. This used to be a much more prevalent idea on the west coast, but now you walk up Madison Avenue and you see these young girls with that cloned, cougar-like face.
>
> (cited in Wiseman, *The Guardian* January 2011)

Heidi's face is that of the Marks and Spencer's girlfriends who reflect 'every women you are', the young girl and the older woman simultaneously. She is every girlfriend: cougar and school girl.

2. Not surprisingly, all the working class girls are cut. In this way it mimics the format and governance of another British reality television programme, *Snog Marry Avoid* (BBC Three, 2008), where 'fakery addicts' are stripped of their accoutrements of glamour – a component of working class femininity – and inducted into the 'natural beauty' of middle class taste.

8 The Friendship Market

1. The blurb by *The Observer* on the front advertises it as 'The hottest thing to hit the dating scene since *Sex and the City*'. The US version is titled *Find a Husband After 35: A Simple 15-Step Action Program*.

2. The groom is sometimes addressed. For example, in the Autumn 2009 edition of *Brides* there was a CD Rom for grooms, and there are wedding blogs like The Man Registry. Wedding forums also have sections for grooms.

3. The contours of Facebook are constantly changing. Since writing this book, every second post in a user's news feed is an advertisement. Yesterday it was a picture of a bunch of bananas advising me – of course – on the latest way to lose weight. Today Tescos ask me to like their latest education project to 'empower' girls in Senegal: 'Join in and help by liking this post: 1 Like = 1 Lesson!' Discourses of activism and feminism combine with charity to encourage me to spread their brand through my friendship networks.

Bibliography

2 Broke Girls, 2011–present. Television series, CBS.

13 Going on 30, 2004. Film, dir. Gary Winick, Revolution Studios.

Access Hollywood 2012. 'Heidi Montag now living a "humble life"', online, available at: http://www.accesshollywood.com/billy-bush/heidi-montag-now-living-a-humble-life_videotab_1421147, accessed 10 Nov 2012.

Adams, G. 2008. 'There's a new genre in Tinseltown, and it's all about female friendship', *The Independent*, 8 Jun, online, available at http://www.independent.co.uk/arts-entertainment/films/news/theres-a-new-genre-in-tinseltown-and-its-all-about-female-friendship-842485.html, accessed 10 Nov 2012.

Adewunmi, B. 2012.'Can a black woman relate to *Girls?*', *The Guardian*, 21 Oct, online, available at http://www.guardian.co.uk/tv-and-radio/2012/oct/21/girls-smart-sassy-brits-groundbreaking, accessed 24 Oct 2012.

Adkins, L. and B. Skeggs eds. 2004. *Feminism after Bourdieu*. Oxford: Blackwell.

Ahmed, S. 2004. *The Cultural Politics of Emotion*. Edinburgh: Edinburgh University Press.

Ahmed, S. 2007. 'Editorial: The Happiness Turn', *New Formations* 63, pp. 7–14.

Akass, K. and McCabe, J. 2000. *Reading the L Word: Outing Contemporary Television*. London and New York: I.B.Tauris.

Alice, 1976–1985. Television programme, CBS.

Andrejevic, M. 2003. *Reality TV: The Work of Being Watched*. New York: Rowman & Littlefield.

Apter, T. and Josselson, R. 1999. *Best Friends: The Pleasures and Perils of Girls and Women's Friendships*. New York: Three Rivers Press.

Apter, T. 2007. *Sisterknot: Why We Fight, Why We're Jealous, and Why We'll Love Each Other No Matter What*. New York and London: Norton.

Aronczyk, M. and Powers, D. eds. 2010. *Blowing Up the Brand: Critical Perspectives on Promotional Culture*. Oxford: Peter Lang.

Arthurs, J. 2004. *Television and Sexuality: Regulation and the Politics of Taste*. Maidenhead: Open University Press.

Arvidsson, A. 2006. *Brands: Meaning and Value in Media Culture*. London and New York: Routledge.

Baby Mama, 2008. Film, dir. Michael McCullers, Broadway Video.

The Bachelor, 2002–present. Television series, ABC.

The Bachelorette, 2003–present. Television series, ABC.

Banet-Weiser, S. 2012. *Authentic: The Politics of Ambivalence in a Brand Culture*. New York: New York University Press.

Barnouin, K. and Freedman, R. 2005. *Skinny Bitch*. Philadelphia, PA: Running Press.

Barnouin, K. and Freedman, R. 2007. *Skinny Bitch in the Kitch: Kick-Ass Recipes for Hungry Girls Who Want to Stop Cooking Crap (and Start Looking Hot!)*. Philadelphia, PA: Running Press.

Barnouin, K. and Freedman, R. 2008. *Skinny Bitch: Bun in the Oven, A Gutsy Guide to Becoming One Hot and Healthy Mother!* Philadelphia, PA: Running Press.

Barnouin, K. and Freedman, R. 2009. *Skinny Bastard*. Philadelphia, PA: Running Press.

Baumgardner, J. and Richards, A. [2000] 2010. *Manifesta: Young Women, Feminism, and the Future*, 10th ed. New York: Farrar Straus Giroux.

Beauty Shop, 2005. Film, dir. Bill Woodruff. MGM.

Beck, U. and Beck-Gernsheim, E. 2002. *Individualization: Institutionalized Individualism and its Social and Political Consequences*. London: Sage.

Berger, J., Blomberg, S., Fox, C., Dibb, M. and Hollis, R. 1972. *Ways of Seeing*. London: Penguin.

Berlant, L. 2008. *The Female Complaint: The Unfinished Business of Sentimentality in American Culture*. London and Durham, NC: Duke University Press.

Binkley, S. 2007. *Getting Loose: Lifestyle Consumption in the 1970s*. Durham, NC and London: Duke University Press.

Black, P. 2004. *The Beauty Industry: Gender, Culture, Pleasure*. London: Routledge.

Blackman, L. 2004. 'Self-Help, Media Cultures and the Production of Female Psychopathology', *European Journal of Cultural Studies*, 7 (2), pp. 219–236.

Bolter, J.D. and Grusin, R. 1999. *Remediation: Understanding New Media*. Cambridge, MA: MIT Press.

Bordo, S. [1993] 2003. *Unbearable Weight: Feminism, Western Culture, and the Body*, 10th ed. Los Angeles, CA: University of California Press.

Bourdieu, P. 1984. *Distinction: A Social Critique of the Judgment of Taste*. Trans. Richard Nice, Cambridge, MA: Harvard University Press.

Bourdieu, P. and Wacquant, L.J.D. 1992. *An Invitation to Reflexive Sociology*. Chicago and London: University of Chicago Press.

Boyle, K. and Berridge, S. 2012. 'I Love You, Man: Gendered Narratives of Friendship in Contemporary Hollywood Comedies', *Feminist Media Studies*, online, available at http://www.tandfonline.com/doi/abs/10.1080/14680777. 2012.740494?journalCode=rfms20#.UZj97Ct35bt, accessed January 2013.

Bratich, J. 2007. 'Programming Reality: Control Societies, New Subjects and the Powers of Transformation', in D. Heller, ed. *Makeover Television: Realities Remodelled*. London: I.B. Taurus, pp. 6–22.

Bratich, J. 2011. 'Affective convergence in reality television: A case study in divergence culture', in M. Kackman, M. Binfield, M. T. Payne, A. Perlman, B. Sebok, eds. *Flow TV: Television in the Age of Media Convergence*. London and New York: Routledge, pp. 55–74.

Braun, T. 2007. *The Philosophy of Branding: Great Philosophers Think Brands*. London: Kogan Page.

Braxton, G. 2006. ' "Girlfriends" feels left out of the clique', *LA Times*, online, available at http://articles.latimes.com/2006/sep/30/entertainment/et-girlfriends30, accessed 10 October 2010.

bridalbootcamponline.com 2012, Waterfront Media, online, available at http://www.bridalbootcamponline.com/publicsite/funnel/index.aspx, accessed 11 Nov 2012.

Bride Wars, 2009. Film, dir. Gary Winik, Firm Films.

Bridesmaids, 2011. Film, dir. Paul Feig, Universal Pictures.

Bromley, R. 2000. 'The theme that dare not speak its name: Class and Recent British Film', in S. Munt, ed. *Cultural Studies and the Working Class: Subject to Change*. London: Cassell, pp. 51–68.

Bushnell, C. 2005. *Lipstick Jungle*. London: Abacus.

Butler, J. [1990] 1999. *Gender Trouble: Feminism and the Subversion of Identity*. New York and London: Routledge.

candacebushnell.com. 2012. 'Shows', online, available at http://www. candacebushnell.com/shows.html, accessed 11 November 2012.

Carby, H. 1997. 'White woman listen! Black feminism and the boundaries of sisterhood', in H. Mirza, ed. *Black British Feminism: A Reader*. London and New York: Routledge, pp. 45–53.

Cashmere Mafia, 2008. Television series, ABC.

Cashmore, E. 2006. *Celebrity Culture*. Oxon and New York: Routledge.

Celebrity Juice, 2008–present. Television series, Talkback Thames.

Cheers, 1982–1993. Television series, Paramount Television.

Clueless, 1995. Film, dir. Amy Heckerling, Paramount Pictures.

Confetti.co.uk 2012. Available at http://www.confetti.co.uk, accessed 12 December 2009.

Constantine, S. and Woodall, T. 2000. *Ready 2 Dress: How to Have Style Without Following Fashion*. London: Weidenfeld and Nicolson.

Constantine, S. and Woodall, T. 2003. *What Not to Wear: The Rules*. New York: Riverhead Books.

Constantine, S. and Woodall, T. 2004. *What You Wear Can Change Your Life*. London: Weidenfeld and Nicolson.

Constantine, S. and Woodall, T. 2005. *Trinny and Susannah: What Your Clothes Say About You: How to Look Different, Act Different and Feel Different*. London: Weidenfeld and Nicolson.

Cook Yourself Thin, 2012. 'Dawn Nelson', online, available at http://www. cookyourselfthin.co.uk/article/cook-yourself-thin-episode-twelve-dawn-nelson.html, accessed 11 Nov 2012.

The Cosby Show, 1984–1992. Television series, NBC.

Cotton, F. and Willoughby, H. 2010. *Fearne and Holly: The Best Friend's Guide to Life*. London: Vermillion.

Cougar Town, 2009–present. Television series, ABC.

Coyote Ugly, 2000. Film, dir. David McNally, Touchstone Pictures.

Dadds, K. 2012. 'Josie Gibson is unrecognisable as she finally reveals her slender physique in form-fitting dress'. *Daily Mail*, online, available at http://www.dailymail.co.uk/tvshowbiz/article-2216718/Josie-Gibson-looks-unrecognisable-reveals-slender-physique-form-fitting-dress.html, accessed 11 November 2012.

Davies, F. 2008. 'Paradigmatically Oppositional Representations: Gender and Sexuality in the L Word', in R. Beirn *Televising Queer Women: A Reader*. London: Palgrave MacMillan, pp.179–193.

Dean, M. 1999. *Governmentality: Power and Rule in Modern Society*. London: Sage.

Deleuze, G. and Guattari, F. [1980] 2004. *A Thousand Plateaus: Capitalism and Schizophrenia*. London: Continuum.

Deleuze, G. 1992. 'Postscript on the Societies of Control', *October*, 59. pp. 3–7.

Devil Wears Prada, 2006. Film, dir. David Frankel, Fox 2000 Pictures.

Doane, M. A. 1987. *The Desire to Desire: The Woman's Film of The 1940s*. Bloomington, IN: Indiana University Press.

Dowdeswell, J. 2009. 'Happy ever after.' *Hello!* 28 Sept, Celebrity news, No 1091, p. 22.

Down in the Delta, 1998. Film. dir, Maya Angelou. Amen Ra Films.

eburyreads 2010. 'Fearne and Holly talk about The Best Friend's Guide to Life', *YouTube*, online, available at http://www.youtube.com/watch?feature=player_detailpage&v=pU8pM2fNAWg, accessed 11 Nov 2012.

Eichenbaum, L. and Orbach, S. 1988. *Between Women: Love, Envy, and Competition in Women's Friendships.* New York: Viking Penguin Inc.

Eng, K. 2004. *Secrets & Confidences: The Complicated Truth About Women's Friendships.* Jackson, TN: Seal Press.

Failure to Launch, 2006. Film, dir. Tom Dey, Paramount Pictures.

The Family Stone, 2005. Film, dir. Thomas Bezucha, Fox 2000 pictures.

Fearne Cotton, The Official Site 2011. 'Fearne Cotton in a Swimsuit...Really', online, available http://officialfearnecotton.com/video/2011/03/18/fearne-cotton-in-a-swimsuit-really/7472, accessed 11 Nov 2012.

Fearne and Holly Go Dating, 2007. Television series, ITV.

Ferris, S. 2008. 'Fashioning femininity in the makeover flick', in S. Ferriss and M. Young, eds. *Chick Flicks: Contemporary Women at the Movies.* New York and London: Routledge, pp. 41–57.

Ferriss, S. and Young, M. 2008. *Chick Flicks: Contemporary Women at the Movies.* New York and London: Routledge.

The 40 Year Old Virgin, 2005. Film, dir. Judd Apatow, Universal Pictures.

Foucault, M. 1991. *Discipline and Punish: The Birth of the Prison.* trans. Alan Sheridan. London: Penguin.

Four Weddings Website, 2009. 'Four Weddings: Your Weddings', online, available at http://skyliving.sky.com/fourweddingsuk, accessed 12 Dec 2012.

Fraser, A. 2012. 'I've Lost a Whole Tom Cruise in Weight', *OK!* 30 October, pp. 54–57.

Fraser, N. 2003. 'From Discipline to Flexibalization? Re-reading Foucault in the Shadow of Globalization', *Constellations*, 10 (2), pp. 160–171.

French, P. 2010. 'Sex and the City 2', *The Guardian*, online, available at http://www.guardian.co.uk/film/2010/may/30/philip-french-sex-and-city-2-review, accessed 11 Nov 2012.

fhm.com. 2012a. 'Holly Willoughby – Ice Maiden'. *FHM*, online, available at http://www.fhm.com/girls/covergirls/holly-willoughby, accessed 11 Nov 2012.

fhm.com. 2012b. 'Fearne Cotton – Inky Marvel'. *FHM*, online, available at http://www.fhm.com/girls/covergirls/fearne-cotton, accessed 11 Nov 2012.

Gerhard, J. 2005. 'Sex and the City: Carrie Bradshaw's Queer Postfeminism', *Feminist Media Studies*, 5 (1). pp. 37–49.

Giddens, A. 1991. *Modernity and Self-Identity: Self and Society in the Late Modern Age.* Palo Alto CA, London: Stamford University Press.

Girlfriends, 2000–2008. Television series, UPN.

Glock, A. 2005. 'She Likes to Watch', *New York Times* Feb 6, late ed. sec. 2, p. 26.

Goldberg, L. 2012. 'TCA: Lena Dunham Says HBO's *Girls* Isn't *Sex and the City*', *Hollywood Reporter*, online, available at http://www.hollywoodreporter.com/live-feed/tca-hbo-girls-lena-dunham-judd-apatow-281483, accessed 11 Nov 2012.

Goodman, E. and O'Brien, P. 2001. *I Know Just What You Mean: The Power of Friendship in Women's Lives.* New York: Fireside.

Goodridge, M. 2003. 'Showtime for Greenblatt', *The Advocate* Sep 30, pp. 46–48.

Greenwald, R. 2004. *The Program: Fifteen Steps to Finding a Husband After Thirty*. London: Time Warner Paperbacks.

Greven, D. 2004. ' "The Museum of Unnatural History": Male Freaks and *Sex and the City*', in K. Akass and J. McCabe, eds, *Reading Sex and the City*. London and New York: I.B.Tauris, pp. 33–47.

Grindstaff, L. 2002. *The Money Shot: Trash, Class and the Making of TV Talk Shows*. Chicago: University of Chicago Press.

Hakim, C. 2011. *Honey Money: The Power of Erotic Capital*. London: Allen Lane.

The Hand that Rocks the Cradle, 1992. Film, dir. Curtis Hanson, Hollywood Pictures.

The Hangover, 2009. Film, dir. Todd Phillips, Warner Bros.

Hantman C. 2009. *30 Days to Finding and Keeping Sassy Sidekicks and BFFs: A Friendship Field Guide*. London: Random House.

Harvey, D. 2005. *A Brief History of Neoliberalism*. Oxford: Oxford University Press.

Hearn, A. 2008. 'Variations on the branded "self": Theme, invention, improvisation and inventory.' in D. Hesmonhalgh and J. Toynbee, eds. *The Media and Social Theory*. London: Routledge, pp. 194–210.

Hearn, A. 2010. 'Reality Television, *The Hills* and the Limits of the Immaterial Labour Thesis'. *triple C-Cognition, Communication, Co-operation*, 8 (1), pp. 60–76.

Heat. 2012. 'In Love and Ditching the Diet', June.

Hello! Magazine 2011. 'Holly Willoughby: Not-so-short but Tweet Birth', 25 April, No. 1171, p. 43.

Hello! Magazine 2012. 'A traditional service for Anna and Ian in their glorious Home Counties wedding', online, available at http://www.helloonline. com/weddings/201204037653/the-wedding-of-anna-hanson-and-ian-black/, accessed 11 Nov 2012.

Hello! Magazine 2012. 'An unforgettable beach wedding for Nick and Nikki', online, available at http://www.helloonline.com/weddings/201204197798/ nick-and-nikki-edwards-marry-in-beach-wedding/, accessed 11 Nov 2012.

The Help, 2011. Film, dir. Tate Taylor, Dreamworks SKG.

The Help Featurette, Available at http://www.imdb.com/title/tt1454029/, accessed 19 August 2012.

Hendershot, H. 2009. 'Belabored Reality: Making It Work on *The Simple Life* and *Project Runway*', in S. Murray and L. Oullette, eds. *Reality TV: Remaking Television Culture*, 2nd ed. New York/London: New York University Press, pp. 243–259.

Henry, A. 2004. *Not My Mother's Sister: Generational Conflict and Third-Wave Feminism*. Bloomington, IN : Indiana University Press.

Hidalgo, M. M. M. 2008. ' "Going Native on Wonder Woman's Island": The Exoticisation of Lesbian Sexuality in *SATC*', in R. Beirne, ed. *Televising Queer Women: A Reader*. New York and Basingstoke, Hampshire: Palgrave Macmillan.

Hill, A. 2005. *Reality TV: Audiences and Popular Factual TV*. London and New York: Routledge.

Hill Collins, P. 2004. *Black Sexual Politics: African Americans, Gender, and the New Racism*. London and New York: Routledge.

The Hills, 2006–2010. Television series. MTV.

hitched.co.uk 2009 'September challenge', online forum, available at http://www. hitched.co.uk/Chat/forums/t/135841.aspx, accessed 11 Nov 2012.

Hochschild A. R. [1983] 2003. *The Managed Heart: Commercialization of Human Feeling.* Berkeley, CA: University of California Press.

Hochschild A. R. 1989. *The Second Shift: Working Parents and the Revolution at Home.* London: Viking.

Hollinger, K. 1998. *In the Company of Women: Contemporary Female Friendship Films.* Minnesota, MN: University of Minnesota Press.

Hollinger, K. 2008. 'Afterword: once I got beyond the name chick flick', in S. Ferriss and M. Young, eds. *Chick Flicks: Contemporary Women at the Movies.* New York and London: Routledge, pp. 221–232.

Holly Willoughby: the official website, 2010. 'The best friends guide to life is out', 14 October, online, available at http://officialhollywilloughby.com/2010/10/14/the-best-friendsguide-to-life-is-out/, accessed 20 Sep 2010.

Holmes, S. 2005. 'Westminster Papers in Communication and Culture', University of Westminster, London, 2 (2), pp. 6–21.

Holmes, S. and Redmond S. eds. 2006. *Framing Celebrity: New Directions in Celebrity Culture.* London and New York: Routledge.

Holmes, S. 2007. ' "Ask the fastidious woman from Surbiton to hand-wash the underpants of aging Oldham skinhead..." Why Not Wife Swap?', in T. Austin and W. de Jongs, eds. *Rethinking Documentary: A Documentary Reader.* Maidenhead, Berks: Open University Press, pp. 59–74.

Holmlund, C. 2002. *Impossible Bodies: Femininity and Masculinity at the Movies.* New York and London: Routledge.

hooks, b. 2000. *Feminism Is for Everybody: Passionate Politics.* London: Pluto Press

I Could Never Be Your Woman, 2007. Film, dir. Amy Heckerling, Templar Films Unlimited.

I Don't Know How She Does It, 2011. Film, dir. Douglas McGrath, The Weinstein Company.

Illouz, E. 1997. *Consuming the Romantic Utopia: Love and the Cultural Contradictions of Capitalism.* Berkeley and Los Angeles: University of California Press.

Illouz, E. 2007. *Cold Intimacies: The Making of Emotional Capitalism.* Cambridge: Polity.

In Her Shoes, 2005. Film, dir. Curtis Hanson, Fox 2000 Pictures.

Isaacs, F. 2003. *Toxic Friends/True Friends: How Your Friendships Can Make or Break Your Health, Happiness, Family, and Career.* New York: Citadel.

Jenkins, H. 2006. *Convergence Culture: Where Old and New Media Collide.* New York and London: New York University Press.

Jermyn, D. 2006. 'In love with Sarah Jessica Parker: Celebrating Female Fandom and Friendship in *Sex and the City*', in K. Akass and J. McCabe eds. *Reading Sex and the City.* London and New York: I.B. Tauris, pp. 201–218.

Jermyn, D. 2006a. 'Bringing out the * in you': SJP, Carrie Bradshaw and the evolution of television stardom', in S. Holmes and S. Redmond, eds. *Framing celebrity: New Directions in Celebrity Culture.* London and New York: Routledge, pp. 67–85.

Jones, M. 2008. *Skintight: An Anatomy of Cosmetic Surgery.* Oxford: Berg.

Jonet, C.M. and Williams, L. A. 2008. "Everything Else Is the Same': Configurations of *The L Word*', in R. Beirne, ed. *Televising Queer Women: A Reader.* New York: Palgrave MacMillan, pp. 149–162.

Kackman, M., Binfield, M., Payne, M.T., Perlman, A. Sebok, B. eds, 2010. *Flow TV: Television in the Age of Media Convergence.* London and New York: Routledge.

Kaklamanidou, B. 2012. 'Pride and Prejudice: Celebrity Versus Fictional Cougars', D. Jermyn, ed. *Celebrity Studies: Special Issue: Back in the Spotlight: Female Celebrity and Aging*, 3 (1) pp. 78–89.

Kate and Allie, 1984–1989. Television series. CBS.

Kavka, M. 2008. *Reality Television, Affect and Intimacy: Reality Matters*. Basingstoke: Palgrave MacMillan.

Kindersley, T. and Vine, S. 2009. *Walking Backwards in High Heels*. London: Fourth Estate.

Knocked Up, 2007. Film, dir. Judd Apatow, Universal Pictures.

Kosofsky Sedgwick, E. 1985. *Between Men: English Literature and Male Homosocial Desire*. New York: Columbia University Press.

Kosofsky Sedgwick, E. 2004. 'The L Word: Novelty in Normalcy', online, available at *The Chronicle of Higher Education* http://chronicle.com/article/The-L-Word-Novelty-in/13751, accessed October 2012.

Laverne & Shirley, 1976–1983. Television series, ABC.

Lavinthal, A. and Rozler, J. 2008. *Friend or Frenemy: A Guide to the Friends You Need and the Ones You Don't*. New York: HarperCollins.

Lawson, N. 2009. *All Consuming: How Shopping Got Us into This Mess and How We Can Find Our Way out*. London: Penguin.

Lazar, M. 2009, 'Entitled to consume: postfeminist femininity and a culture of post-critique', *Discourse and Communication*. 3 (4), pp. 371–400.

Levy, A. [2003] 2005. *Female Chauvinist Pigs: The Rise of Raunch Culture*, 2nd ed. New York: Free Press.

Lipservice, 2010–2012. Television series. BBC3.

Lipstick Jungle, 2008–2009. Television series. NBC.

Lorde, A. 2009, *I Am Your Sister: Collected and Unpublished Writings of Audre Lorde* R. P. Byrd, J. B Cole, B. Guy-Sheftall, eds. Oxford: Oxford University Press.

Lotz, A. 2006. *Redesigning Women: Television after the Network Era*. Champaign: University of Illinois Press, 2006.

Lovell, T. 2000. 'Thinking Feminism With and Against Bourdieu', *Feminist Theory* 1 (1), pp. 11–32.

Lugones, M. 2003. *Pilgrimages/Peregrinajes: Theorizing Coalition Against Multiple Oppressions*. Lanham, MD: Rowman & Littlefield.

Lyle, S. 2008. '(Mis)recognition and the middle-class/bourgeois gaze: A case study of Wife Swap', *Critical Discourse Studies*. 5 (4), pp. 319–330.

McClintock, A. 1995. *Imperial Leather: Race, Gender and Sexuality in the Colonial Contest*. New York and London: Routledge.

McRobbie, A. 2004. 'Notes on What Not to Wear and Post-Feminist Symbolic Violence', *The Sociological Review*, 52 (2), pp. 99–109.

McRobbie, A. 2009. *The Aftermath of Feminism: Gender, Culture and Social Change*. London: Sage.

The Mary Tyler Moore Show, 1970–1977. Television series, CBS.

Mathieson, T. 1997. 'The Viewer Society: Michel Foucault's "Panopticon Revisited" ', *Theoretical Criminology*, 1 (2), pp. 215–234.

Mead, Rebecca. 2007. *One Perfect Day: The Selling of the American Wedding*. New York: Penguin.

Mean Girls, 2004. Film, dir. Mark Waters, Paramount Pictures.

Milligan, A. 2010. *Brand It Like Beckham: The Story of How Brand Beckham Was Built*. London: Marshall Cavendish.

The Mirror, 2008. 'Exclusive: Fearne Cotton and Holly Willoughby on men and marriage.' online, available at http://www.mirror.co.uk/celebs/latest/2008/08/14/exclusive-fearne-cotton-and-holly-willoughby-on-men-and-marriage-115875-20696256/, accessed 11 Nov 2012.

Mistresses, 2008–2010. Television series, BBC.

Mohanty, C. 2003. *Feminism Without Borders: Decolonizing Theory, Practicing Solidarity*. Durham: Duke University Press.

Mulvey, L. 1975. 'Visual Pleasure and Narrative Cinema', *Screen*, 16 (3), pp. 6–18.

mumsnet. com. 2012. 'is there anything i can do about my mum-tum?? '*Mums Talk*, online forum, available at www.mumsnet.com/Talk/style_and_beauty/1527936-is-there-anything-i-can-do-about-my-mum-tum, accessed 11 Nov 2012.

Murray, S. and Ouellette, L. eds. 2009. *Reality TV: Remaking Television Culture*. New York/London: New York University Press.

Myss, C. 1996. *Anatomy of the Spirit: The Seven Stages of Power and Healing*. New York: Three Rivers.

nasdreas. 2011. 'Paris Hilton Insults Lindsay Lohan by Proxy', *YouTube*, online, available at http://www.youtube.com/watch?v=pQLUcjEhcUY, accessed 12 October 2012.

Negra, D. 2009. *What a Girl Wants? Fantasizing the Reclamation of Self in Postfeminism*. London and New York: Routledge.

Ngai, S. 2005, *Ugly Feelings*. Cambridge, MA and London: Harvard University Press.

Nunn, H. and Biressi, A. 2010. 'A Trust Betrayed: Celebrity and the Work of Emotion', *Celebrity Studies*, 1 (1), pp. 49–64.

O'Hagan, A. 2010. 'Sex and the City is Ugly on the Inside', *Evening Standard*, online, available at http://www.thisislondon.co.uk/film/review-23839220-sex-and-the-city-2-is-ugly-on-the-inside.do, accessed 11 Nov 2012.

OMGthatcom, 2011. 'Paris Hilton Takes a SHOT At Lindsay Lohan', *YouTube*, online, available at http://www.youtube.com/watch?v=apNN0tZRukU, accessed 20 Oct 2012.

Orbach, S. 2009. *Bodies*. London: Profile Books.

Orbach, S. 2009b. 'Interview with Decca Aitkenhead', *The Guardian*, 11 May.

Ortega, M. 2006. 'Being Lovingly, Knowingly Ignorant: White Feminism and Women of Color', *Hypatia*, 21 (3), pp. 56–74.

Oullette, L. and J. Wilson, 'Women's work: Affective labour and convergence culture', *Cultural Studies*, 25 (4–5), pp. 548–565.

Palmer, G. 2011. 'Organic Branding: The Self, Advertising and the Life-Experience Formats', in B. Skeggs and H. Wood, eds. *Reality Television and Class*. Basingstoke: Palgrave Macmillan, pp. 132–143.

Paris Hilton's My New BFF, 2008–2009. Television series, MTV and ITV2.

Paris Hilton's My British BFF, 2009. Television series. ITV2.

Perrier, M. 2012. 'Letting go of kindness: Towards an Ethics of Conflict for Feminist Theory', Conference Paper Given at *Forthcoming Feminisms*, Leeds, UK November 2012.

Pickard, A. 2010. *The Guardian*, online, available at http://www.guardian.co.uk/film/filmblog/2010/jun/04/sex-and-the-city-2-fans,accessed 11 Nov 2012.

Poison Ivy, 1992. Film. dir. Katt Shea. New Line Cinema.

Pratt, M. 2008. ' "This is the Way We Live...and Love!": Feeding On and Still Hungering for Lesbian Representation in *The L Word*', in R. Beirne, ed. *Televising Queer Women: A Reader*. New York: Palgrave Macmillan, pp.136–147.

Pratt, M. 1991. 'Arts of the Contact Zone', *Profession*, pp. 33–40.

Predelli, L. N. and Halsaa B. 2012. *Majority-Minority Relations in Contemporary Women's Movements: Strategic Sisterhood*. Basingstoke: Palgrave MacMillan.

Prime, 2005. Film, dir. Ben Younger, Prime Film Productions LLC.

Ringrose, J. and Renold, R. 2010. 'Normative cruelties and gender deviants: The performative effects of bully discourses for girls and boys in school', *British Educational Research Journal*, 36 (4), pp. 573–596.

Ringrose, J. 2013. *Postfeminist Education? Girls and the Sexual Politics of Schooling*. London and New York: Routledge.

Riviere, J. 1986. 'Womanliness as a Masquerade', in V. Burgin, J. Donald, C. Kaplan, eds. *Formations of Fantasy*. London: Methuen, pp. 35–44.

Roberts, M. 2007. 'The Fashion Police: Governing the Self in *What Not to Wear*', in D. Negra and Y. Tasker, eds. *Interrogating Postfeminism: Gender and the Politics of Popular Culture*. London and Durham: Duke University Press, pp. 227–248.

Rose, N. 1996. *Inventing Our Selves: Psychology, Power, and Personhood*. Cambridge: Cambridge University Press.

Rosin, H. 2012. *The End of Men: And the Rise of Women*. New York: Riverhead Books.

Ryan, L. 2007. 'Frenemies at Work', *Businessweek*, online, available at http://www.businessweek.com/careers/content/jun2007/ca20070614_437227.htm, accessed 11 Nov 2012.

Said, E. 1978. *Orientalism*. London: Routledge.

Sandhu, S. 2010. 'Sex and the City 2, review', *The Telegraph*, online, available at http://www.telegraph.co.uk/culture/film/filmreviews/7764817/Sex-and-the-City-2-review.html, accessed 11 Nov 2012.

Scott & Bailey, 2011–present. Television series. ITV.

Sex and the City, 1998–2004. Television series. HBO.

Sex and the City, 2008. Film, dir. M.P. King, New Line Cinema.

Sex and the City 2, 2010. Film, dir. M.P. King, New Line Cinema.

Sgroi, R. 2006. 'Consuming the Reality TV Wedding', *Ethnologies*, 28 (2), pp. 113–131.

Shapiro B. S. 2009. *Toxic Friends: The Antidote to Women Stuck in Complicated Relationships*. London: St Martin's Press.

The Simple Life. 2003–2007. Television series, Fox and E!

Single White Female, 1992. Film, dir. Barbet Schroeder, Columbia Pictures.

Skeggs, B. 1997. *Formations of Class and Gender: Becoming Respectable*. London and New York: Sage.

Skeggs, B. 2004. 'Context and Background: Pierre Bourdieu's analysis of class, gender and sexuality', in L. Adkins and B. Skeggs, eds. *Feminism after Bourdieu*. Oxford: Blackwell, pp. 19–33.

Skeggs, B. and Wood, H. 2008. 'Spectacular morality: 'Reality' television, Individualization and the Remaking of Working Class', in D. Hesmondhalgh and J. Toynbee, eds. *The Media and Social Theory*. Oxon: Routledge, p. 177–193.

Skeggs, B. 2010. 'The Value of Relationships: Affective Scenes and Emotional Performances', *Feminist Legal Studies*, 18 (1), pp. 29–51.

Skeggs, B. and Wood, H. eds. 2011. *Reality Television and Class*. Basingstoke: Palgrave Macmillan.

Skeggs, B. and Wood, H. 2012. *Reacting to Reality Television: Performance, Audience and Value*. London and New York: Routledge.

Skinny Bitch. 2012. Online, available at www.skinnybitch.net, accessed 11 Nov 2012.

Smith-Shomade, B. E. 2002. *Shaded Lives: African-American Women and Television*. New York: Rutgers University Press.

Smith-Shomade, B. E. 2007. 'Target Market Black: BET and the Branding of African America', in S. Banet-Weiser, C. Chris, A. Freitas, eds. *Cable Visions: Television Beyond Broadcasting*. New York and London: New York University Press, pp. 177–193.

Snog Marry Avoid, 2008–2013. Television series, BBC Three.

Sobchak, V. 1999. 'Toward a Phenomenology of Nonfiction Film Experience', in J. Gaines and M. Renov, eds. *Collecting Visible Evidence*. Minneapolis, MN: University of Minnesota Press, pp. 241–254.

The Spice Girls, 1997. *Girl Power!* London: Zone/Chameleon Books.

Springer, K. 2008. 'Divas, Evil Black Bitches, and Bitter Black Women: African American women in postfeminist and post-civil rights popular culture', in C. Brunsdon and L. Spigel, eds. *Feminist Television Criticism: A Reader*, 2nd ed. Maidenhead, Berkshire: Open University Press, pp. 72–92.

Superbad, 2007. Film, dir. Judd Apatow. Columbia Pictures.

Sweet Home Alabama, 2002. Film, dir. Andy Tennant. Beuna Vista Pictures.

Tanenbaum, L. 2003. *Catfight: Rivalries Among Women, From Diets to Dating, From the Boardroom to the Delivery Room*. New York: Perennial.

Taylor, J. 'Interview with Holly Willoughby', *The Daily Mail*, online, available at http://www.dailymail.co.uk/home/moslive/article-2114854/Holly-Willoughby-I-used-strip-undies-time–I-believe-say-again. html#ixzz25xsYgEmF, accessed 11 Nov 2012.

Taylor, L. 2011. ' "I'm a girl, I should be a princess": Gender, Class Entitlement and Denial in *The Hills*', in B. Skeggs and H. Wood, eds. *Reality Television and Class*. Basingstoke: Palgrave Macmillan, pp. 119–131.

Thinspiration, online, available at http://thinspiration-pictures.blogspot.co.uk, accessed 14 May 2013.

Ticineto Clough, P. ed. (with Jean Halley), 2007. *The Affective Turn: Theorizing the Social*. Durham, NC and London: Duke University Press, 2007.

Tyler, I. 2006. 'Chav Scum: The Filthy Politics of Social Class in Contemporary Britain' *Media/Culture*. 9 (5), online, available at http://www.journal.media-culture.org.au/index.php/mcjournal, accessed 11 Nov 2012.

Tyler, I. 2008. ' "Chav mum, chav scum": Class Disgust in Contemporary Britain', *Feminist Media Studies*. 8 (1), pp. 17–34.

Tyler, I. and Bennett, B. 2010. 'Celebrity Chav: Fame, Femininity and Social Class', *European Journal of Cultural Studies*, 2010. 13 (3), pp. 375–393.

Vogue.co.uk 2011. 'Sarah Jessica Parker Unveiled', *Vogue*, online 14 Sep, available at http://www.vogue.co.uk/videocategory=exclusives&id=10666, accessed 11 Aug 2012.

Waiting to Exhale, 1995. Film. dir, Forest Whitaker. Twentieth Century Fox.

Walkerdine, V. 2011. 'Shame on You! Intergenerational Trauma and Working-Class Femininity on Reality Television', in B. Skeggs and H. Wood, eds. *Reality Television and Class*. Basingstoke: Palgrave Macmillan, pp. 225–236.

Warn, S. 2006a, 'Introduction', in K. Akass and J. McCabe, eds. *Reading The L Word: Outing Contemporary Television*. London and New York: I.B.Tauris, pp. 1–8.

Warn, S. 2006b, 'Radical Acts: Biracial Visibility and The L Word', in K. Akass and J. McCabe, eds. *Reading The L Word: Outing Contemporary Television*. London and New York: I.B.Tauris, pp. 189–198.

Weber, B. 2009. *Makeover TV: Selfhood, Citizenship and Celebrity*. Bloomington, IN: Duke University Press.

Weisberger, L. 2003. *The Devil Wears Prada*. London: Harper Collins.

Wernick, A. 1991. *Promotional Culture: Advertising, Ideology and Symbolic Expression*. London: Sage.

What Not to Wear, 2001–2005. Television series, BBC.

Wifeswap, 2003–present. Television series, Channel 4.

Wiseman, E. 2011. 'The year-zero face: Is 36 the perfect age for a woman?', *The Guardian*, online, available at http://www.guardian.co.uk/lifeandstyle/2011/jan/16/year-zero-face-plastic-surgery, accessed 11 Nov 2012.

Wiseman, R. 2002. *Queen Bees and Wannabes: Helping Your Daughters Survive Cliques, Gossip, Boyfriends, and Other Realities of Adolescence*. New York: Three Rivers Press.

Wolf, N. 1993. *Fire With Fire: The New Female Power and How It Will Change the 21st Century*. New York: Random House.

Wolf, N. 2009. 'Carrie Bradshaw: Icons of the decade', in *The Guardian*, 22 December.

The Women, 2008. Film. Picture House Entertainment.

Wright, J. 2005. *Perfect Bride: The Complete Beauty, Diet and Exercise Countdown*. London: Hamlyn.

Yager J. 2002. *When Friendship Hurts: How to Deal with Friends Who Betray, Abandon, or Wound You*. New York: Simon & Schuster.

Yeğenoğlu, M. 1998. *Colonial Fantasies: Towards a Feminist Reading of Orientalism*. Cambridge: Cambridge University Press.

youandyourwedding.com 2012. '2013 Brides to be…Weekly weigh in! Let's get motivated!', online forum, available at www.youandyourwedding.co.uk/forum/weight-loss-for-your-wedding/2013-brides-to-be-weekly-weigh-in-lets-get-motivated/367704.html, accessed 11 Nov 2012.

You Are What You Eat, 2004–2007. Television series, Channel 4.

Index

Printed and bound in the United States of America